"A magnificently researched book.... Lauren K. Thompson goes straight to the letters and diaries of the rank and file, allowing the reader to see how grisly veterans sought truces to cope with the brutalities of war. *Friendly Enemies* is both a poignant and practical story of men asserting their humanity in the relentless and unforgiving struggle of survival."

—Peter S. Carmichael, author of *The War for the Common Soldier: How Men Thought, Fought, and Survived in Civil War Armies*

"This first study of fraternization during the American Civil War reveals that the topic yields more than anecdotes to color campaign narratives—it provides much-needed insight into soldier resistance and survival, trade networks, and veteran memory."

—Lorien Foote, author of *The Gentlemen and the Roughs: Violence, Honor, and Manhood in the Union Army*

"Lauren Thompson explores Civil War episodes shrouded by myth—those moments when Billy Yank and Johnny Reb exchanged banter, coffee, and tobacco instead of lead. Surveying the entire war, she explains that brave and otherwise dutiful soldiers fraternized with the enemy to assert their individuality. Significantly, she stresses the racial dimensions of these meetings. Only white soldiers fraternized, vowed they could restore peace, and recalled their exchanges years later to foster reunion and white supremacy."

—Jason Phillips, author of *Looming Civil War: How Nineteenth-Century Americans Imagined the Future*

Friendly Enemies

Studies in War, Society, and the Military

GENERAL EDITORS
Kara Dixon Vuic
Texas Christian University

Richard S. Fogarty
University at Albany, State University of New York

EDITORIAL BOARD
Peter Maslowski
University of Nebraska–Lincoln

David Graff
Kansas State University

Reina Pennington
Norwich University

Friendly Enemies

Soldier Fraternization
throughout the
American Civil War

LAUREN K. THOMPSON

University of Nebraska Press
LINCOLN

© 2020 by the Board of Regents of the University of Nebraska

Portions of this book originally appeared in "Escaping the Mechanism: Soldier Fraternization during the Petersburg Campaign," *Civil War History* 63, no. 4 (Dec. 2017): 349–76 and reappear here with permission of the Kent State University Press.

All rights reserved

The University of Nebraska Press is part of a land-grant institution with campuses and programs on the past, present, and future homelands of the Pawnee, Ponca, Otoe-Missouria, Omaha, Dakota, Lakota, Kaw, Cheyenne, and Arapaho Peoples, as well as those of the relocated Ho-Chunk, Sac and Fox, and Iowa Peoples.

First Nebraska paperback printing: 2023

Library of Congress Cataloging-in-Publication Data
Names: Thompson, Lauren K., author.
Title: Friendly enemies: soldier fraternization throughout the American Civil War / Lauren K. Thompson.
Other titles: Soldier fraternization throughout the American Civil War
Description: Lincoln, NE: University of Nebraska Press, [2020]. | Series: Studies in war, society, and the military | Includes bibliographical references and index.
Identifiers: LCCN 2019042718
ISBN 9781496202451 (hardback)
ISBN 9781496233394 (paperback)
ISBN 9781496221629 (epub)
ISBN 9781496221636 (mobi)
ISBN 9781496221643 (pdf)
Subjects: LCSH: Soldiers—United States—Social life and customs—19th century. | Soldiers—Confederate States of America—Social life and customs. | Fraternization—United States—History—19th century. | United States. Army—Military life—History—19th century. | Confederate States of America. Army—Military life. | United States—History—Civil War, 1861–1865—Social aspects.
Classification: LCC E607 .T56 2020 | DDC 973.7/3013—dc23
LC record available at https://lccn.loc.gov/2019042718

Set in Garamond Premier Pro by Mikala R. Kolander.

To Mommy
for taking me to the battlefields
To Mom Max
for believing in me
To John
for loving me unconditionally

Contents

List of Illustrations .. ix
Acknowledgments .. xi

Introduction .. 1
1. Fraternity and Resistance .. 17
2. Discourse .. 35
3. Trade .. 63
4. Information .. 85
5. Ceasefires .. 111
6. Memory .. 137
Conclusion .. 165

Notes .. 169
Bibliography .. 189
Index .. 203

Illustrations

1. *Rainy Day on Picket* by Edwin Forbes .. 39
2. *The Picket* by Edwin Forbes .. 41
3. *The War in Tennessee—Union Pickets Approached by Rebels in Cedar Bushes* by C. E. T. Hillen .. 53
4. *Federal Entrenchments in Front of Vicksburg* .. 69
5. *Pickets Trading between the Lines* by Edwin Forbes .. 80
6. *News from Home* by Edwin Forbes .. 87
7. *An Incident of the War* by Arthur Lumley .. 90
8. *Meeting of Union and Rebel Pickets in the Rappahannock River* by Mr. Oertel .. 92
9. *Reading the News* by Edwin Forbes .. 101
10. *Atlanta, Georgia (Vicinity). Federal Pickets before the City* by George N. Barnard .. 125
11. *Petersburg, Virginia. Earthworks in Front of Petersburg* .. 129
12. Civil War veterans .. 140

Acknowledgments

This book took more dedication and determination than I could have ever imagined. Somehow, I mustered the discipline needed to research, write, edit, and secure the means to publish, present, and fund this project. That grit was only possible through the assistance and support of mentors, scholars, colleagues, friends, and family. I will be forever grateful to three people in particular for their counsel and guidance throughout this journey. First, and foremost, Dr. Maxine D. Jones deserves more credit than I can put into words. Her selflessness and tireless efforts to ensure my success gave me strength throughout every step of the process. She gave me even doses of reassurance and tough love. It was through her advice and wisdom that I found the confidence to do what others told me was impossible. Dr. Jones taught me a crucial lesson in our field: how to rise above adversity and failure. "Mom Max" also taught me the most valuable step in life: to know your worth. From the person I was when I met her as a first-year PhD student to the woman I am now, I owe her the credit. I am thankful she took a chance on me. I can only hope to one day embody her optimism, grace, and strength. Second, I would like to thank Peter S. Carmichael. When I studied with Dr. Carmichael at West Virginia, he gave me the topic of fraternization and assured me it would be something worth pursuing. It is because of Pete, and his training, that a book centered on soldier fraternization now exists, and I am indebted to him for his continued support. Finally, none of this would be possible without the mentorship of James H. O'Donnell III. "Dr. O" took me under his wing at Marietta College and never stopped believing in me. It was at Marietta that Jim told me, "Lauren, you can and should get your PhD." Since that conversation in Thomas Hall, I never looked back. This book became a reality because of his confidence in my abilities as an academic. I thank Dr. O for believing in the hardworking, history-loving girl from Pittsburgh.

Thank you to the University of Nebraska Press for taking on my vision and bringing it to fruition. This book was only possible through the incredible support of my editor, Bridget Barry. From our first meeting at the OAH in St. Louis in 2015 until now, I will be forever grateful for her professionalism, expertise, and diligence. I am so unbelievably fortunate she saw something in me and stuck with me through this process. It is often hard to find positivity and confidence while in the thick of revisions—I thank her for bringing both. I could not imagine working with anyone else. I would also like to thank Emily Wendell for assisting me with the publication logistics. She kept me centered while going through the final steps before publication. I am equally thankful to the scholars who reviewed my manuscript. They pushed me to think deeply about these men and their experiences. Their insightful critiques made this book so much stronger. Additionally, I am so very appreciative to those on the UNP review board for their approval of my manuscript. And, to all the folks at University of Nebraska Press—my project editor, Elizabeth Zaleski; my copyeditor, Ginny Perrin; the marketing team; the cover design artist; and anyone who had their eyes and hands on this creation, I thank them for their efforts with this project.

I am indebted to the number of scholars who offered critiques and advice. Jason Phillips deserves much praise for his continuous support of my study of soldier fraternization. From commenting on my paper at SCWH to his suggestions on my manuscript organization, I hold Jason's scholarship in the highest regard and am so very grateful for his expertise. This book is stronger because of him and for that I am most thankful. Lorien Foote assisted with suggestions but, even more importantly, gave me confidence through mentorship and friendship. She always takes the time to support a junior scholar like myself. I am lucky to have her in my corner. Her scholarship and kindness inspire me. I am much obliged to Barbara Gannon for singing praises about this project in the final review. Although underserving of such approval, I will be forever appreciative of her endorsement and thank her for the continued support over these years. A heartfelt thank you to George Rable for assisting me with sources and sharing accounts of fraternization from his soldier manuscript index. George's enthusiasm for my topic and support throughout has been most helpful in navigating the waters of Civil War scholarship. Much appreciation goes to Lorri Glover for supporting me along the way. Lorri commented on this project at the OAH and then, two years later, welcomed me to St. Louis when I landed my tenure-track job at McKendree. She helped me gain access to the Saint Louis University Library during the summer to revise this manuscript. I am also very grateful for Diane Miller Sommerville and her mentorship over the past few years. Diane chaired my panel at SMH and since that time has been a friend and someone I admire. Thank you to James Broomall for commenting on portions of this project in Ottawa and for inviting me to present this research at Shepherd University. Parts of this manuscript originally appeared as an article in *Civil War History*, entitled "Escaping the Mechanism: Soldier Fraternization during the Petersburg Campaign, 1864–65," used with permission from Kent State University Press. I am so very grateful to Kevin Adams for seeing my potential and offering his critique and selfless guidance with that article, and ultimately, this book. Lesley Gordon and Brian Craig Miller both deserve recognition for their editorial efforts and seeing the article through from submission to publication. For the anonymous reviewers and any other scholars that offered feedback, may they accept my gratitude for giving their time and making this book a stronger piece of scholarship.

My research would not have been possible without funding from the Mellon Foundation, United States Army Heritage and Education Center, and Florida State University. I would like to thank the Virginia Historical Society for the Andrew Mellow Fellowship. Most notably, Frances Pollard and Ham Dozier deserve a special thank you for their assistance and support during my time in Richmond. My research on the Army of Northern Virginia would not have been possible without their generosity. I would also like to thank the Army War College for awarding me the Matthew C. Ridgway Grant. My time in Carlisle was essential for gaining the perspective of Union soldiers, and I could have spent an entire summer reading their vast collection of soldier manuscripts. Thank you to the historians and staff at the United States Army Military History Institute (USAMHI) for their expertise and financial assistance. The Florida State University History Department awarded me a handful of travel grants. Because of their funding, I was able to research at the Alabama Department of Archives and History, Mississippi Department of Archives and History, New York Historical Society, New York Public Library, and University of Southern Mississippi Special Collections. I would like to thank the archival staffs at the following locations: Emory University's Manuscript and Rare Book Library, State Archives and Library of Florida, Missouri History Museum Library and Research Center, The National Archives, and Historical Society of Pennsylvania. Their expertise on the collections and friendliness during my time researching was a massive help in securing evidence for this book. Bev and Tom Lowry deserve special recognition. Their massive undertaking of Union Court Martial cases, known as the Index Project, Inc., was essential in locating cases on fraternization at the National Archives. I thank them for accepting my inquiry and sharing their index project, and kindness, with me.

I would especially like to thank the faculty at Florida State University who took part in shaping this project and my abilities as a historian. My dissertation committee deserves much gratitude for their edits, guidance, and continued support. Professors Jennifer Koslow, Andrew Frank, Kurt Piehler, Katherine Mooney, and Maxine Montgomery used their expertise to strengthen this project, and I am very grateful for their advice in working toward a book manuscript. A special thank you to Jen Koslow and Patrick Byrne for allowing me to stay with their family, Bubby and Ellen, in New York. I would like to thank Kurt for believing in my project and his letters of recommendation, which contributed to this project's funding. Andrew provided his expertise on nineteenth-century scholarship and challenged me to think critically about fraternization. Also at Florida State, professors Suzanne Sinke and Johnathan Grant were always there for me in both teaching and counsel.

This project began in the summer of 2009 in Fredericksburg, Virginia. As a seasonal interpretive park ranger at Fredericksburg and Spotsylvania National Military Park, I would spend my days off combing through the bound volumes at Chatham. I read books on the campaigns in between tours at Chancellorsville Visitor Center and the Wilderness Exhibit Shelter. In the evenings, I would sit along the banks of the Rappahannock and mull over the war and the soldiers. It was in these moments that a lowly master's student developed an idea for a book. Over the past decade, as I dealt with setbacks and frustrations, I would always think back to those Virginia summers to remember why I started. My time at Fredericksburg also blessed me with two scholars who supported my vision. Greg Mertz trained me in interpretation, and I am a better scholar and teacher because of it. He also taught me the value of synthesizing the military and social approaches when studying the war. I thank him for reminding me to never stray too far from the battlefield and for always having my back. Eric Mink's knowledge of battles and individual soldiers motivates me. It is something I strive to match, but surely will not, in my own thinking and writing. I thank him for being my go-to park expert and for answering all my questions about soldiers and images. I am so very grateful for his friendship.

No one quite understands the book writing adventure like your colleagues. If anyone can empathize and provide camaraderie it is these amazing human beings. David Goldberg deserves his own section for how much he means to me. We started together in Woodburn G-13 at WVU and who would have dreamed a decade later we would be in the Midwest living our best lives. I thank him for getting me through my lowest points and for alleviating my stress with laughter. He is an incredible scholar and teacher, I am so lucky to have him as a best friend. Joe Rizzo completes our triumvirate, and I am equally grateful to him. Joe's regular phone calls, company on conference trips, and humor allowed me to see the joy in this journey. He and I were together every step of the way—from Virginia Battlefields in our Green and Gray, to the AHA in our suits. A special thank you to my colleagues from West Virginia and Florida State, particularly Cara Snider, Brandon Williams, Kevin Kokomoor, Kyle Harris, and Josh Butler. Thanks to them, this process was more endurable, and their continuous encouragement allowed my dream to become a reality.

I would also like to thank a group of colleagues in my field, notably Megan Bever, Angela Jill Cooley, Laura June Davis, Angela Elder, Timothy Fritz, Misti Nicole Harper, Scott Hubbard, Matt Hulbert, Greg Jones, Laura Mammina, Christian McWhirter, John Mitcham, Lindsey Privette, Angela Riotto, Matt Stanley, Dave Thomson, Trae Welborn, and Charles Wexler. It takes a special group to navigate graduate school, the job market, and our early careers together. I am so appreciative of their collegiality, encouragement, and friendship. Many of us presented on panels together, shared reading lists, and roomed at conferences. A special thanks to Laura Mammina for adopting my little "Yankee" and making him a part of her family. I would like to thank Megan Bever for inviting me to present this research as part of the Sherwood Speaker Series and for her hospitality while in Joplin. And, thanks to Laura June for rooming with me at AP and being my closest confidante. All of these incredible people offered support and reassurance through this book process and for that I will be forever appreciative. I only hope I can return the favor, and I most certainly look forward to what the future holds for our cohort.

My team at McKendree University is simply outstanding. I am blessed to be employed alongside some of the most incredible scholars and teachers I have ever met. I will forever be indebted to Shelly Lemons for choosing me. She is the best department chair and colleague I could ever ask for. I am indebted to her for her unwavering support in the completion of this book. Thanks to her for picking up my slack when this book took priority and, most of all, for being my teammate and friend. Also, a massive thank you to my friends and colleagues at McKendree, especially Christine Bahr, Melissa Barfield, Brenda Boudreau, Jessica Campbell, Ann Collins, Nichole DeWall, Brian Frederking, Jen Funk, Debbie Houk, Kevin Kao, Paula Martin, Rich Murphy, Duane Olsen, Neil Quisenberry, Sara Trask, Paul Worrell, and Kevin Zanelotti. I appreciate their patience and kindness throughout this process. They welcomed me to McKendree with open arms and always encouraged the importance of this book, even with our teaching and service priorities. I can only hope this book makes an impact on our campus and shows my dedication to continuing my career with all of them as a Bearcat. Before landing my tenure-track job at McKendree, I taught at two different schools as a visiting professor. At Pitt-Johnstown, I am so grateful for the mentorship and support of my colleagues there, particularly, Kay Reist, Jeremiah Coldsmith, Chris Cook, and Ross Kleinstuber. Last, but most certainly not least, I am thankful to the faculty at Marietta College, particularly Matt Young, Mike Tager, and Katie McDaniel. They were responsible for planting the seeds of inquiry and have continued to be there for me since.

As an academic, it is often difficult to find people who stick with you. I actually do not blame them. I would not want to listen to me ramble on about soldiers either. However, there are a few people that stuck with me from start to finish, and I cannot fully articulate my debt to these individuals. Tiffany Baker and John Grandage took me under their wing in Tallahassee and supported me through every challenge. My workouts with Tiffany and our numerous dinners with John allowed me to escape the grind, and, through it all, they never stopped believing in me. I also value the kindness and support of great friends like Monterae Carter, Mack Betton, Ariel Harmon, Emilie Lynch, my running buddies, my gym friends, my St. Louis friends, and my 2111 Family in Tallahassee. Their unwavering affection replenished my spirit and allowed me to complete this book. And, to all my students, both former and current, whose encouragement and humor kept me optimistic—I do this for them.

It is my hope this book and my passion in the classroom will inspire them to do incredible things and never be afraid to do what is right.

I would like to express the utmost gratitude to my family. When I decided to pursue my PhD and write my book, my family never showed me anything but support in these decisions. I am very thankful for my Philadelphia family for their care and praise throughout this journey. They opened their home to me in Philly for research but also welcomed me to the "Junction" every summer for rejuvenation and lots of laughter. If there is one person whose selflessness and strength allowed me to follow my dreams, it would most definitely be my mom. She fostered my passion for the Civil War. For my thirteenth birthday I wanted to go to the 135th reenactment of the Battle of Gettysburg. And, of course, she made it happen. We took trips to Antietam, Fredericksburg, Williamsburg, and Baltimore. She taught me the value of history. My mom, also, modeled the characteristics of drive, self-discipline, and perseverance. She took on two full-time careers to put my brother and me through school and always put our needs above hers in the hope that we would have a better life. She is my inspiration. Both she and Maxine Jones are the strong, independent women that I can only one day hope to become and to whom this book is dedicated.

I also had an incredible surprise along the way. I moved to St. Louis to start a new tenure-track job and begin revising my dissertation. But, those were not the only new beginnings. I met and began a new journey with a man who understands me and loves me unconditionally. When John came into my life, I never looked back. There are not enough words to express my gratitude and love for this man. Aside from showing me the love I never thought possible, he balances me with his flexibility and patience. He gave me the space to write, wiped my tears when my anxiety became too much, restored my confidence when I felt like an imposter, and remained unwavering in his affection as I balanced teaching and writing. He is my rock and the love of my life. There is no one else I would rather have by my side as I cross the finish line for this endeavor. I am grateful, and lucky, he chose me. This book is also dedicated to him.

Friendly Enemies

Introduction

In August 1862 twenty-one-year-old Morris Brown Jr. volunteered to fight for the Union Army and mustered into Company A of the 126th New York Volunteer Infantry. Before the war he attended Hamilton College in New York and was a member of the Chi Psi fraternity. During the Battle of Gettysburg, Brown captured both a number of Confederates and a Confederate flag. Later that fall, with the rest of the Second Corps Army of the Potomac, his unit camped on the Rapidan River in Virginia. "Picket duty is quite interesting here. We are so close to the rebs that we are talking & blackguarding each other continually," Brown wrote in a letter to his mother. At many points throughout the war, enemies were only separated by a few hundred yards of water or field; a permeable boundary, neither battlefield nor camp. Brown continued,

> The other night I could hear one swearing away because he did'nt have any shoes, blankets, or overcoat.... The next morning he saw me eating my breakfast and yelled out & asked me what I had to eat. I told him and asked him to come over & eat breakfast with me. he said he would do it if I would let him go back, which I agreed to. Down on the ground went his gun & over he came, & oh! you ought to have seen him eat & drink coffee. Well we talked & chatted quite a while when he concluded that he would go back & away he went.[1]

Tragically, later that spring Brown was killed in action during the Petersburg Campaign, but posthumously received the Congressional Medal of Honor for his bravery at Gettysburg. Private Brown, a volunteer soldier who demonstrated the utmost level of courage and valor, also disobeyed the order that prohibited any contact with the enemy.

Confederate soldier William Harris Clayton of the Seventh Georgia Infantry fought in the Army of Northern Virginia against the Union Army of the Potomac for which Morris Brown fought. Like Brown, Clayton suffered a wound in June 1864, but he survived the war. Like their foe, men who fought for the Confederacy also took part in fraternization and continuously wrote about it in their letters and diaries. Clayton traded newspapers with a Union soldier during the Peninsula Campaign in June 1862. He actually sent the *New York Herald* he received, in exchange for a *Richmond Dispatch*, with a letter to his father. However, Clayton was not so lucky and was caught upon returning back to his picket line. "It [the exchange] has got me in a little scrape but I will risk the chances. I am now under arrest on account of exchanging papers and talking with the Yankees while on picket," Clayton admitted to his father.[2] Private Clayton's encounter confirmed the illegality of these behaviors. Why, then, would men risk their standing in the army or even their lives to trade with men they were moments earlier trying to kill? Evidently having breakfast and trading newspapers with the enemy proved beneficial for these privates.

Men who fraternized described it as enjoyable, peaceful, and beneficial. Depending on the soldier, fraternization provided different opportunities. For some men, it was a way to get a warm cup of coffee or tobacco during a sleepless shift on picket duty. For others it alleviated boredom and satisfied their curiosity about a "Yank" or "Johnny." Many men saw it as way to stop the relentless picket fire while in the trenches. Some soldiers used it as a way to gain information about the war by acquiring enemy papers. At the heart of all these reasons, however, was the notion of choice. Men fraternized because the military hierarchy and the harsh realities of warfare caused an identity crisis for citizen soldiers. Soldier accounts emanate uncertainties because of the major gap between what men expected from war and what they actually experienced. Men saw military service as a way to strengthen and display their independence, but quite the opposite happened. In February 1861 Floridian Mark Lyons was full of anticipation to fight for Southern independence. "Nothing discourages me. I feel that it will be my duty to fight. I care not if I be the last man," he exclaimed.[3] A year later he lamented, "I would like very much to get home as the life of a soldier does not suit me, merely from the fact that I have always controlled my own actions but in my present circumstances I am only a piece of the mechanism, moved by the will of others."[4] The juxtaposition between Lyons's initial eagerness and his disillusionment the following year proves he had little understanding of what military life would be like, particularly in regard to the grinding subordination. Soldiers often compared their lot in the rank and file to that of a machine, animal, or slave. "Only a little more than two more years and then *Hurrah*, I'll be my own master again," expressed Illinoisan George Sinclair.[5] Similarly, Virginian William B. Kidd thought, "How I do long for the time to come when I shall not be under military law and be a free man again."[6] Men who based their identity on control of their environment found themselves in a system that regulated every aspect of their lives. When citizen soldiers experienced war, and its limits, they tested restrictions. Soldiers redefined themselves by constructing outlets to help them withstand mental and physical hardships. Men sought a variety of methods for escape, such as attending religious sermons, drinking, and, most notably, forming bonds with comrades. When men were in small groups and close to their enemy, soldiers identified with one another and formed fraternal bonds. Men could quickly shift their perception of the enemy from one of fear and hatred to one of empathy and commonality. Fraternization thus allowed soldiers to test boundaries of authority and equipped men with a sense of how much freedom they actually had.

This thorough investigation of fraternization employs the extensive literature on the common Civil War soldier. In his definitive scholarship on this topic from the mid-twentieth century, Bell Irvin

Wiley depicted the war from a perspective other than high command. Both *The Life of Johnny Reb: The Common Soldier of the Confederacy* (1943) and *The Life of Billy Yank: The Common Soldier of the Union* (1952) shed light on the daily life of common Civil War soldiers. Through his thorough examination of their letters and diaries, Wiley paved the way for scholarship on the soldier experience. In the late twentieth century, historians James McPherson and Reid Mitchell continued to study the Civil War from the soldiers' perspective in attempting to understand why they fought. In his work *For Cause and Comrades: Why Men Fought in the Civil War* (1997), McPherson claims that the majority of men enlisted and continued to fight because of deeply seated political ideologies. Mitchell, in *Civil War Soldiers: Their Expectations and Their Experiences* (1988), employs a cultural approach in arguing that a shared American culture surfaced as men faced their enemy, combat, and death. These historians, rather than focusing solely on campaign strategy and battles, political administrations, or the decision making of the high command, synthesize the broader narrative amid their focal point: men in the ranks. Following their lead, studies of Civil War soldiers over the last thirty years have blossomed in both breadth and depth as historians have approached these men from several sociocultural angles. By using ideologies of nationalism and independence in conjunction with social constructions of race, class, and gender, historians have further diversified the common soldier experience. Through studies on secession, emancipation, religion, and masculinity, historians have provided intricate insight on the ideologies that caused men to enlist, withstand physical and emotional strain, and ultimately fight and die for their country.[7]

Most significant for understanding fraternization, a group of these scholars investigate not just *why* but *how* soldiers fought. This concept is described by historian Aaron-Sheehan Dean thus: "They [soldiers] did not necessarily control every aspect of their worlds, and they did not always fully understand the situations they found themselves in or the effects of their actions, but they willfully shaped the course of the war."[8] In keeping soldiers as the fundamental focus and expanding on the assertion that they managed their daily lives as individuals, these scholars maintain that soldiers did not just react to their circumstances but created them. In terms of Confederate soldiers, historians demonstrate how, despite privation and consistently being outnumbered, Southern men developed their own motivational factors. Jason Phillips, author of *Diehard Rebels*, suggests men grasped control amid the uncertainty of war because a portion of strong-willed Confederates truly believed they were unconquerable.[9] Similarly, in his extensive study on the Army of Northern Virginia entitled *General Lee's Army*, Joseph Glatthaar shows how Confederate soldiers withstood difficulties through the awareness that the Confederacy's existence was contingent on their army's survival.[10] For Union soldiers, scholars argue that men who enlisted to preserve the republic upheld their duty in taking action. Earl J. Hess brings forth the many factors that enabled soldiers to endure combat in his book *The Union Soldier in Battle*. Self-control, relationships with comrades, and conceptions of honor, Hess argues, allowed men who fought in Union armies to maintain their duty.[11] In *What This Cruel War Was Over* Chandra Manning argues that when Union troops encountered African Americans they pushed for an end to slavery and were responsible for redirecting the war aim toward emancipation.[12] Lorien Foote reveals how Union soldiers' socioeconomic status led to competing definitions of manliness. In her study *The Gentlemen and the Roughs*, Foote argues that, when confronted with the limits of military discipline, many soldiers asserted their manhood through exhibiting restraint, while others did so through resistance.[13] Most recently, in his in-depth study of how soldiers experienced war, Peter Carmichael demonstrates how the contingencies of soldiering can be lost when historians place too much weight on the dichotomies of courage and cowardice, loyalty and disloyalty, and so on. In *The War for the Common Soldier* he argues that men exhibited their "hard-nosed pragmatism" through flexible and spontaneous responses to their circumstances.[14] This incredibly rich body of scholarship highlights nuances in the common soldier experience and serves as a foundation for this investigation of soldier fraternization.

I employ a similar methodology to understand why soldiers fraternized and how they benefitted from these seemingly strange incidences. To place soldiers' actions as the primary focus, I undertook an extensive reading of their letters and diaries to understand how they experienced the war. Men who fraternized wrote about these occasions in their letters home and personal diaries. This study casts a wide net to include the voices of both Union and Confederate soldiers from nineteen states in the Union and ten of the eleven Confederate states.[15] I did not limit the scope of this project to one army, one theater of the war, nor one year of the war because I wanted to analyze how fraternization evolved throughout the war. As tactics changed, the way soldiers fought and responded to war changed too. I narrowed the scope of fraternization by homing in on the points when armies were in close proximity to one another, both in camp and in battle, for a significant period of time. Soldiers who fought during these campaigns and were not imprisoned, hospitalized, or on furlough provided the highest percentages of contact with the enemy. Instances of fraternization came from Union men who served in the Armies of the Potomac, Tennessee, James, Cumberland, and Ohio; and Confederate men who served in the Armies of Northern Virginia, Tennessee, and the Department of the Mississippi. I also focused solely on soldier versus soldier fraternization. Today, the term *fraternization* holds a different meaning than at the time of the Civil War. The modern U.S. Army definition of fraternization, found in Army Regulation 600–20, pertains to interactions with civilians or the "relationships between soldiers of different rank."[16] Interactions between soldiers and civilians during the Civil War happened because of and resulted in a different set of circumstances than those I chose to focus on. Fraternization between officers and privates in the same army also does not fit the framework for this study. Similarly, fraternization between prisoners and their guards, which represents a captor-versus-captive relationship, encompasses a different set of variables. This study centers on moments where soldiers exercised their power of choice only when both parties were on equal footing.

Who, then, was a fraternizer? This study provides over three hundred different instances of fraternization from the wartime accounts of 150 soldiers. Of this group, approximately 70 percent took part in these interactions, while the other 30 percent witnessed them. It should be noted that those who observed fraternization analyzed the scenes objectively and rarely, if ever, criticized their comrades who did. The overwhelming majority of these men were infantry; however, roughly a dozen cavalrymen and artillerists fraternized as well. Approximately one-fifth of those who fraternized were noncommissioned or lower-ranking officers. While these men were in charge of their posts on picket duty, they too took part in exchanges with the enemy. And, about one-third of those who fraternized did so on more than one occasion. Irish and German soldiers fraternized alongside their native-born comrades. Sixty percent of these soldiers wrote these accounts in letters sent home. But, no one type of recipient was in the clear majority. Letters were evenly distributed to female family members (wives, mothers, sisters) and male family members (fathers, brothers, friends). Many soldiers would spare family members, particularly women, the vivid details of battle, but had no hesitations sharing details of their interactions with the enemy.[17] Finally, approximately 80 percent of those who fraternized were volunteer soldiers. Because fraternization was a form of resistance, men who did could be unfairly characterized as uncommitted conscripts. This analysis of fraternization, however, proves that the majority of those who engaged in it showed significant ideological motivation. A few dozen were ardent secessionists and emancipationists. The majority of them were politically moderate and driven by their commitment to seeing the war through. Oftentimes in the same letter, soldiers would document their experiences fraternizing and their disdain for cowards and those who shirked their duty. Thus, in most cases, the standard fraternizer was a volunteer private infantryman who was candid about his frustrations with army life but also about his dedication to his service and country.

Fraternization, though, was exclusively between white men. By the end of the war, approximately 180,000 African American soldiers had served in the United States Colored Troops (USCT) in Union Armies. The sight of black men in uniform represented a direct threat to white supremacy. Southern masculinity was contingent on the existence of racially based chattel slavery. All the ways in which Southern white men defined their masculinity they simultaneously denied to men of color. Southern "slave codes" prohibited men of color from owning property, bearing arms, traveling, marrying, and literacy.[18] Antebellum white men measured their manhood on their ability to protect their dependents.[19] Southern slaveholders deprived black men of that right as they separated, sold, abused, and raped their wives, daughters, and mothers.[20] Although slaves constructed their own meanings of manhood and developed methods to resist this treatment, brutal punishment and methods of torture left black men and women with very little control over their own bodies.[21] On the battlefield, fighting for a society that prohibited black men their masculinity, Southern soldiers stood opposite former slaves. Southerners' dehumanization of black men filled them with strong emotions of "sheer race hate."[22] Confederate soldiers vehemently opposed the USCT, as their presence indicated both the antithesis to their own manhood and a new social order they deeply feared. Thus, fraternization was a ritual denied to black men, and would be indicative of race relations in postwar America.

In addition to understanding who fraternized, this study also identifies the conditions that led to and developed from these occurrences. Fraternization did not happen in a vacuum. Something prompted it, and men gained something from it. Men needed an escape, and they crafted ways to push back against the system. Fraternization became a method of self-preservation. For example, in order to lessen continuous fire, soldiers negotiated ceasefires with their enemy. New Yorker Sylvanus A. Markham proclaimed, "I was out yesterday and we made an agreement with the Johnnies in front of us not to shoot at each other unless we was ordered to advance so we lay there all day without firing at each other we would get out of our pits and walk around and talk with each other at a distance sometimes talking with each other you would think we were the best of friends."²³ Soldiers also suffered physically from starvation, scurvy, lice, heat exhaustion, frostbite, and dysentery on a daily basis. "I regret to state that in some instances our men stripped the dead bodies of the enemy stark naked and in other instances dug up bodies that had been buried to get their clothes," a Virginian admitted to his wife.²⁴ Freezing temperatures and fatigue could be lessened by acquiring a cup of coffee from the Union troops on the opposite river bank. Similarly, drunken officers, men who furnished substitutes, and stay-at-home politicians troubled soldiers on both sides. Conversations and even meetings between enemy pickets allowed men to express these mutual frustrations. As Anson B. Shuey told his wife, "They [Confederates] said to us that they would be agreed to hang Jefferson Davis and Abraham Lincoln together."²⁵ Emotionally, many soldiers dealt with anxiety and depression brought about by homesickness, the loss of comrades, and the anticipation of future sacrifices. "About this time, homesickness appeared in camp, and quite a number of strong men fell victim of the disease and died," lamented John Daniel Follmer.²⁶ One way soldiers could determine if their sacrifices were making an impact was through obtaining newspapers from the enemy. News of campaigns outside their camps and developments within the political administrations gave men knowledge and information about the war. Collectively, fraternization demonstrated soldiers' abilities to use and adapt to their environment.

A complete investigation of fraternization, as the sole focus, has not yet been conducted by leading Civil War scholars. Because fraternization was a common event in soldiers' daily routines, scholars who work with soldier manuscripts often come across mentions of it. En route to other arguments, scholars analyzed what these incidents meant. In his book *Reluctant Rebels*, historian Kenneth Noe claims, "Human sympathy, a sense of shared suffering and neglect, and the desire for scarce coffee, in short, could occasionally bring combatants together, but those factors only went so far in mitigating later enlisters' fervent hatred of the yankee."²⁷ Noe acknowledges fraternization but argues it did not change soldiers' opinions of one another.

Friendly Enemies does not suggest fraternization changed the course of the war or that it caused a mass exodus of soldiers from their ranks. If anything, because fraternization was about the individuals who partook in the exchanges, it reinvigorated soldiers' inner selves and allowed them to continue fighting. Phillips, in *Diehard Rebels*, eloquently demonstrates how prewar propaganda stereotyped enemies in the most abstract ways and that it was not until they met up close on the battlefield that they actually faced one another. However, Phillips claims that this proximity and soldiers' observations of one another's circumstances "reinforced Confederates' low opinions of the other side and confirmed stereotypes."[28] I, however, find, based on the evidence in soldiers' accounts, that when soldiers observed one another up close, the similarities in their conditions and daily routines prompted feelings of empathy and actually broke down stereotypes. In regard to fraternization, Phillips states, "This unusual behavior existed but most interaction across the lines was anything but cordial."[29] Although enemies shared bullets more often than coffee and tobacco, these instances cannot be overlooked. I agree with Noe and Phillips: fraternization did not result in connections between enemies that caused men to rethink or even abandon their duty. The significance of fraternization, however, was in the purpose it served for the individual soldier. These chapters show how committed soldiers were able to remain dedicated because of opportunities, like fraternization, to fight the war on their own terms.

An accurate study of Civil War soldiers cannot begin in 1861. Men came to war with traditions, experiences, and values from a world before they were soldiers. Therefore, Chapter 1 sheds light on why men fraternized. Upon enlisting, men immediately experienced challenges to their individualism and mastery. War pushed men to the physical and emotional limits. What resonated in many soldiers' letters and diaries were frustrations over the rigid class divisions in the military hierarchy. Soldiers blamed their plight on politicians, who started the war but stayed home, and officers, especially those promoted not for experience but for their connections at home. Men managed these setbacks by repeating learned behaviors from antebellum society, and tailored them to fit their wartime environment. First was the notion of fraternity. Both middle- and working-class men sought spaces of relief physically separate from their bosses and labor. This recreational sphere, according to sociologist E. Anthony Rotundo, was "unbound by rules and spontaneous" and mixed "combat with friendship, rivalry with nurture, competition with camaraderie."[30] When men went to war, homosocial relationships with their comrades, particularly in camp, allowed men to air their frustrations and essentially restore their spirit. Picket duty was a physical escape outside the surveillance of officers, which added an element of secrecy, like fraternal lodges or drinking halls absent of bosses. The fraternal sphere organically shifted beyond the picket line and extended to include the enemy. Second was the practice of resistance. Men tested the limits erected to control them. Because intercourse with the enemy was strictly forbidden, fraternization served as a subtle form of dissent that allowed soldiers to push back against the high command. Therefore, when armies came into close contact with one another for extended periods of time, men utilized the spaces for fraternity and resistance.

Chapter 2 focuses on how certain conditions aligned for enemies to meet and how the first widespread instances of fraternization transpired. After General Robert E. Lee's Army of Northern Virginia defeated General Ambrose Burnside's Army of the Potomac in mid-December 1862, soldiers in these armies remained camped opposite one another for the next five months. The winter of 1862–63 was the worst of the war for the Army of the Potomac. Even though the Confederate Army's morale was at a high point, southern soldiers felt the full effect of war as they sat in the city of Fredericksburg, cold and hungry. When men from both armies went to the Rappahannock River for their turn on picket duty, they had strict orders against firing on the enemy. Therefore, antagonists remained virtually unarmed and separated by only one hundred yards. First, men observed one another's daily routines. For many men, this was the first time they saw a "Yank" or a "Johnny" up close. Then, they began to shout at one another across the river. Jocular banter about one another's commanders, leaders, conditions, and stereotypes ensued. Simultaneous to the fraternization between the armies in Virginia, General Ulysses S. Grant's Army of the Tennessee approached General John C. Pemberton's Confederate Department of the Mississippi at Vicksburg. Despite being a siege, soldiers positioned across from one another shared jokes and conversation, too. Following Pemberton's surrender at Vicksburg, the Confederate Army of Tennessee and the Union Army of the Cumberland pursued one another through Eastern Tennessee, resulting in the Battle of Chickamauga. As armies navigated the rivers and mountainous terrain, they caught glimpses of one another, met in between the lines, and talked. What these encounters prove was that, despite being from different states and in different armies, the development of fraternization occurred whenever armies were close to one another.

The conversation between enemies broke down barriers as men began to empathize with one another's mutual circumstances. Chapter 3 highlights the extraordinary trade network that developed in 1862 and continued throughout the remainder of the war. Basic needs came first. Soldiers used what they had to trade with their enemy, most commonly, Union coffee for Confederate tobacco. Sometimes, particularly during sieges, soldiers would trade food. During Vicksburg, Union soldiers would offer hardtack to Pemberton's men, who suffered from starvation. When General Braxton Bragg's Army of Tennessee besieged General Grant's Union troops inside the city of Chattanooga, men found relief through trading rations prior to the battle in November 1863. At Petersburg, Union men would even exchange whiskey if they had it. Because men met in between the lines to trade, they often conversed about deeper matters than the jokes and wit that initiated the exchanges. Enemies shared thoughts on home, hopes for peace, and their mutual displeasure with the leadership and high command. Men often agreed that if it was left up to them, the war would be over. Interestingly though, despite soldiers' continual "talks of peace," they did not suggest over what terms. When fraternizers had candid conversations about the war, Northern and Southern men never discussed slavery. Fraternization demonstrated the reparation and protection of white male camaraderie at the expense of race.

Chapter 4 focuses on the exchange of information, specifically through newspapers. Soldiers spent ample time contemplating their position, the efforts of other armies in the field, and affairs on the home front, such as Conscription Acts, the Emancipation Proclamation, and the election of 1864. News about political administrations and changes in the high command usually found their way to men through the camp rumor mill. One way to offset these swirling uncertainties was through papers, namely those from the enemy. Papers from the other side, more than their own, aided men in determining if their sacrifices were making an impact. Of all the different types of fraternization, officers cracked down on the trade of newspapers most. As Virginian John Dooley admitted, "the latest newspapers, so that many important designs, which should be covered by the veil of secrecy from the enemy, reach them through trafficking and the imprudence of editors that published unwarranted details."[31] Over half of the court-martial charges for fraternization leveled against Union soldiers were for their attempts to exchange newspapers with the enemy. Despite the risk, men continued to construct ways to make their duty manageable.

Unlike at earlier points in the war, siege warfare forced men to withstand unrelenting enemy artillery and infantry fire. Chapter 5 depicts how fraternization evolved from a trade network to a survival method. It was amid the siege environment that men constructed the most meaningful form of fraternization: the intricate and continual arrangement of ceasefires. When Grant's assaults on Pemberton's army halted in May 1863, soldiers dug earthworks for protection and dealt with continuous fire throughout a six-week siege. It was from these conditions that antagonists arranged ceasefires and managed ways to trade during burial truces. Although the armies in the East gained most of the attention, it was in the western theater at Vicksburg where soldiers first sought ways to lessen dangers by calling these truces. When General Joe Johnston's Confederate Army of Tennessee tried to halt General Sherman's pursuit toward Atlanta in the spring of 1864, men tried to honor ceasefires, specifically after the Battle of Kennesaw Mountain on June 27. In mid-July, Sherman's troops crossed the Chattahoochee River, and one of the most widely documented occurrences of fraternization took shape. Enemies stopped firing, met in the river to trade, and engaged in swimming parties. A month later, as Sherman's men closed in on General John Bell Hood's Army inside Atlanta, men attempted to lessen constant fire on the front lines. It was through such erratic circumstances—shifting troops, leaders, and terrain—that men seized any semblance of stability. As frustrations, anxieties, and casualties mounted, men in the western armies used their environment and, most importantly, their enemy to make daily life easier and clutch opportunities to escape the incessant danger during the last year of the war. Simultaneously, men gridlocked at Petersburg for eleven months dealt with side effects of siege warfare. The leadership of both armies required their men to endure life in the trenches with the hope that the election of 1864 would play out on their side's favor. Even when the high command cracked down on fraternization through very rigid penalties and public court-martial sentences, soldiers continued to assert their autonomy through these means. What this chapter also highlights is the exclusivity of fraternization. The Confederate reactions to seeing members of the USCT on picket duty foreshadowed hostilities toward people of color in postwar society. And, some Union soldiers spoke negatively about their comrades of color while acknowledging ceasefires with their enemy. Union and Confederate soldiers fraternized not just because of their shared "Americanness," but also because of their whiteness.

Similar to the reasons why analyses of Civil War soldiers cannot start in 1861, they cannot conclude in 1865. Chapter 6 follows soldiers into their lives as veterans and adds another layer to recent scholarship that places veterans at the center of postwar memory studies.[32] Veterans' shaped Civil War memory by writing about their recollections of fraternization in their unpublished memoirs. Former soldiers returned to battlefields and etched their reminiscences. It served as closure for some, and for others a way to cope. But, when men wrote about friendly interactions with the enemy, it caught the attention of reconciliationists. Many periodicals, veterans' magazines, and newspapers during the last quarter of the nineteenth century promoted shared honor and sacrifice that united the North and South. These themes came at the expense of debates over causation, the collapse of the Confederacy, and, most importantly, emancipation and Jim Crow–era race relations. Thus, stories of fraternization served as ideal propaganda for promoting sectional unity and protecting white supremacy.

A thorough examination of fraternization reveals how enemies interacted with one another amid the bloodiest war in U.S. history. Because this project focuses on the points where men showed amnesty and empathy toward one another, it does not, however, claim that enemies did not also have deep-rooted hatred for one another. These instances depict a lighter side of war but are not intended to lessen the inhuman brutality nor minimize the death of 620,000 Americans. If anything, the fact that such actions arose out of such carnage highlights the exceptionalism and intrigue of fraternization. Some of the most miraculous accounts of fraternization occurred at the deadliest campaigns. What this investigation claims, rather, is that men did not simply respond to war but instead fought war in both nontraditional and understated ways. By using these interactions as a lens to understand the common soldier, fraternization demonstrates how men managed their duty by restoring the independence military life indisputably suppressed. Those who fraternized were not cowards, deserters, or bounty jumpers, but loyal soldiers. When they found themselves surrounded by privation, disease, and death, men responded by modifying prewar traditions to fit their current state and, in turn, made their daily lives safer and more tolerable. In doing so, soldiers realized that, although their enemy's ideology may have differed from their own, their hardships were actually quite similar. This common bond not only deconstructed soldiers' preconceived stereotypes about their enemy but resulted in the fact that, as historian James I. Robertson Jr. argues, "America has never known a war where fraternization ran so rampant."[33] Of course, both sides spoke the same language, fundamentally allowing men to converse. They were also of the same race and Western European ethnicity, which, at the most basic level, allowed men to feel a connection because they looked the same. Men on both sides shared relatively similar religious convictions. They also grew up in a participatory, although partisan, democracy and viewed themselves as citizens in a republican government. Taken as a collective, it is understandable why they fraternized: soldiers matched one another in who they were and how they fought and experienced war. At the forefront of these shared characteristics was their resourcefulness. Men used anything—and anyone—to stay alive, and that surprisingly included the enemy.

I

Fraternity and Resistance

> I will remain in the war and see the fight out. After that however, no more soldiering for me—I will allow those who bring the war about fight it out the next time.
>
> —Lieutenant JAMES MCBETH, 131st New York Infantry

In 1861 Private Wilbur Fisk enlisted in Company E of the Second Vermont Volunteer Infantry. After working in a Lowell Mill and then as a self-educated teacher, Fisk fought for his country to "expiate the crimes of the South." He ardently opposed slavery and secession. "God does not love slavery; there is no slavery in heaven. God does not love rebellion; rebellion could not live there. He hates oppression and oppressors," he preached. After the Battle of Chancellorsville in early May 1863, Fisk's regiment, as part of the Sixth Army Corps of the Army of the Potomac, remained encamped near the city of Fredericksburg. While on picket duty along the Rappahannock, Fisk had a long conversation with his enemy about the war. "They were frank and candid in their talk," Fisk said, "and expressed feelings in regard to the war very similar to those expressed by the boys on this side. They were tired of it they said and our boys responded with an amen." As in other meetings, men on both sides agreed that if it were up to them, they would all go home and let their commanders fight it out. Fisk added, "They told us if we would use a certain sign when we met on the battlefield, they would spare us." Enemies then exchanged newspapers and letters to be mailed. A Confederate who stayed longer received a blanket from one of Fisk's comrades. Upon departing, they shook hands and bid one another farewell. "I couldn't help thinking it a great pity that we should have to shoot such good hearted fellows," Fisk remarked. Although steadfast in his ideology and a veteran of major battles, Fisk participated in exchanges that were "contrary to orders" with men who weeks earlier tried to kill him and his comrades. Even stranger, in his reflection on this interaction, he felt sympathetic to his enemy. Fisk expounded, "A few bad men have conspired to destroy our government, thus drawing thousands of others into the vortex of rebellion, and, for the iniquity of these comparatively few, millions who have no personal feelings of animosity, must meet in arms and in cold blood slay each other."[1] What Fisk understood took most people until long after the war, if ever, to understand: a rich man's war and a poor man's fight. No matter how much they differed in viewpoint, after fraternizing with the enemy, Fisk shared fellow feelings toward them. These interactions developed because of a very significant rift between common soldiers and the men who led them. Many lower-ranking officers knew nothing more about military leadership than they did. Elites who brought about the war now critiqued their efforts on the battlefield while furnishing substitutes. Military life exacerbated class divisions and tested the ideologies men fought to protect. Soldiers, however, countered by tailoring the coping strategies they learned as citizens to fit their wartime needs.

Civil War soldiers were born during a period characterized by massive political, economic, and social change. During the Antebellum period in American history, the simultaneity of universal white male suffrage and the Market Revolution renegotiated citizens' relationship with their government. Aided by advancements in transportation, manufacturing, and communication, this period saw mass participation in partisan politics.[2] As a result, cultural conceptions of masculinity, independence, and competition evolved too. Men worked to achieve more in terms of political participation, earnings, education, and, in most cases, ownership of capital.³ Most men embraced social mobility with the hope to one day be self-employed. They wanted to be free from control and measured their worth by the number of dependents they had.⁴ This brought men into competition with other independent men. Historian Michael Kimmel suggests, "American men define their masculinity, not as much in relation to women, but in relation to each other. Masculinity is largely a homosocial enactment."⁵ When Civil War soldiers reached adolescence during the 1850s, they witnessed a generation of self-made men come into competition with one another.⁶ While Democrat and Republican leaders feuded over the issue of slavery, the masses of white men listened. Men who paid serious attention to politics interpreted sectional propaganda and political mudslinging as an avenue for the opposition's control at their personal expense. "Manhood is less about the drive for domination and more about the fear of others dominating us, having power or control over us," argues Kimmel.⁷ Debates in newspapers, speeches, and social halls across the country resonated deep within the hearts and minds of white men in the 1850s. Whether a yeoman farmer or a small shop owner, men felt personally invested in these national events and internalized any sectional infringement on their ability for economic growth. When heightened sectional tensions culminated in war, men volunteered because they felt their self-interest was contingent on the fate of their nation.⁸ The majority of Civil War soldiers knew quite clearly why they enlisted and continued to fight. Southern men, whether slaveholders or not, fought for the protection and expansion of a slave labor society, which guaranteed the continuation of white male supremacy. Northern men fought to replace the extension of slave labor with wage labor so that ingenuity and entrepreneurship could thrive.⁹ At the very core of these sectional ideologies was the belief in individual autonomy, or freedom of control over one's self. However, most volunteers did not yet recognize these notions were incompatible with soldiering.

Men came to war to showcase their independence and prove their masculinity, but military authority impeded their pursuits. Ideology and sentimentalism could "not accommodate the extremes of the military world" argues historian Peter Carmichael.[10] Military life severely limited a soldier's control. "You get stiff and insensible; you seem to move mechanically because those before and behind are moving and the string of automatons is pulled unconsciously along. You feel like you are in a dream," wrote a North Carolinian.[11] Soldiers found themselves caught in a continuous cycle of inspection, drill, manual labor, picket duty, and the seemingly endless march. "I do not think of much now it is about the same old story it is eat drill and sleep, drill eat and sleep and sleep drill and eat," wrote an Illinoisan.[12] "The most individualistic society on earth now demanded that its free men submit to the control of others and subsume themselves into units that acted with the efficiency and precision of a machine," argues historian Lorien Foote.[13] Subordination ran counter to their own self-interest. In his extensive study of the Army of Northern Virginia, Joseph Glatthaar states, "Almost everything about the army sought to strip away any semblance of individuality and rights."[14] For example, Virginian John Shipp sarcastically lamented, "Since we have been here we amuse ourselves by throwing up breastworks, cutting down trees, and walking 10 miles a day . . . a soldier[']s life is always gay."[15] Men of the rank and file were in a space where other men dictated every aspect of their lives, every hour of their days. "Men had valued their autonomy so much that they went to war when they felt it was threatened," Reid Mitchell explains. "Military life itself, however, proved a powerful threat to men's self-esteem. Military discipline required their autonomy to be curtailed."[16] It was a catch-22. "I tell you what it is a man's life, when he enters the army, is not worth a row of pins," wrote James McBeth of the 131st New York Infantry. "He is a mere tool—all his actions—and his life subject to the compromise of his superior officer."[17] This gap between expectations and reality is best described by Gerald Linderman: "The war regularly betrayed the confidence with which Union and Confederate soldiers sought to fight it; much that they encountered was at odds with their expectations."[18] The inflexible military hierarchy represented both the most significant and consistent limitation to soldier autonomy.

Men who fought to prevent the enemy from limiting their virtues felt their own command structure strip them of their dignities. For Confederates, however, many soldiers found great motivation from the high command, for example, soldiers in the Army of Northern Virginia. Historians agree that the presence of Generals Lee, Jackson, and Longstreet glorified the Confederate war effort and motivated men in the ranks.[19] Lee served as a beacon of motivation to his troops, but not every Southern man fought in his army, and a majority of the men in his army did not interact with General Lee or his corps commanders on a daily basis. Instead, Confederate soldiers took direct orders from their regimental commanders. Many of these noncommissioned officers held positions because of their family connections rather than their performance on the battlefield. Some had little to no military experience. "Having come from civilian pursuits and entering a war for the defense of their rights," maintains Glatthaar, "rebel troops were particularly sensitive to anything that smacked of inferiority or second-class status."[20] When discipline came from men who appeared to be appointed through nepotism, Confederates felt alienated.

This disconnect only grew when these officers received material comforts and furloughs. "We came off picket guard soon this morning. Last night we slept in hogsheads on the banks of the river but the officers (3 Lieut. Saunders, Dick, and Taliaferro) slept in a good brick house. What a difference between the officers and the privates as the fact I have mentioned above will show," a Virginian observed.[21] Regimental officers had better living conditions, access to the best food and drink, and most importantly, were the first to be granted furloughs. Nothing warmed the hearts of the men more than the prospect of going home to see their loved ones. James Montgomery Lanning of the Eighteenth Alabama wrote, "I feel somewhat melancholy on account of failing to get permit to go home; hope it will not be long till I get a furlough for 30 days."[22] Rank-and-file Confederates saw furloughs as a reward for following their duty, but when their requests were continually denied and officers approved, bitterness ensued. "The furlough system was put into operation to let the officers go home. That is all they keep up this system for. Every officer in our brigade has gone home in the last six months," expressed Granville Belcher of the Fifty-Seventh Virginia in a letter to his wife.[23] Soldiers longed to visit home but instead watched their commanders do so, while they were left to suffer privations in winter camp.

Union soldiers felt similar disillusionment with the leadership, in terms of favoritism and preferential treatment, but also, for slightly different reasons. Union men often felt their lives were at risk because of their officers' incompetency. "From want of confidence in its leaders and from no other reason, the army is fearfully demoralized. The politicians forget that our soldiers are all intelligent men equally capable with themselves of distinguishing between a brave leader and a sagacious strategist. A general growl has followed the new appointment and fresh defeats are anticipated. The men feel that their lives are trifled with. Desertions are frequent and dissatisfaction general, and without concealment," groaned a Union soldier regarding the appointment of General Joseph Hooker.[24] Men in the ranks felt the commanders seemed to be more concerned about competing with one another than with their well-being. "As long as military and political jealousy is allowed, full sway of the rebellion will never be put down. Never! Not one of our generals that have begun to make themselves popular and shown that they were men for the times," exclaimed a Union soldier.[25] Another disconnect stemmed from the diverse makeup of Union men, both in culture and social class. Officers' inability to relate to their men also prohibited them from understanding how to train and lead their men. Some soldiers learned by exhibiting restraint, for others it was by aggression. Officers' means of control varied between using gentlemanly candor and brute force. "We learned some things we did not know about the life of a soldier, and trust we are better for the knowledge gained. We have a greater degree of confidence in our officers than we had starting out, although we note the lack of education, and frequent exhibitions of bad judgment as well as the many indications of ill temper and brutality," stated John Daniel Follmer. He continued, "The officer is to be courteous and gentlemanly, but some of ours seem to never have learned the trade and are more at home in a saloon brawl."[26] This dichotomy of restrained versus martial manhood affected the experience of those who served. Historian Lorien Foote argues, "Some officers used army discipline as a tool to promote the values and attributes they deemed essential for manhood; for other officers and enlisted men, army discipline impinged on some elements of their manly identities and they sought ways to resist."[27] Thus, officers who sought to control their men by "harsh external discipline" only offended already wary soldiers.[28]

Nothing, however, angered a soldier more than when his officers were drunk. John Price Kepner of the Sixth Pennsylvania Infantry wrote, "I have no desire to be numbered in the list of officers of our Regiment who, without a single exception, are no more than gamblers and drunkards."[29] Many Federal soldiers, like Kepner, remained cynical throughout the war about officers' special treatment and lack of concern for their well-being. "Had an excellent sermon from the Chaplain, in which he read the riot act against drunken officers— the only pity was that so few of them were present to profit by what he said," observed a Pennsylvania infantryman.[30] After the defeat at Chancellorsville, Henry Welch expressed, "There never was a very great victory gained by a set of drunk officers. The General that commanded our brigade was so drunk that he could not sit on his horse. And the Division General had got so much down that he had all he could attend to keep from falling off his horse."[31] Confederate soldiers felt similar disillusionment about drunkenness among the leadership. "The officers could get all the whiskey they wanted and could carry their carousals late into the night proving the truth of what Shakespeare said 'What is the captain is but a hollow word, in the private is flat blasphemy' this theory has been practiced in all cases that have came under my observation thus far in the show," wrote John West Haley. "Officers set the example and when the men follow it, they must be set up as targets of ridicule. Oh consistency."[32] Haley noted a double standard among officers in that they punished privates for drunkenness when they themselves were guilty of such behavior even more frequently than the men they commanded. When the men that led them tested moral and military boundaries with rampant drunkenness, privates felt frustration over the hypocrisy. But, officers were not the only party responsible for their sentiment.

Common soldiers also felt controlled by the politicians and bureaucrats who drew them into war and let them do the fighting. Those who avoided the service, especially because of their wealth, fervently angered soldiers in the ranks. "Had every able bodied man shouldered his musket and come to the front when you did, this war would have closed long since, and today instead of being seated on the ground writing on a cartridge box, while the cold rain is pattering on our bunk over our head; we could all have been at home enjoying peace beneath our proud confederate banner," expressed John Wesley Culpepper.[33] A major divide existed between those who fought and those who stayed home. Men who commented on and critiqued the armies from safe and comfortable distances deeply frustrated soldiers. For example, Illinoisan William Cross Hazelton wrote, "If the 'gentlemen' at home who are crying 'forward to Richmond' will come into the field with their muskets we will go forward with them. Yes, more, we will take the front; but they will remain at home don't let them drive our generals into attempting that which they cannot perform, thus sacrificing the lives of their soldiers."[34] Soldiers like Hazelton felt that most of these stay-at-homes used their commentary about the war for political gain. "They [politicians] experience no danger from the ignorance and bull headedness of these military commanders. It is only the poor soldier that is made the sacrifice," wrote James McBeth.[35] Politicians who appointed, and critiqued, commanders did so at a safe distance, while soldiers like McBeth were put in harm's way. Similarly, New Yorker Silas Auchmoedy elaborated, "There are a great many such who are a great deal more able than I was who are now having their fine times while I and a great many others are standing all kinds of hardships and are ready to fight and even shed blood for their liberties. Shame on such. If I were in their place I would hide myself and turn hermit."[36] This disgust, articulated by Auchmoedy, grew even more intense when Union soldiers read opinions from Northern Democrats. These were men, also known as "Peace Democrats," or "Copperheads," who wanted an immediate end to the war and advocated recognizing the Confederacy as an independent nation. Soldiers took particular offense to Northern Democrats because they were overly critical of the Lincoln administration, their campaigning, and the war itself.[37] "I was sorry to hear that there are so many copperheads up there. They are our bitterest enemies. They are too cowardly to fight us face to face, but hand about and injure our cause all they can by plotting and talking treason," expressed a New Yorker.[38] Men on both sides felt enraged at and disconnected from those at home who were not making sacrifices and, in turn, were sabotaging soldiers' efforts to win the war.

The Confederate Conscription Act of 1862 frustrated Confederate volunteers, particularly because the act exempted from service Southern men who owned twenty or more slaves. Floridian Joshua Hoyet Frier labeled this "one of the meanest specimens of class legislation that ever disgraced the statue books of modern civilization."[39] The slaveholders who wrote and signed declarations of secession developed a loophole that prevented them from serving, at the expense of Southern yeoman farmers. About those who took these exemptions, South Carolinian David Logan Jackson expressed, "If there were many, or enough possessed of the right kind of patriotism at home, as well as in other places, there would not be so much distrust and cowardly submissive feelings as there is pervading the country; the trifling scoundrels at home who are depreciating our currency, are doing more against our cause than all of Lincoln[']s fleets and armies."[40] When loss and privation plagued their morale, Southern soldiers lamented the class divide the most. "Pa I certainly am tired of this war. I see a great deal on our side that I think is wrong. Not that I have become a Union man in the least. I would be willing to give all that I have or expect to have to be liberated from this war[,] but since the wealthy class has gotten out they are refusing to take substitutes," expressed Virginian Joseph Griggs. "I tell you it is very discouraging to the soldiers[,] for they are out of the war and their substitutes are gone."[41] And for men who continued the fight, it polarized them against those who had brought the nation to war and then criticized from the sidelines. Soldiers came to the realization that those without training and those who stayed home, solely because of their social standing, dictated soldiers' current state and, ultimately, determined their fate.

These resentments compounded soldiers' physical and mental strain. Factors such as battle, labor, and illness further diminished control over their bodies. Nothing in their civilian lives could have prepared soldiers for the nature of combat and horrors of war. Because soldiers rarely knew the high command's campaign agenda, they constantly feared the unknown and felt their safety was subject to the officers' orders. After soldiers experienced combat, they soon realized how little control they possessed. James McBeth wrote, "It is astonishing what little consideration military commanders have for a man's life—they seem to consider that these men are given to them for the sole purpose of slaughter and that the greater number slaughtered the more glory is due them. The test of generalship among them seems to be the number of men killed in a battle—not what good has been accomplished by it."[42] Like McBeth, both Union and Confederate soldiers witnessed men in their units, usually friends from the same hometowns, fall victim to bullets, disease, or enemy prisons. "Life is uncertain anywhere but far more in the army than it would be in our peaceful and quiet homes," a Pennsylvanian wrote to his wife. "The soldier is not only slaughtered upon the battle field, but he is ever exposed to diseases accumulated by the exposures of camp life, which is bringing thousands of our brave soldiers to an untimely grave."[43] Fear of disease, especially during the winter months, deepened the depression that settled over camps. Many soldiers suffered from illness and wounds, often multiple times. Although those who survived became hardened veterans who found strength in one another, these soldiers could not help but feel that their fate was left up to chance. A soldier's continual encounters with death and suffering instilled a harsh realization that at any moment he could be the next casualty. Because an idle mind often exacerbated these fears, boredom particularly plagued soldiers mentally in camp. Monotony of winter encampment, long marches, and repetitive drills did not mollify anxiety for soldiers who nervously awaited the next campaign. Boredom also caused melancholia and homesickness. In his 1861 diary William B. Kidd wrote, "Staying in camp is a dull business at all times. Time passes off dull and heavily. Seems to be twice as long as it really is. I feel sad and gloomy. How I wish I could be at home with my wife."[44] Soldiers worried about their dependents because distance disturbed their ability to remain in control of the only world they had known prior to military life. South Carolinian soldier Tally N. Simpson wrote to his sister Mary, "A soldier's life to all appearances is one of idleness. He carries himself lazily about and performs reluctantly the duties which necessarily devolve upon him. Far away from home sweet home and the loved ones there, surrounded mostly by strangers, and always in anticipation of a bloody struggle with the enemy, he sees but little pleasure in the things transacted in camp."[45] The reality of soldiering was a far cry from what citizen soldiers had first envisioned, and men struggled to make sense of their place in the war. Something had to give.

When limitations and sometimes outright failures struck soldiers, men constructed methods for handling these obstacles to their independence. Men did not need to formulate these strategies from scratch, however, but rather reinvent what they had already learned from experiencing obstacles and failure as children and adolescents. Before men volunteered to fight for the Union or the Confederacy, they had learned ways to manage setbacks. Childhood for most young boys growing up in antebellum America was made up of an education, either at work or in school, surrounded by other boys. From a young age, boys compared themselves to one another as they interacted beyond the surveillance of parents. When boys entered a space free from authority and seized their first experiences of autonomy, they took part in games, traditions, and rituals. The major way boys and adolescents dealt with challenges to their freedom was through the care of women. Boys went to their mothers, or perhaps older sisters, for support and restraint. Because women in the mid-nineteenth century were the center of the private sphere, boys, and even adolescents, sought relief and comfort in the home. Eventually their challenges became more frequent and, as a part of reaching adolescence, young men transitioned to independent men. But this was not easy, as "the misfortune of being young and misexperienced in the ways of the world . . . a young man that leaves the parental roof . . . [suffers] the buffs and sneers that a cold and selfish world throws at him," said Federal infantryman Thomas Bell.[46] Because independent men still needed some kind of support, they turned to male friendship. Homosocial relationships allowed men to share comfort, support, thoughts about women, and fears. Because the demands of the public sphere often kept men at significant distances from their women, men created relationships with other men in order to express their emotions. Anthony Rotundo claims male friendships and organizations provided an outlet for emotional expression without "threatening the individual autonomy or the psychological armor that were basic parts of a man's public identity."[47] Thus, men sought one another's company, empathy, and advice to bolster their confidence and self-esteem. When men felt defeated, they yearned for a place where they could reestablish their self-worth by replacing failures and frustrations in the public sphere with male camaraderie.[48]

Male friendships oftentimes took place within organized fraternal societies. Lodges provided refreshment in a peaceful, private space separate from an uncertain, troublesome public world. In mid-nineteenth-century America fraternal society membership grew in correlation to the middle class. Historian Mark Carnes points out, "The rise of fraternal ritual is evidence of man's ability to create cultural forms to mediate the demands of society."[49] Middle-class men constructed a brotherhood out of white male solidarity. Chapters of the Freemasons, Odd Fellows, and Sons of Temperance established bonds between workers across trades as an escape from the conflicts of everyday work life. Prewar participation in brotherhood societies and fraternal organizations exhibited the significance of homosocial relations. Through connections built in local lodges and in capital cities, society members created networks of trust, friendship, and communication that facilitated political activity. In uniting men across class lines, fraternal lodges served as spaces of equality outside the realm of a deeply hierarchical society. In her study on Virginia's lodges, historian Ami Pflugrad-Jackisch notes, "Many fraternity members saw their lodges as a refuge from the political and economic turmoil that went on just outside the lodge-room door."[50] However, as the sectional conflict grew and divided the nation, the lodges began to divide as well. Communications between lodges showed dedication to fraternalism but were not able to avoid the sectionalism that plagued the nation at large. Many lodges quarreled over whether the lodge should promote industrialism or artisan labor. Lodges in border states argued over the morality of slavery and the significance of slave labor. Despite the dissolution of the Union and, as a result, some lodges, the fraternal tradition would resonate during the war as citizen soldiers faced a different set of demands.[51]

When citizens became soldiers, they recreated a space for relief and fraternity. Particularly because of the absence of women, men relied on homosocial relationships for comfort. If they could, soldiers reformed or visited lodges while enlisted. While at Camp Fuller in Rockford, Illinois, Richard Prowse admitted, "A lot of us went down to the city Thursday evening to the lodge also last night there is two masonic lodges here we have been to both. I tell you my dear, I find comfort talking with the masons for in them I have friends that I aren't afraid to trust. When all the other friends fail the masons are always ready."[52] Prowse sought comfort in fellow Freemasons to alleviate frustrations with the new demands of soldiering. However, for the majority of men, once they moved out, their near proximity to lodges was unlikely. More common, and arguably the most significant factor that kept men in the ranks, were the relationships they forged with other men in their units. In camp, particularly at night, soldiers retreated to their space of reprieve. After joking around the fire and airing their frustrations, men felt their spirits replenish.[53] In some instances, the boundaries of the fraternal space extended across enemy lines. Just as men coalesced through white male sovereignty when they entered lodges in prewar society, soldiers were able to set aside ideological differences at certain times during the war. Soldiers characterized their fraternalism with the enemy as beneficial, comforting, and peaceful—an escape from the anxiety, suffering, and death. Historian Dana D. Nelson argues, "Men's social spaces came increasingly to rely on rituals to constitute the affective exchange of brotherhood."[54] Across enemy lines men continued these rituals of exchanges: banter, handshakes, and sharing a drink and a smoke. This fraternalism simultaneously employed the other tradition from their civilian lives, resistance.

In addition to homosocial relationships, the other major way men managed frustrations was through resistance. When events of the 1850s climaxed in the election of Abraham Lincoln in November 1860, Southerners saw their control dissipate, and they resisted through secession, which in turn represented a challenge to Northerners. Southern secession was the ultimate expression of active and direct resistance, and Northern soldiers responded by enlisting to stop it. These men, who rushed to enlist with the hope of reclaiming their power, were about to have it stripped away. "A private has but little chance of knowing what movements are or what they are for. His only duty is to receive orders and obey them. I first launched out to gain a livelihood for myself and (as then I thought) to be independent but alas the folly that ambition often leads to," expressed Thomas Bell.[55] These men were ill prepared for life in one of society's most hierarchical institutions. Gerald Linderman contends, "Small town individualism and egalitarianism contributed nothing to military discipline. Volunteers on both sides fiercely resisted subordination to a military hierarchy."[56] Not only did competition in the public sphere teach men growing up in antebellum America how to measure their independence but also how to cope with its limits. One of the most significant ways adolescents tried to withstand challenges to their individuality was by pranks, petty theft, and other minor misbehaviors. As soldiers, men rationalized their world by grasping opportunities to control their circumstances. Historian Aaron Sheehan-Dean argues, "Soldiers worked out the strategies that would allow them to retain their dignity and autonomy while in military service."[57] For both Union and Confederate soldiers, one of those strategies was resistance against authority.

Fraternization with the enemy was strictly prohibited. Armies continuously passed ordinances against meeting with the enemy. "Information has been brought to these headquarters whereby it appears, that a portion of the pickets, detailed from this command, are in the habit while on post of laying aside their equipment, and straying from their posts, of holding personal intercourse with the enemy's pickets, contrary to orders and in some instances of actually trading and bartering goods with the enemy," stated regimental commanders in the Tenth U.S. Army Corps. "Pickets are forbidden to hold any communication, whatsoever, with the enemy."[58] Interestingly, during burial truces or passages of information across the lines, officers would meet under white flags. Commanders gave their men the gruesome and awful duty of identifying and burying their fallen comrades. To make things worse, while the common soldiers handled mutilated corpses, they witnessed their officers meet and drink with the opposing officers. "In the afternoon a flag of truce went out with a party to bury the dead and bring in the wounded. Our officers and rebel officers met on the picket line and drank together. After this was done they shook hands and separated," described John West Haley of the Seventeenth Maine.[59] Similarly, South Carolinian Tally Simpson noted, "Brid Genl Patrick, USA, with several of his aides-de-camp, came over under flag of truce. Papers were exchanged, and several of our men bought pipes, gloves, etc. from the privates who rowed the boats across."[60] When soldiers emulated this exchange, officers cracked down on the very behavior they exhibited, creating yet another double standard, compiled upon several other privileges.

Fraternization thus served as a relatively respectable form of resistance, and the benefits were tangible. Soldiers exhibited several types of dissent. Men refused to work, drill, and fight. Others resorted to drinking, brawling, and cursing at their officers. Some of the most radical forms of resistance were bounty jumping, murder, and suicide. Desertion warrants the most attention, as it was both a quantitative indicator of morale and synonymous with cowardice. Because desertion became such a problem at certain points of the war, court-martial sentences for it ranged from public humiliation to death by firing squad.[61] "One man was shot this evening by military order, in Wilson's Brigade. It seemed to create a high sensation among the men. We are having a quantity of desertions since the fall of Vicksburg," wrote a Confederate.[62] The majority of soldiers who grew frustrated with their generals and conditions, however, never dared to desert or resort to drunkenness and violence because they feared the stigma of insubordination. Two characteristics of nineteenth-century manliness, mostly among middle-class white men, were self-control and restraint.[63] Fraternization protected these traits and soldiers' reputations because they viewed them as expressions of civility. Soldiers wrote openly about their experiences fraternizing in their letters home. They witnessed scenes of fraternization and never spoke negatively about the men involved. This was not the case when men witnessed violent disorderly conduct. Most were very critical of dangerous behavior and expressed their disdain, or omitted the details, in their letters and diaries. Fraternization, on the other hand, was an intermediary pushback against authority and, based on their reactions in letters home, deemed acceptable by their fellow comrades and their families. It was an act of resistance that allowed soldiers to maintain both their personal dignity and military duty. As a "hidden transcript," or set of actions that take place beyond direct observation by power holders, soldiers used their environment, which included the enemy, in order to push back against military rule.[64] As historian Wayne Lee suggests, "Just as in society, military subcultures develop when individuals make choices, improvise, and sometimes deviate . . . when confronted with uncertainty."[65] Men who filled the ranks of Union and Confederate armies did not have to reinvent how they handled challenges but, instead, modified their prewar coping mechanisms to fit their wartime circumstances. "As in their efforts to take control of their lives and careers in the civilian world, soldiers came to understand that they did not have to be passive victims of battle. They had the opportunity to take hold of the experience and mold it to familiar and manageable forms," claims historian Earl Hess.[66] Because Northern and Southern soldiers both saw war as an extension of their quest for independence, they sought similar ways to adapt when the unforgiving realities of military life challenged that mission. Whether intentionally or subconsciously, soldiers' actions, like fraternization, were pragmatic responses to unthinkable turmoil. As a way to mitigate war's effect on their bodies and psyches, soldiers reestablished the fraternal bonds and rituals of dissent they practiced in civilian life.

2

Discourse

We pushed our pickets as far as a small stream called Turkey Creek. The rebel pickets being immediately on the other side. We were within speaking distance, and as it was understood on both sides that there should be no firing, unless an advance was made in force, we had quite a sociable time with them. They asked what regiment we were. We told them. "Well," said they, "You are brave fellows but you are in the wrong army!" They sang us some songs about stars and bars. Our boys replied by singing some songs in which the rebels and their leaders were not spoken of in the most complimentary terms.

—William Cross Hazelton, Eighth Illinois Cavalry Regiment

Several tactical and geographical elements aligned in order for communication and interactions between enemy soldiers to take place. First, above all else, was the meeting of armies. If armies were camped at a distance or only came together for a battle and then retreated in separate directions, men did not come close enough to fraternize. But, when soldiers remained in proximity to one another for an extended period of time, they were able to closely observe their enemy. Soldiers realized that their own daily hardships—extreme temperatures, fatigue, combat—were the same as their enemy's. Consequently, when the high command positioned men at a close distance, fraternization became more frequent. Second, the military practice of using picket lines allowed for fraternization. In the early years of the war, before the onset of siege tactics, those stationed to picket duty were given strict orders to prevent an engagement with the enemy. Their duty was to protect the main body and notify their commander if their enemy made any significant movement. Men went on picket duty during winter encampment and during the time in between major battles. By separating a regiment or a few companies of privates from the main body, the high command essentially constructed a space for fraternization to happen. In plain sight, enemies observed one another's daily routines of drill, inspection, and leisure. In a letter to his sister, Confederate soldier Francis Edward Bayol of the Fifth Alabama wrote, "We could see the Federal flag and camps distinctly. The enemy's and our pickets were in a few hundred yards of each other, it was the order whilst we were there, that pickets should not shoot each other."[1] When soldiers had ample time to observe their enemy in concrete form, they realized that they were not all that different from one another. The realization that their enemy's circumstances varied little from their own further enhanced their curiosity about each other.[2] However, when battle tactics evolved into siege warfare, leadership ordered soldiers on picket duty to continuously fire. Soldiers followed these orders and, as a result, had to be on constant guard. Picket duty thus transitioned to a space of combat and fear. Some soldiers attempted to restore the fraternal spaces they had enjoyed by continuing communication with the enemy and subsequent peacefulness.

Last, armies often needed a permeable boundary where meetings and trade could transpire, allowing for fraternization. Many times, this space was a river or stream, but sometimes it was an open field with sloped ground, a small ravine, or even a wooded area. This "third space" neither fully divided nor conjoined men from opposing sides. It was a neutral zone. It was a penetrable boundary waiting to be tested. Soldiers developed a set of "signs" to denote the absence of officers and the willingness to meet. Robert Gaines Haile of the Fifty-Fifth Virginia wrote, "The Yankee pickets and ours are on very friendly terms. They are not more than two or three hundred yards apart. I had not been there long before one of the Yankees advanced, waves his cap, and made signs for someone to meet him."[3] Thus, the high command overlooked the consequences of placing men who speak the same language and suffered similar circumstances close to one another for a long period of time.

The first point in the war where these conditions aligned was on the banks of the Rappahannock River during the winter of 1862–63. If there was ever a battle in the American Civil War where men questioned their expendability, it was the Union Army of the Potomac at Fredericksburg. The attack on Marye's Heights on December 13, 1862, exposed strategic flaws in frontal assaults, and men in the ranks paid the ultimate price. "I saw some soldiers who had been wounded this evening, they say that Antietam was nothing to this," lamented a Pennsylvania cavalryman.[4] On that day, the Union Army sent seven divisions of men, divided into sixteen brigades, wave by wave uphill over open ground in an attempt to break the Confederate position behind a stonewall.[5] Union soldiers not only watched the leading divisions disintegrate but also saw men coming back into the town wounded and crippled as they crossed the pontoon bridges. Federal soldiers in the subsequent divisions immediately met artillery and stepped on the bodies of the wounded as they crossed the field. Union soldier William Reed Moore bemoaned, "It was simply dreadful. Utter discouragement, four days fighting and exposure, demoralization, defeat, everything to make us miserable."[6] After nightfall on the thirteenth, Union soldiers were pinned on the field for two days until General Burnside ordered a retreat into the town and fled back across the Rappahannock. Over the next few weeks, families across the nation read the names of the fallen, making 1862 one of the gloomiest Christmases in American history. Soldiers began winter encampment in the very spot they had arrived in November before the battle, which gave them ample time to replay the images of battle throughout the freezing Virginia nights.

At the beginning of 1863, men in both the Army of the Potomac and the Confederate Army of Northern Virginia had a lot to think about. They shared several of the same hardships. Boredom and the monotony of camp life did not make things easier for these men. "Our food has been pretty bad lately. Considerable number of fights in camp recently. We are bored, bored, bored," wrote a Mississippi private.[7] To keep men busy, officers ordered them to conduct drills, inspections, manual labor, and picket duty, which only angered those who had to do useless tasks. Routine labor led men to become even more disgruntled with their position in the army, particularly because their idle minds wandered toward home. Historian of the battle George Rable writes, "Of all the problems that plagued both armies, the pangs of loneliness hit some men the hardest."[8] For the soldiers who joined their respective armies in 1862, this was the first winter they spent in camp and away from their families. Regardless of victory or defeat, homesickness struck soldiers and affected them in different ways. "They get a little sick and then they get thinking about home and then you might as well give them up," detailed a New Yorker. "One for instance, Dick Carney, now he looks like an old man of 75. He has lost all his ambition if he has had any."[9] Younger, unmarried soldiers did not feel the burden as much as soldiers who left their wives and children. "It is my constant prayer and desire that all may be well with my loved ones," one soldier hoped, "and that it will not be long till we again may be united to live the remainder of our days in peace and happiness. I hope when the winter closes peace may be made and all honorably discharged from the service to go home to stay with our dear loved ones."[10] Some soldiers coped with homesickness by praying for peace and envisioning life after the war. Other soldiers resisted by deserting their ranks and returning to their families. Connecticut soldier Charles Griswold wrote to his sister, "All talk of going home, of deserting, anything but fighting. I have not seen as much patriotism here as I could put in my eye."[11] Some soldiers developed an alternative form of resistance.

Both Union and Confederate regiments took a twenty-four-hour shift about every nine days on the banks of the Rappahannock along a one-and-one-half-mile range of shoreline, with about thirty men at each quarter-mile interval.[12] Picket duty gave the soldiers a break in the daily routine. Soldiers saw this as a chance to escape

FIG. 1. Men were exposed to harsh elements while on picket duty. Edwin Forbes, *Rainy Day on Picket*, ca. 1876. Library of Congress Prints and Photographs Division. Morgan collection of Civil War drawings, LC-USZ62-79168.

the constant surveillance of officers during the drill-inspection regimen. Although soldiers welcomed the chance to avoid this routine, picket duty had difficulties of its own. Historian A. Wilson Greene asserts, "Picket duty presented the men's most taxing obligation during these late December days."[13] While on picket duty, soldiers were cold, wet, tired, and hungry. "I had to go on picket twelve miles farther without any thing to take except a few crackers and my horse and I stayed out on picket for 36 hours and it rained half of the time. Everyone has to stay awake on picket the whole time," wrote Pennsylvania cavalryman Levi Lewis.[14] On picket duty soldiers were not allowed to sleep, so they would try to rotate brief shifts to rest. "Out of the 96 hours that we was on picket, I only slept 4 hours and that was the first night," admitted one Yankee.[15] During his service on court-martial duty, Albert Peck wrote, "We tried a great many cases, among which were for sleeping on post while on picket duty. The penalty for sleeping on picket post was death and we had to pass such a sentence on some cases."[16] As Peck depicted, although picket duty allowed for a break from drilling, the long arm of officer control did extend to those on the line. Most significantly, the lack of sleep coupled with loneliness gave soldiers ample time to think, particularly of home. "Still on picket all alone thinking of my dear lonely wife and sweet little daughter; do they think of me? May it be the will and pleasure of God to speedily terminate this war and reunite us again," disclosed an Alabamian.[17] Although it gave them time away from camp, picket duty often worsened soldiers' physical and mental grit.

Bored, cold, and exhausted men sat across from one another without any imminent sense of danger. Soldiers had strict orders against firing on the enemy in order to prevent an unwarranted engagement. Frequently men would note these observations in their letters home. New Jersey soldier Richard S. Thompson wrote, "You cannot imagine how strange it looks to see the outposts of these contending armies sitting within easy pistol shot of each other day after day and yet no firing."[18] Men could walk about freely and observe one another from a close space. "We go in at

FIG. 2. Union soldier on picket duty along the banks of the Rappahannock River. Edwin Forbes, *The Picket*, September 9, 1863. Library of Congress Prints and Photographs Division. Morgan collection of Civil War drawings, LC-DIG-ppmsca-20646.

night and send the men out on the bank of the river on post (and they will not fire on a single man). Their pickets and ours are in plain view in short musket range, but both sides have orders not to fire," wrote sharpshooter William Montgomery.[19] Connecticut soldier Charles Griswold described the proximity thus: "We were on picket yesterday directly opposite the city, could hear the rebels shout in their frolics and see them snowball, could hear their bands play. Tis only a stone's throw across the river from one picket to another."[20] As soldiers studied the daily routines of their enemy, curiosity evolved into an identification with them. "Our station on picket duty was on the bank of the Rappahannock opposite the famous little city, Fredericksburg. We could see the rebels on the other side of the river very distinctly, not only pickets but others, playing ball, etc," a New Yorker told his wife. "They seem quite lively & talkative, but we are not allowed to talk with them; otherwise we should keep up quite a conversation as we can easily hear them across the river. They frequently sing out, as we are marching in squads to relieve posts, 'close up.'"[21] Soldiers on both sides realized they had comparable conditions and daily routines. "An Alabama picket is opposite of ours. I think it's the 2, 13, 15, 73rd Alabama regiments. The 14, 17, 18, and 21st Miss. Regiments did picket in the city and below," detailed Massachusetts soldier Roland E. Bowen.[22] Soldiers, like Bowen, began to categorize their enemy as individuals who belonged to specific states and units—as opposed to one large, generic group. The enemy became more personal and familiar. "We took position on the left of the line. The rebs were in plain sight on the opposite bank and we should no doubt have carried on a conversation with them if the roaring of the water which at this point ran very swift and over rocks had not prevented us from hearing anything in the shape of talk," noted John West Haley. "Once when the officer of the day came down on our side, we heard the rebel sentinel sing out 'officer of the day, turn out the guard!' they presented arms and then returned to their camp fire."[23] Soldiers perceptions and identifications of one another soon developed into communication.

Soldiers extended the social practices enjoyed in their respective camps across the river to include the enemy. Conversation in the form of witty banter was, in most cases, the first interaction and set the foundation for all subsequent exchanges. Historian E. Anthony Rotundo terms the practice "verbal jousting," which allowed men to "prove their shrewdness" through content that was "a playful contempt for one's fellows."[24] "The Rebels were doing picket duty on the opposite side, which is only a stone's throw across, we could talk to each other, and a great many good jokes are cracked between them and us, songs were sung of all kinds," one soldier documented.[25] As a way to poke fun at one another, enemies joked about their opponents' shortcomings, which in most cases were the subpar conditions of Confederates and the poor generalship of the Federals. "The Yankees say that we have a new general in command of our army & his name is General Starvation & I think for once they are about right," wrote William Montgomery.[26] One of the most repetitively recorded jokes of the time was the Confederate slogan, "It will be a hard road to Richmond with a Longstreet to travel, two Hills to climb, and a Stonewall to get over" in reference to their commanders.[27] In reference to Professor Thaddeus C. Lowe's Union reconnaissance balloon, a Fredericksburg civilian, Mary S. Hill, observed, "We went the next day to the Rappahannock, where the men of the 6th Louisiana were on picket; yanks on the other side. While on the river watching the 'Tiger' floating over, I heard the following conversation: Yank, 'Did you see our balloon?' (They had sent up three.) 'Why didn't you send one up?' 'We do, but it wants no gas. It is called Jeb Stuart, and knows where you are, and how many.'"[28] Men verbally tested one another. George Mitchell of the Fifth New York wrote:

> One of them sung out to Al Van Orden (who was on picket yesterday morning) at the same time holding up a canteen, "say johnny I'll trade you this canteen full of good whiskey for a plug of tobacco"—that's something I've run short on myself replied Al.—"I'm sorry to hear that" says johnny. "I was just screwing my jaw in shape for a good chaw, what do you do when you aint got any tobacco and cant get it."—"go without it" replied Al. johnny, "but if youll come half way over I'll meet you and will have a drink together."[29]

Private Van Orden's conversation with the Confederate demonstrated a witty soldier vernacular. Thomas Mann described this discourse: "Badinage and repartee were freely swapped and though never taking on a very serious character or showing any temper except with a sarcastic cast."[30] Soldiers did not view these jokes as threatening but rather symbolic of a shared masculine ritual. "The picketing is done on both sides on the best of terms, they converse across the river to each other and joke the same as if both belonged to the same army, and were fighting for the same cause," articulated George Mitchell.[31] The friendliness between pickets allowed Mitchell to realize the similarities between him and the enemy he was taught to hate.

For many soldiers, this discourse between them and their enemy marked their first interaction with someone from the opposite section. These men had based their understanding of the enemy only on hearsay and partisan stereotypical depictions. Soldiers referred to each other as "Billy" and "Johnny." They concurrently mocked "Jeff Davis" and "Abe Lincoln." "The Rebs ask us if we don't want some cotton, and we say no we have got plenty of wool," said a Union private.[32] Soldiers poked fun at conventional conditions such as the Union soldiers' warm coats and good rations. Sharpshooter Wyman White wrote, "They kept asking us 'Say Yank, When are you all coming over here with your eight days rations? We are awfully hungry over here!'"[33] Southerners were known for their jokes and sectional slurs, while Northerners were known for shouting humorous vulgarities.[34] Music was often the key that opened the door to acquaintance and provided the basis for continuing association.[35] "Perhaps our band would play 'Home Sweet Home' when it would likely be answered by 'The Mocking Bird,'" noted a rebel soldier.[36] Northern troops joined in the singing of Southern songs like "Dixie" and "Bonnie Blue Flag."[37] Banter between enemies highlighted sectional prejudices, hardships of camp life, and soldier jargon. Most importantly, it drew enemies together and established a foundation for more intricate means of communication.

Conversations, and how soldiers had them, developed too. If the space was water, soldiers communicated by passing letters on small boats. Joseph Hopkins Twichell, chaplain of the Seventy-First New York, wrote, "Our position opposite the enemy and in sight is the occasion of some interesting incidents. Letters tied to boards, or the boards themselves inscribed, are occasionally sent across both ways according to the wind."[38] If land separated the picket lines, soldiers decided to physically venture into the neutral zone in order to communicate. Henry Martyn Truehart of the Seventh Virginia Cavalry wrote, "We are on duty every other day, alternately, as pickets and as reserve pickets. Our pickets and those of the enemy, stand from 200 to 500 yards apart, and about 150 to 200 yards apart along the line. They frequently come up and wave paper at us, and on our making signs that we will not shoot they come half way and we meet and have a talk, always shaking hands on meeting and parting."[39] Almost always, the handshake represented the closure of the meeting and recognition that men were one another's equals. Similarly, Edgeworth Bird wrote:

> The firing of the pickets at each other had been pretty well stopped. It several times happened that they would wave white handkerchiefs to each other, and meet half way out and talk. Ryan, Dawson and someone else went out on invitation by a wave of handkerchiefs and had a long talk with five or six Yankees; had quite a pleasant chat about matters in general and some about the war. When they parted, our men told them, while shaking hands, they'd be glad to see them at Manassas again—at which they winced but didn't kick up.[40]

Unfortunately, the respite and familiarity these peaceful moments brought, would not last.

When the temperatures rose and the roads dried in late April 1863, General Hooker drew General Lee's army out of Fredericksburg by holding a defensive position a few miles west of the city. Soldiers exhibited remarkable courage but sustained more loss at the Battle of Chancellorsville in May 1863. Chancellorsville was General Lee's greatest victory and another devastating defeat for the Army of the Potomac. Simultaneous to the campaign on the Rappahannock River, however, the Union Army of the Tennessee besieged General John C. Pemberton's Confederate Army in the city of Vicksburg along the Mississippi River. Men in these armies were from different states, with different commanders, but forged relationships strikingly similar to those developed by their comrades in Virginia. Soldiers' letters and diaries depicted frequent fraternization during the Siege of Vicksburg and between the Battles of Chickamauga and Chattanooga. Different armies composed the ranks of both Union and Confederate forces at these campaigns. At Vicksburg, the Union Army of the Tennessee fought against the Confederate Department of the Mississippi. During Chickamauga, the Union Army of the Cumberland faced the Confederate Army of Tennessee and a corps from the Army of Northern Virginia.[41] This shift in both leadership and troops in the western theater created unstable conditions and different, yet equally frustrating, factions. Soldiers who fought in campaigns outside of Virginia did so under unique circumstances as they navigated different forms of terrain and practiced siege tactics before the armies in the East had done so. The western armies played a vital a role in the grand strategy because the high command required them to cover vast territory, control rivers, and secure important cities. The Confederate armies in the West set up defensive positions to secure their transportation, communication, and supply networks, while Union armies infiltrated deep into Southern territory in an attempt to disrupt these war-making centers.[42] As a result, both Union and Confederate soldiers experienced shortages and felt the privations of overextended supply lines. Soldiers constantly had to remake themselves as they were asked to do the unfathomable. As armies, tactics, and strategy shifted, so too did their day-to-day conditions, and, in order to make up for the difficulties, soldiers sought relief in ways that made sense to them.

The Vicksburg Campaign opened on December 26, 1862, when General William Tecumseh Sherman's XV Corps attempted to assault Vicksburg directly. General Ulysses S. Grant's frontal assault, known as the Battle of Chickasaw Bayou, ended in a defeat for his army when Pemberton's men repulsed the Union advance. Not only was this the first decisive defeat for the Army of the Tennessee but, most significantly, it indicated to Grant, his subordinates, and his men that Vicksburg would not succumb without a Confederate stance. Grant went back to the drawing board, while those at home read of his defeat alongside the major Union defeat in Fredericksburg. Growing antiwar sentiment on the Northern home front angered men in the Army of the Tennessee. Isaac Jackson of the Eighty-Third Ohio wrote, "I hope the people have become fully aroused to their sense of duty and will attend to the double eyed traitors at home while we attend to the open armed enemies of the country down here."[43] Unfortunately, Grant's next plan did not alleviate their sinking morale. In order to gain the heights on the east side of the city, Grant attempted to get across the delta by digging a canal north of the city. This proved to be difficult because of the low, muddy ground, and everything became filled with water. Men on picket duty stood in waist-deep water, and mud delayed supply trains.⁴⁴ According to historian of the campaign Steven Woodworth, "The winter on the Mississippi was like the Continental Army's winter at Valley Forge—discouraged by recent setbacks, betrayed by antiwar agitation on the home front, miserable in their cold wet encampments and dying. Yet this hard experience toughened them and forged them together into a unified and confident fighting force."⁴⁵

One of the most difficult circumstances for men in the Army of the Tennessee was the climate and geography, which tainted water supplies and crippled men with illnesses they had never been exposed to. Men who fought in the Union Army of the Tennessee were first-generation Germans, Chicago laborers, and farm boys from Ohio, Indiana, Illinois, and Iowa. "When we first came down here a great many men were sick and a great many died," Isaac Jackson told his brother.⁴⁶ The majority of soldiers had never experienced the humid swamps of Mississippi and instantly fell victim to dehydration, diarrhea, and heat exhaustion. George C. Burmeister of the Thirty-Fifth Iowa recorded, "The heat is getting almost intolerable, the drops of perspiration are rolling down my body when I am lying still. I am afraid that the heat, the poor water, the meager rations, and the hard work will prove very deleterious to the health of our men."⁴⁷ The winter months, although they provided relief from the heat, did not lessen illness because soldiers who navigated the swamps could not get dry. "As a result," wrote John Loveless, "there is a good many of our boys sick with the chronic diarrhea and fever together and some three or four has died with it and there is five besides that can't live not more than two days with it now in the hospital."⁴⁸ For soldiers, the fear of succumbing to illness constantly loomed and caused them as much anxiety as facing the enemy. "The health of the army does improve much in some regiments, but others are burying their boys every day. Our medical department is much out of order and many are there who have died out of neglect and proper care," noted George K. Pardee of the Forty-Second Ohio while camped at Ballard's Farm outside Vicksburg. Pardee continued, "We have poor places to camp, poor water to use, and a great many little things to contend with. We can all look out for bullets and many of us not get hurt, but we cannot take care of our men and protect ourselves from sickness with all the inconveniences we have to contend with."[49] Invisible microbes tore through the ranks more often than bullets.

With the arrival of spring, troop health improved and the army could maneuver the terrain, allowing for the Army of the Tennessee to do what it did best—conducting an offensive campaign. General Grant moved his army south of Vicksburg along the western bank of the Mississippi while simultaneously moving Union gunboats down the river to offset Confederate artillery and extend their supply line. The Army of the Tennessee then crossed the Mississippi River at Grand Gulf on May 1. John V. Oliver of the Tenth Missouri wrote, "We marched to the river 45 miles below Vicksburg, crossed the river below the gulf on our transports that run the blockade some time ago. This I consider one of the best moves that has been made in the southern army."[50] Before moving toward Vicksburg, Grant sent a portion of his army northeastward to drive General Joe Johnston's Confederate Army of the Tennessee out of Jackson, Mississippi. This maneuver left Pemberton's Army of the Mississippi virtually surrounded in Vicksburg without the possibility of gaining reinforcements from elsewhere. Grant was ready to move westward to Vicksburg and launched a series of frontal assaults on Pemberton's forces. Douglas Richie Bushnell of the Thirteenth Illinois wrote on May 24, "We have made two general assaults on their works and in all instances been repulsed, our losses have been considerable."[51] Instead of continuing frontal assaults, Grant ordered the Army of the Tennessee to "dig in," and thus began the siege of Vicksburg.

For the next six weeks, both Union and Confederate soldiers experienced a style of warfare where a new set of conditions evolved for both the besiegers and the besieged.[52] Because Grant's army held the waterways, roads, and railroads that surrounded Vicksburg, Pemberton's men suffered tremendous food shortages. John Earnest wrote, "Besides this we lived on less than a quarter rations—ate pea bread, mule meat, and rats."[53] Grant knew that by encircling

Vicksburg, time would eventually cause Pemberton's army to capitulate. Mississippian soldier William Pitt Chambers described the severity when he wrote, "When the siege began, we were receiving one-third a ration of meat, and about two thirds of a ration of meal. This was soon greatly reduced. In lieu of the cornmeal, we had cow peas ground and made into bread. . . . Then the bread ceased all together . . . instead of bacon, about 3 or 4 ounces of *mule meat*."[54] Water supplies were also critical in the humid summer climate. "In addition to this, water was scarce and part of the time ponds were the only accessible sources of supply and these were often stirred by hundreds of beef cattle and so hot it almost scalded the throat when swallowed," described J. P. Cannon.[55] Felix Walthall also complained about the lack of water and that the officers were the only ones with access to it. Walthall wrote, "The only drinking water we had, had scum on top of it."[56] With poor water and food came illness. "I have not been well since I have bin hear though I keep going when a man gets sick hear nobody believes that he is sick until he is dying some of our officers do not care no more for you than if you were so much dust and our regimental surgeon has marked some men for duty one day and they die the next," admitted Larkin Weaver to his father.[57] The combination of the shelling and encroachment of the enemy, coupled with starvation, led to a major drop in morale. Confederates knew it was only a matter of time before the Union Army broke through or they starved to death. Chambers captured the essence of these multiple factors when he wrote, "In our regiment a willingness to capitulate soon became quite prevalent. They realized that they were starving; they saw themselves surrounded by a force five times greater than their own; they beheld the enemy entrench himself and build stronger and better forts than ours; and they saw their comrades being shot down every day."[58] Demoralized soldiers like Chambers awaited their fate and exhibited their strength by weathering the storm. Despite this intense combat, men on opposing sides fraternized.

From late May through Pemberton's surrender on July 4, Union and Confederate troops disobeyed orders against contact with the enemy. Fraternization during the siege of Vicksburg materialized because Grant's troops maintained a position within shouting distance of the Confederate Army. Enemies began conversing as early as May 21, as observed by a citizen of Vicksburg, Emma Balfour. While on the lines making cartridges, Ms. Balfour wrote, "Last night after the firing ceased as the Yankees passed in speaking distance of our ranks, our men called out, 'Lend us some coffee for supper, won't you, we will pay you when Johnston comes.' They replied, 'Never mind the coffee, but Grant will take dinner in Vicksburg tomorrow.'"[59] Similarly, Union soldiers reported conversation, as in the case of Illinoisan Chesley Mosman, who wrote, "Skirmishers yell, 'What's the caliber of your gun?' Reb, 'Yankee Caliber.' 'You shoot too high. Little Lower.' 'So that will do.' 'Got Vicksburg yet?' 'How do you like Jeff Davis?' 'Hold a candle for that man to see to shoot by.'"[60] At Vicksburg, soldiers exhibited the same mockery and verbal jousting as at Fredericksburg. Union soldier Theodore Upson wrote, "The Johnnys would call to our men that they were waiting for them to capture the city, and our men would tell them they were in no hurry—that they were prisoners feeding themselves. Sometimes our boys would throw hardtack over the works telling them they did not want them to starve entirely, and the Johnnys would say 'Come to my house Yank when the war is over and I will give you a square meal.'"[61]

This banter, unlike that at Fredericksburg, was not during an encampment but amid a major siege. Men on both sides had orders to fire anytime they saw the enemy. Despite these orders, men took it upon themselves to talk to the enemy. This behavior among soldiers presents an important development. When men were in proximity to one another, regardless of the threat, they conversed. "We are in hearing distance of the enemy as they often come across the words. On one of these occasions, a Yank wanted to know if our rations were not near out. To which one of the 1st Missouri replied; 'O, Dicks, did you ever read the Bible where God gave manna to the children of Israel when in the desert?'" reported Theodore Fisher. "To which the Yank responded; 'O, Johnnie, did you ever read in the Bible where Moses was put in the Bulrushes he couldn't get out either, could he?' 1st Missouri; 'O, yes, a nice young lady came and took him out, you know.'"[62] Fisher went on to write that he hoped Johnston's army would take them out of Vicksburg. These conversations, although less jovial than those during picket duty, highlighted a soldier tendency to interact with the enemy. Because the fighting was continuous, however, soldiers used fraternization to develop a new set of benefits exceptional to siege warfare. These developments are covered in following chapters.

In mid-July a transitionary phase between campaigns ensued, as both armies reorganized and the veterans of Vicksburg marched eastward. After the Union Army of the Tennessee paroled units of Pemberton's Army, the Confederate Department of the Mississippi moved to Jackson in order to link up with General Braxton Bragg's Army of Tennessee. Grant's success at Vicksburg earned him the rank of major general, and General-in-Chief Henry Halleck appointed him commander of all armies in the western theater. Under the advice of Grant, Halleck then appointed William Tecumseh Sherman to command the Army of the Tennessee.[63] Corps from the Army of the Potomac and the Army of Northern Virginia came to Tennessee in the late summer of 1863. The Tennessee Campaign, commonly known as the battles of Chickamauga and Chattanooga, demonstrated how terrain, supply lines, and cohesion between commanders made the difference between victory and defeat. There was more soldier fraternization at Chattanooga than Chickamauga. However, the outcome at Chickamauga set the stage for how and why the Army of Tennessee besieged Grant's forces in the city of Chattanooga. Also, as when General William Rosecrans's Army of the Cumberland navigated the intricate mountainous terrain in pursuit of Bragg's army, they caught glimpses of their enemy, and fraternization occurred.

When Rosecrans's troops began their pursuit toward Chattanooga, they thinly spread out in order to cover the narrow valleys, steep mountain passes, and winding Tennessee River. Inevitably, enemies came into contact with one another at points along the river and streams. George S. Lea of the Seventh Mississippi wrote, "Only four regiments here and have the river to guard for several miles above and below. Our lines is one bank of the river and theirs on the other side. Frequently talking from one side to the other it is a violation of orders but some will do it. They curse us call us damn rebs come over and get coffee, etc. We can see every movement they make and it looks as they did not care. Speak of driving us from our position in a few days very sanguine of success."[64] The Seventh Mississippi fought at Vicksburg and was part of the detachment to assist Bragg. Lea most likely participated or at the very least witnessed fraternization during that campaign. On the other hand, Francis Sherman of the Eighty-Eighth Illinois, part of the Army of the Cumberland, did not fight at Vicksburg but fraternized with Confederates. In a letter to his father Sherman admitted, "The pickets are in plain sight of each other and are continually calling to each other. The other night came the cry across the water, 'Hello, Yank, where is Rosey?' Yank: Upon the hill back there. What do you want to know for? Secesh: Why Bragg has sworn to kill him. Yank: How's he going to do it? Secesh: By running him to death chasing him.' This is all the amusement the boys have on either side, as strict orders are given not to fire on each other."[65] The lighthearted banter, articulated by Sherman, served as a momentary respite from the constant marching and anxiety brought about by the impending battle. More importantly, Sherman's fraternization demonstrated the organic nature of these conversations. Interactions between antagonists developed simultaneously in multiple armies, in different theaters of the war.

When armies encircled one another, enemies faced one another at very close range, with orders to fire. Specifically, at Chattanooga, Atlanta, and Petersburg, both veteran and newly conscripted soldiers alike exhibited the inclination to communicate with their enemy, despite the danger. The majority of fraternization during the Battle of Chattanooga took place prior to the major fighting on November 23–25, 1863. Even though the Army of Tennessee's main body remained on the heights surrounding Chattanooga, the picket lines extended down the slopes and close to the Union line. For exam-

FIG. 3. Union and Confederate soldiers at close distances in the mountains of Tennessee. C. E. T. Hillen, *The War in Tennessee—Union Pickets Approached by Rebels in Cedar Bushes*, December 12, 1863. Library of Congress Prints and Photographs Division. LC-USZ62-96124.

ple, Jabez Banbury described, "I am just ordered on picket with my regiment, a severe task as we had no sleep last night and but little the night before but we will have plenty to keep us awake tonight as our picket line will be but a few rods from the enemy's."[66]

As at other places, soldiers began to speak across the lines. While besieged in the city of Chattanooga, Illinoisan Frederick Hess wrote, "The pickets talked together and made fun. The rebels want to know how the women was getting along in the town and if they hadn't all left yet."[67] Similarly, Joshua Callaway told his wife, "Our pickets and those of the enemy are very close together but do not fire at each other, though they talk together, swear at each other, etc."[68] Soldiers' perception of the enemy changed incrementally. Prewar propaganda described men from the opposite section in the most radical forms. As Jason Phillips puts it, "abstractions of the enemy influenced soldiers' images of the war and its contingencies."[69] Not until soldiers viewed their enemy up close did they realize their similarities, and, as military historian Gerald Linderman argues, "They grew to respect and even admire the enemy."[70] For example, John Kennerly Farris described his experience fraternizing in front of Lookout Mountain as: "Our pickets and the federal pickets stand in sight and speaking distance of each other but never molest each other, but on the other hand are as friends as though they belonged in the same army."[71] As the war churned on, Farris's account depicted how enemies developed a mutual respect for one another. With an inevitable battle looming and both sides visibly war-torn, men stood opposite from men with similar principles of sacrifice and duty.

For the Union armies in Tennessee, they carried momentum as the year 1863 came to a close. After the monumental victory in late November 1863, Grant kept his men in Chattanooga to take full advantage of its resources. Grant, promoted to lieutenant general, took command of all Union forces and relocated to Virginia in order to help the Army of the Potomac take Richmond and destroy Lee's Army of Northern Virginia. The Lincoln administration appointed General Sherman in command of the western armies—Armies of the Tennessee, Cumberland, and Ohio. These three armies proved their worth at Chattanooga. James Henry McBride described the relationship between the armies as "a kind of rivalry existing between Grant, Thomas', and Hookers troops to see who would do the best and they all fought like tigers."[72] Historian Steven Woodworth argues that the Army of the Cumberland and the Ohio adopted the "can-do attitude" shown by the Army of the Tennessee.[73] The morale for the Union troops in Chattanooga was the opposite of their enemy in Dalton. Despite their appreciation of the appointment of Joe Johnston as commander, the loss at Chattanooga demoralized many soldiers in the Army of Tennessee during their winter encampment in Dalton, Georgia. "Our troops are much dispirited and out of heart. A great many of our soldiers have quit and gone home, and others speak pretty boldly of doing so and many will make their words true. But the signs of the present are very depressing upon the already depressed soldier," wrote Farris. "A great many are nearly naked and others are without blankets and all without tents except a few of the lucky."[74] Farris's account summed up the physical and emotional strain on the soldiers in the Army of Tennessee. To make matters worse, the divide between the officers and enlisted men continued to grow. Edward Brown wrote, "Christmas has been disagreeable because the superabundance of drunkenness among those with whom military law forces me to abide. I have never known so much drunkenness among them before."[75] This behavior made it even more difficult for men to salvage any respect that remained for their superiors. "The Col. Commanding the brigade was beastly drunk and so was the colonel commanding the regiment and the officer of the day. Oh the scenes of yesterday were awful to contemplate. . . . guards and officers were cursed and abused by drunken officers . . . no regard was paid to any law or regulations whatever," vented Farris.[76] The breakdown in order caused once patriotic and loyal soldiers to yearn for peace. Chambers, a veteran of Vicksburg, wrote, "An apathy seems to have fallen on our armies and stilled the energies of our people."[77] The sinking morale, as at many other points during the war, was soon replaced by anxiety as the temperatures rose and the roads dried.

Johnston and his Army of Tennessee had to hold their position in the hills northwest of Atlanta. However, General Sherman planned to take his 100,000-man force through Georgia to take Atlanta.[78] In order to do so, instead of frontal assaults, Sherman ordered continuous attacks against Johnston's left flank. He continually positioned his men between Johnston and Atlanta. Thus, Johnston could not "wait out" the summer but instead had to engage and pursue Sherman. This strategy, when launched in May 1864, played out in a series of battles in Georgia at Dalton, Resaca, Adairsville, New Hope Church, Dallas, and Picket's Mill.[79] A Confederate joke shared during fraternization with Union soldiers was, "'Who commanded the Federal Army?' answer, 'General Sherman.' 'Who commanded the Rebel Army?' answer, 'General Sherman, because when he moved, they had to move.'"[80] Despite the quick pace of Sherman's pursuit, soldiers took it upon themselves to shape their environment by reaching out to the enemy on friendly terms. For example, Mississippian Joseph Rand wrote, "Made peace with the Yankees for a while. Talked with them about a half hour."[81] The absence of hostilities made for a "nice day" and set the scene for conversation to take place. For example, New Yorker Charles Houghton, who felt discouraged from not receiving pay in months and from the heat, wrote, "I am on picket today and the rebels are on the other side we talk and joke with them all of the time."[82] Houghton's account provides further evidence of the correlation between demoralization and fraternization and the subsequent relief it provided.

When Sherman split his forces, sending the Ohio and Tennessee Armies to the East and the Army of the Cumberland directly toward Atlanta, this merriment ended almost as quickly as it began. A new set of circumstances arose when the Atlanta Campaign came to fruition on July 22 at the Battle of Atlanta and resulted in a siege that lasted until September 2, 1864. Throughout the month of August, while Union infantry attacked Confederates in Georgia at Ezra Church, Utoy Creek, and Jonesboro, their cavalry attempted to cut Confederate supply lines at Dalton and Lovejoy's Station.[83] Additionally, Union artillery consistently bombarded Atlanta. Confederate soldiers felt the full sting of the siege. On July 18, Jefferson Davis removed Joe Johnston from command and replaced him with General John Bell Hood. The removal of Johnston frustrated the wartorn Army of Tennessee. "About 1 p.m. a circular was brought around the lines and read, imparting the sorrowful news that our beloved commander had been removed and General J. B. Hood placed in command," bemoaned J. P. Cannon. "This a great blow to our cause and has cast a gloom over the whole army. Strong men wept, while others cursed, and not one approved the change. We think it is a terrible mistake of our President. No man in the Confederacy, not even the great Lee himself, could take the place of General Johnston in the confidence and love of the army of Tennessee just at this critical time."[84] Most men loved General Johnston and were very angry about the change in leadership. Southerners' demoralization over Johnston's removal coupled with the siege conditions, in and around Atlanta, only worsened morale. On August 8 Georgian James W. Watkins wrote, "We are seeing hard times. We are on duty every day or night we have been in the ditches 18 days and we have to eat and sleep right in the ditches all the time it rained so hard that everything that we had got wet. There is a grate many of ours men running a way every nite and a grate many is sick in the hospital."[85] Like Watkins, Confederates characterized their experience at Atlanta by the wet, filthy, and lice-ridden trenches they lived in.[86] For example, Lea wrote, "We have to lie in the wet ditches till all of us look as a dog just out of a rabbit hole. Instead of being white we are all red."[87] Lea was at Vicksburg but described Atlanta as "The hardest times now that we have ever seen. Men being killed and wounded every day. I would give a great deal for the campaign to stop much less the war. Oh it is a terrible time with us and I am afraid the worse has not come yet."[88] Lea, a three-year veteran, indicated the difficulties and anxieties soldiers faced during the last year of the war. However, these soldiers in Georgia were not the only armies besieged in the summer of 1864.

When the Petersburg Campaign began in mid-June 1864, General Grant's Army of the Potomac had already spent the previous two months pursuing General Lee's Army of Northern Virginia from the Rappahannock to the James River. Prior to the Overland Campaign, in May 1864, the two armies were at good strength and morale. The Battles of the Wilderness, Spotsylvania, and Cold Harbor left soldiers exhausted from the months of fighting. Due to the fast pace of the Overland Campaign, the armies did not have a chance to rehabilitate the wounded nor bury the dead. After the disaster at Cold Harbor, General Grant ordered his army to bypass Richmond and move south to meet up with Butler's troops outside of Petersburg. General Lee anticipated an attack at Richmond, and while it seemed as a better immediate option for the Union Army, Grant was thinking long term. He knew that the city of Petersburg supplied and fed the Confederate capital because of its position on the James River. When Lee heard Grant's army was on the move, he immediately sought to secure the roads leading into Richmond. On June 14 the Army of the Potomac crossed the James River by pontoon bridge and, by the morning of June 17, the bulk of the Union Army was south of the James.[89] When Lee found out that General Beauregard abandoned his position, he stated, "We must destroy this Army of Grant's before he gets to the James River. If he gets there it will become a siege, and then it will be a mere question of time."[90] Lee's predictions would become a reality when, despite having the advantage of interior lines, his army miscalculated Grant's intention and would soon be cut off from the lower south and surrounded by Union forces.

In the summer of 1864, these armies experienced full-scale siege for the first time. Unlike the previous spring on the Rappahannock, men were under constant fire at Petersburg. Confederate Council A. Bryan mentioned, "If a man shows the tip of his finger they crack away at him—our lines of breastworks are not any more than 150 yards apart and every day adds to the list of killed and wounded."[91] Soldiers on picket duty were no longer in the open but hidden in entrenchments between the main lines of opposing forces with "gopher holes" about 150 feet ahead of that picket line.[92] "Picket duty occupied our time as we lay at Bermuda Hundred, and this duty became very strenuous. It is one thing to lose one night of sleep each week during a series of several weeks; it is quite another to give up sleep regularly every alternate night for several weeks in succession," described William Reed Moore.[93] It was also difficult to get rations and supplies to those on picket duty. Bryan observed, "Where as our pickets now are if the enemy charges us it will be impossible to get out they are in front of our breastworks about 40 yards and in short range of the enemy's whole line—what water they carry in has to last them until they are relieved (24 hours) and it becomes so hot in the tin canteen you can hardly drink it. They have holes about 3 feet deep that they have to lie in and they have to use it as a privy."[94] Soldiers' daily routine in the Virginia trenches consisted of building earthworks, standing guard, and attempting to find comfort amid all the chaos. Despite persistent fatigue, thirst, and threat of imminent danger on the picket line, men sustained communications with the enemy.

The trench lines at Petersburg allowed antagonists to observe one another at close range. James Beard noted, "We are very close to the rebs here in many places the picket lines is not over ten yards apart. They are Mississippians and belong to Pickets Division they are smart clean looking fellows."[95] This proximity allowed Beard to humanize the enemy opposite of him. Familiarity enabled soldiers to speak to one another. Daniel Emerson Hurd wrote, "We went down opposite the city on picket duty and chatted with the rebel pickets on the other side 'hello, reb,' 'hello, yank,' etc."[96] In a letter to his parents, William Winkleman documented, "We are now on picket duty every other day and our pickets are so close with the rebel pickets that we talk together very easy. I stood right facing a rebel picket and he would always bid us the time of the night like nine oclock Yankees, ten oclock Yankees." Winkleman continued, "Sometimes they would tease us by calling us bull beef because they captured several hundred steers from us at Chandhore Valley Railroad but then we catch them by saying 'SHERMAN!' because he attacked them afterwards and captured a great many more."[97] Winkleman's experience on picket duty demonstrated that, while outside the realm of officer discipline and surveillance, time and time again, soldier discourse took on a life of its own.

Similar to conversations between antagonists at other points in the war, on picket duty at Petersburg the mood was often jocular. While on the front lines, Virginian James Thomas Perry noted, "My post was a pit about 250 yards to the right and Southwest of the site of Ware Bottom Church. The Yankees were remarkably quiet all night. There was only one of the usual exchanges between the pickets that I heard in which the Yankee had the advantage—ours making a noise in imitation of a calf and the Yankee telling him to come over for he had a cow for him to suck."[98] Consistently, Union and Confederate soldiers poked at one another's leaders, commanders, and regional differences. "On picket we heard a loud crack, we looked around to see a high pine tree in the ravine. The Johnnies shouted 'what the devil you coming over there, springing another mine? And we replied 'no, nothing but the props falling out from under the confederacy! Old Abe is splitting rails to transport Jeff Davis to Europe on!," noted George Hubbard in his diary.[99] Jokes often mocked generals and politicians but, more importantly, demonstrated an awareness of their opposition's mutual lot in the ranks. William Ray of the Iron Brigade stated, "The Rebs and our boys got into conversation this evening, our boys cheering for Abe and they for Jeff. And our boys for Little Mac and they the same. They seemed to be pleased when we cheered for him. Then our boys cheered for Butler and they said to hell with him and so on."[100] Men commonly inquired as to where the others were from. "One of them said 'hello you're a fine looking chap' and I said 'hello johnny' he laughed at that he asked me where I was from and I told him I was a Philadelphia boy, he said he was both in Phila. across from the arch street theatre he was a courier a dispatch carrier for generals," said John L. Smith. "He was a nice looking fellow I told him that Mobile was taken for fun and he said no sir! He belonged to the 2nd Florida and he was a Sergeant and said a good many things too numerous to mention. Another Reb came up and this one said 'we will meet again.'"[101] These scenes of enemies talking as old friends, then returning to their positions to fight against one another, certainly demonstrate the exceptionalism of these fraternal bonds. In these fleeting moments soldiers quickly shifted from friend back to foe.

When the leadership placed soldiers near one another for an extended amount of time, men keenly observed their enemy. Once soldiers encountered their enemy in small groups, they became more relatable. As a result, soldiers' understanding of one another became more personal. Men were able to situationally compartmentalize their relationship to the enemy. Soldiers differentiated between times when they were in large columns trying to kill one another and occasions when groups from both sides were isolated from their main bodies under similar conditions. This tendency explains why interactions did not cease when siege tactics required soldiers to constantly fire on picket duty but also why men were able to have these conversations with the enemy and return to fighting them. Soldiers' discourse marked their ability, in certain instances, to identify with one another. Interestingly, jokes and banter shared between the lines was only the first step in building a mutually beneficial system outside the range of officer control. Conversation was the bridge on which soldiers built an even more enticing characteristic of fraternization: a trade network.

3

Trade

Over the breastworks went Rebel and Yank and met between lines and commenced laughing and talking and you would have thought that old friends had met after a long separation. Some were talking earnestly together, some swapping coffee for tobacco, some were wrestling, some boxing, others trading knives.

—LeGrand James Wilson, Assistant Surgeon, Forty-Second Mississippi

Our pickets are in sight of those of the enemy nearly all along the lines. They are continually firing upon each other. Many interesting incidents occur between them. They are in talking distance and are frequently carrying on conversations. The Warwick Creek separates them and the other day one of our men made a proposition to one of the Yankees to meet him half way and converse a little to themselves. It was accepted, so rafts were made and they met in the middle of the creek. They swapped coats & pocket books. Our picket gave the other one a palmetto button for a splendid canteen. He next gave him some tobacco for coffee. The major came down about that time and caught them together. Picking up a gun he ordered his man back to his quarters and told the Yankee that if he did not get back pretty quick he would shoot him. You had better believe he left.

—Private Tally N. Simpson, Third South Carolina Vol. Infantry

Near Gaines Mill, Virginia, in the summer of 1862, Confederate captain Robert Gaines Haile wrote, "I had not been there long before one of the Yankees advanced, waves his cap, and made signs for someone to meet him. He also asked how we were off for provisions. Ferguson replied that we had an abundance of everything except coffee, that article was not as abundant as we could with. The Yankee then told him he would bring him some of that if he would accept it. In about an hour, he returned and sure enough brought both paper and coffee."[1] Haile's encounter depicted the great lengths to which the Union soldier went to honor his promise and bring his enemy coffee. The material goods in many ways stood as a symbol of good intentions. Soldiers exchanged what little resources they had at their disposal, most notably coffee or tobacco. The Union naval blockade prevented Confederate privates from drinking coffee on a regular basis, just as the Southern tobacco crop did not typically make it into the hands of Union privates. Thus, fraternization became a way to obtain these commodities—particularly as both coffee and tobacco comforted men and helped alleviate fatigue. Soon it became known that picket duty presented opportunities to obtain these items. For example, South Carolinian David Logan Jackson wrote, "Our regiment has considerable picket duty to perform now, our Yankee friends are generally very pacific towards us proffering to give us coffee for tobacco, or sweet potatoes."[2] For some men, however, obtaining these commodities did not end the meeting. It often was the starting point and, thus, not the sole reason behind the barter. Walter F. Moring described, "Yankee pickets in full view of us—talk with them nearly all the time—Charley Carr trades a newspaper to one for sugar and coffee. One of our men waded across the river and made the exchange on the other banks—two Yankees came down and we had a long talk."[3] Men smoked and drank coffee, greasing the wheels of sociability. The trade established a space for emotions to be shared. Repeatedly, during these meetings, men expressed that if it were up to the rank and file, the war would be over. The development of trade networks evolved into fraternal spaces where men empathized with one another's hardships and acknowledged that affinity through "talks of peace."

The most frequently documented scene of fraternization on the Rappahannock, after the Battle of Fredericksburg, was the trade of coffee and tobacco. The need for these commodities was the primary attraction to fraternization, first of all, because it was winter and, second, because they helped alleviate sleepiness. After trading, a Mississippian professed, "For tobacco, our pickets trade coffee, an essential drink if one is to keep awake and warm."[4] To offset fatigue Confederates longed for coffee, and Federals yearned for tobacco to smoke. In order to get these items across the river, soldiers constructed miniature sailboats. "On the banks of the river, just below the city, we have a signal station. Being down there, the other morning, I observed what appeared to be a shirt-tail stretched between two sticks, which were attached to a log of wood, floating in the middle of the river," wrote Egbert Rogers.[5] Rogers's description indicated men used what they had—pieces of clothing, wood scraps, sticks on the river bank, and so on to make the trade possible. Men often named their boats "Billy" and "Johnny" or "The Monitor" and "The Merrimack," all in good fun. Anson Shuey wrote, "Our pickets and the rebel pickets talk together nearly all the time, and they make little boats and our men sent coffee over to the rebels and they sent tobacco in return."[6] Soldiers looked forward to picket duty in the hopes a little boat would come over with a fresh supply of energizing material. "A Mississippian had a small boat about three inches deep and two feet long, with a rudder and sail affixed and everything in trim. We took it down to the river, waved our hand [at the Yankees], and received the same signal in return," detailed South Carolinian Tally Simpson. "We then loaded her with papers and sent her across. She landed safely and was sent back with a cargo of coffee."[7] Boats allowed men to get these highly coveted commodities and trade notes. In his observations of the exchanges, Confederate Chaplain James Sheeran wrote, "At various places along this line our boys were amusing themselves by sending across the river their little schooner, laden with tobacco and other commodities to the yankee pickets who lined the banks of the Rappahannock, receiving in exchange for Yankee papers, coffee, etc."[8] Sheeran then went on to claim, "I sent a note over in one of our little schooners, inquiring if there were any Catholic Chaplains in Hooker's Army, and received from a Yankee Colonel an affirmative answer."[9] Sheeran's actions, even as a noncombatant, showed how the trade of commodities allowed men to identify with those on opposite sides.

Once word spread among men in the ranks, soldiers went to picket duty hoping to trade. Union men spoke positively about their experience trading with the enemy. "The Rebels were exceedingly communicative and cordial, and anxious to exchange the weed for the more wholesome luxuries of hardtack and coffee," exclaimed a New Jerseyan.[10] On the opposite side of river, the Confederates had a similar type of experience. As described by Private Henry P. Garrison of the Eighteenth Mississippi Infantry in a letter to his cousin, "The boys told me that they were having a good time with the Yankees while on picket—trading with them every day, swapping tobacco for coffee."[11] Many accounts, like Reeves's and Garrison's, characterized fraternization as positive and happy, a major change from the depictions of battle. Men used words such as "jovial," "good," and "peaceable" to describe these interactions. "We are above the City of Fredericksburg on the River we are kept on picket duty all the time. Times are quiet hear and peaceable we are very close to them (that is the Yankees) very small river between us we very often talk to each other change tobacco for coffee," described an Alabamian. "They are very anxious for peace they think this war will soon end which I hope will be true for I am tired enough of it I want to get back home once more I am very tired living in the woods."[12] Fraternization became popular; it flowed continuously through the different shifts. "Our boys would go over two or three times a day as long as we were out," wrote Henry B. Wood.[13]

Because fraternization became so frequent during the early months of 1863, the high command passed special ordinances against it. When General Joseph Hooker took over control of the Army of the Potomac, he instituted laws prohibiting fraternization. General Robert E. Lee issued two orders: one was to destroy all boats found anywhere, and the second was to arrest any Yankee found in Confederate lines.[14] "Orders most stringent have been read to the army within a few days past," declared Virginian John Dooley, "forbidding any communications upon the part of our pickets with those of the enemy."[15] When Guy Everson sent a boat of papers toward Union lines, "they were detected and the boat was captured. The officer had gone with the boat to the headquarters of General Patrick."[16] Officers attempted to catch men who fraternized by ordering roll call in the middle of the day. Soldiers witnessed arrests on the picket line. "Two of our men went over some days ago with tobacco to exchange for coffee and sugar but when they reached the other bank the Yankees marched them off and they have not been seen since," wrote Murdoch John McSween.[17] To an officer, soldier fraternization was an indicator that he did not have control over his men. And like other forms of forbidden resistance, those caught fraternizing faced a court-martial.

Lieutenant George Kessel of the Sixty-Second New York Infantry was charged with two violations: "Relieving the enemy with victuals," which was in violation of the 56th article of war, and "Holding correspondence with, and giving intelligence to the enemy," in violation of the 57th article of war.[18] On April 9, 1862, while in command of his picket guard, Kessel allowed his men to send sugar and coffee in a small boat across the Rappahannock to the enemy pickets. Additionally, Kessel allowed his men to send printed and written information on those boats as well. Private Michael Collins served as a witness and claimed, "I have heard officers on duty there prohibit their men from communication with the enemy. I saw him on the banks of the river with two or more men and was present there when a boat sailed from this side." When asked, "Would you believe him capable of willfully giving aid and information to the enemy?," defense witness Captain William Ackerman of the Sixty-Second New York stated, "I don't believe he would." The court ruled guilty on all charges, and Kessel was sentenced to be cashiered and to forfeit all pay and allowances that were then or would become due to him thereafter from the United States. Brigadier General Frank Wheaton served as president of the court and concluded: "The Court is thus lenient as it does not doubt the loyalty of the accused but believed that lack of judgment led to the commission of the crime he stands convicted." The ruling of the court, in particular the court's recognition that it did "not doubt the loyalty of the accused," speaks to the broader implications of fraternization.[19] Compared to desertion, insubordination, and other more radical forms of dissent, fraternization did not carry the stigma nor the penalties of disloyalty.

Most soldiers, however, got away with fraternizing. Under the cloak of concealment men felt empowered by their resistance. Men's candor about fraternization in their letters and diaries, both about knowing it was illegal and their choice to partake in it, demonstrated they were not ashamed of their actions. In closing accounts of fraternization with notations such as "this visiting is positively against orders," soldiers admitted a sense of pride in doing it.[20] Soldiers made it a point to denote that fraternization happened away from officer presence. "This sending things across the river goes on when the officers are absent," a New Jerseyan told his sister.[21] This conscientious disregard of orders represented soldiers' pushback against the military hierarchy. Because their enemy was doing the same, these interactions represented a fraternal subculture exclusively for those of the rank and file. However, the trade across the Rappahannock was easier to facilitate due to orders against firing. As the tactics evolved, and men were asked to hunker in trenches, both the besiegers and the besieged had seemingly little reason to risk their lives to honor these trades.

Miraculously, men continued to exchange goods at the sieges of Vicksburg, Chattanooga, Atlanta, and Petersburg. Due to the tightening of supply lines, fraternization aided an immediate need of certain commodities. But, soldiers now fraternized amid orders of continuous firing. Men, in turn, carved out spaces for these transactions to occur. "Adaptability, more than any other trait," claims historian Peter Carmichael, "best describes how Union and Confederate soldiers navigated their world on a daily basis."[22] At night, under the mask of darkness, soldiers at the front would meet in the neutral zone in between one another's lines. When the fraternization occurred at Fredericksburg, it had been weeks since the fight-

FIG. 4. The intricacies of these earthworks demonstrate how men were separated from their officers and positioned close to their enemy. *Federal Entrenchments in Front of Vicksburg*. Library of Congress Prints and Photographs Division. LC-DIG-ppmsca-35295.

ing had ceased, and it was clear to the men that fighting would not occur again until the spring. During sieges, however, men shifted back and forth between fighting and fraternization, sometimes several times in the same day. Soldiers who fraternized at sieges had the ability to quickly shed the emotions of battle.

General Grant's Army of the Tennessee attempted to break through the Confederate line at Vicksburg. On May 22, 1863, General Pemberton's Confederates repulsed the attack. Grant's casualties included 502 killed, 2,550 wounded, and 147 missing, in comparison to roughly 500 Confederate casualties.[23] That very evening, while their comrades lay dying around them, men put down their guns, talked, and traded with the enemy that hours earlier they had tried to kill. "Soon dark comes & being so hushed, our boys begin to talk across to the enemies pickets, who are about 200 yards off," and "one of our boys met a federal picket on half-way-grounds and held a conversation with him and got a yankee paper, some coffee, etc," observed Missourian Robert Caldwell Dunlap.[24] "The federal privates told our boys that 'these men with their shoulder straps on could not compel them to make another charge on our works.'"[25] After the deadly day of fighting, this group of soldiers did not blame their enemy for the loss of comrades and their current state. Rather, as suggested by the Union soldier's remark, their commanders were responsible. This behavior suggests many infantrymen became desensitized to combat and did not take the damage inflicted by their enemy personally but instead understood it was a soldier's duty.

These quick transitions between fighting and fraternizing continued throughout late May when the heaviest fighting during the campaign took place. "Conversations occur nightly between friends on the opposite sides. Two Missionary brothers held a conversation very friendly—one sent the other coffee and whiskey. Then the [*sic*] parted with an oath and an exclamation from one that he would 'blow the other's head off tomorrow.' How unnatural all this is. The commanders' object to this intercourse, but it is impossible they say in two armies so near to prevent it altogether," wrote civilian Emma Balfour.[26] Her consternation over fraternization demonstrates why these interactions seem so odd. To an outsider, it was impossible to fathom how enemies tried to kill one other, mingled as old friends, and returned to firing. Theodore Upson documented his participation in these exchanges from a soldier's perspective. "We have pushed our skirmish lines up till we are pretty close to the Johnnys. A Johnny called, 'Say Yank, got anything to trade?' When I got to him there were two more lying down behind the rock. I said, 'Do you want to capture me?' 'No, we won't hurt you. Got any coffee?'" wrote Upson. At this point, Upson gave the Confederates a pound of coffee and they in return gave him a log of tobacco and an Atlanta paper. The exchange concluded with a handshake and the Confederate said, "Good Luck Yank! Come again sometime. I hope you won't git hurt in any of our fights."[27] Upson analyzed the situation in his diary. "The soldiers of both sides seemed to have lost any feelings of hatred towards each other, and our boys say it was nothing unusual for men on both sides to come out of their works and trade and talk with each other," explained Upson.[28] The more frequently fraternization happened, the less surprising and more predictable it became. In addition to telling his wife about his health and the weather, T. H. Kemp of the Fourteenth Mississippi Regiment wrote, "This morning I drank a cup of sweetened coffee with a Yankee."[29] For Kemp, fraternization was not a mark of dishonor or embarrassment. Instead, he viewed it as interesting and worthy of sharing with his wife, but also a standard part of the day.

The situation for the Department of the Mississippi grew desperate by the first week of July. "We endured all the hardships that ever mortal man did for 48 days and nights. We had to give up for the lack of provisions to live upon. Everything was eaten that would sustain life during the siege we were forced to surrender," confessed Mississippian James Palmer.[30] When the Union line became separated from them by only a parapet, Confederate soldiers knew surrender was virtually inevitable. William Chambers penned, "The long, hot dreary days and nights of toil and danger were telling on the men. Emaciated by hunger, worn out by constant watching and utterly skeptical as to any promised hopes of relief . . . how useless it was to prolong the struggle."[31] Because Confederates were so weakened from hunger, a counterattack on the approaching Federal troops was seemingly impossible. When General Pemberton surrendered on July 4, 1863, fraternization did not end with the fighting. Once the white flags rose from the parapets, Union troops came over their works and met with Confederates in the neutral zone. Steven Woodworth acknowledged, "Along the perimeter, Union and Confederate troops intermingled and fraternized freely, talking over the siege."[32] We might think that both the pang of surrender and the destruction of Vicksburg would be enough to keep Confederates away from the enemy who defeated them. However, the opposite occurred, and men intermingled freely. "The wharf is filled with Confederate and Federal soldiers as if no hostilities ever existed between them," expressed Missourian Theodore Fisher.[33] After six weeks of terrible siege, soldiers surprisingly wanted to spark up conversations. Isaac Jackson wrote to his siblings, "All during the day the forts on both sides covered with men, parties met halfway between the forts and had quite a social time indeed."[34] Perhaps the Confederates' tendency to make amends was mostly because they knew Union men had rations. "Rebels in good spirits. Trading coffee for sugar with the rebels and having a good deal of sport with them," wrote Isaac Vanderwarker III.[35] Despite the massive defeat that signified an end to Southern control of the Mississippi River, Confederate soldiers appeared to celebrate the end of hostilities. Vermonter Albert Merrifield highlighted the intermixing during the surrender: "The remainder of the day was occupied by the officers in making out the certificates or papers of the surrender, while the soldiers on both sides were allowed to meet midway between the parapet, exchanging papers and bread and chatting as friendly as though all had been pleasant and peaceful for the six weeks just passed."[36] Merrifield's observations suggest Confederates' relief over the end of fighting and access to Union goods temporarily outweighed the loss of Vicksburg.

From August 1863 through the end of the war, infantrymen in the largest armies spent a significant amount of their fighting days as part of a siege. However, prior to besiegement, as demonstrated by the armies at Vicksburg, when armies pursued one another across the landscape, they often caught glimpses of one another. Rosecrans's army had to traverse the Cumberland Plateau and the Smokey Mountains, specifically a long ridge that extended eighty-five miles south of the Tennessee River called Lookout Mountain.[37] This region, known as "the southern heartland," linked the Appalachian Mountains and the upper South to Atlanta and the lower South via the vital railroad junction at Chattanooga. Thus, Bragg's army could not guard every road leading to Chattanooga, and the Army of the Cumberland crossed the Tennessee virtually untouched. When men in these armies traversed these winding roads, and small groups of enemies encountered one another, they sought and exchanged commodities to alleviate fatigue. John Kennerly Farris, who felt the effects of poor rations and clothing, observed, "They trade with each other exchanging coffee for tobacco and they would be carried on extensively, but it is against orders for them to talk to each other."[38] Chesley Mosman, who also fraternized at Chickamauga, experienced a similar situation to that of Farris when he wrote, "The pickets of each army go down to this stream for water and it not infrequently happens that squads of men from each side go down at the same time and in cases of this kind they confront each other face to face about five paces apart, the little stream separating them. A good deal of chafing generally occurs and they swap paper, knives, and trade coffee for tobacco."[39] In this scene, the soldiers used mementos to signify the meeting. When the traditional items were not available, men swapped anything they had on them. A few days later, Mosman stated, "Many of our boys went to the right of our brigade picket line and talked to and traded with the enemy's pickets. Pen knives and coffee are in great demand in the southern confederacy. I went after rations. Paid $6.00 for a hat."[40] Because Mosman wanted food, which Union armies typically had, the extent to which weakened supply lines affected the troops was evident.

The trade en route to Chickamauga was out of convenience, whereas the trade at Chattanooga occurred out of necessity. For the Union Army of the Cumberland, the month of October 1863 was characterized by hunger. During his retreat to Chattanooga, Rosecrans abandoned his supply lines, and Bragg held the roads that led to Atlanta and Nashville. Additionally, Bragg's army entrenched itself on the high ground at Missionary Ridge and Lookout Mountain.[41] As a result, the Army of Tennessee surrounded the Army of the Cumberland at Chattanooga. For the next four weeks, the Union troops failed to receive proper food. The Army of the Cumberland became quickly demoralized because of the lack of rations, exposure to the elements, and the fear of the sacrifices needed to assault their enemy on high ground. Ohioan David Ayers described that "I consider that I am nothing but a slave and a target in the hands of a gigantic [?], nothing else."[42] The expression "nothing but a slave" symbolized the lack of agency Union troops faced while surrounded at Chattanooga. Historian of the campaign Peter Cozzens writes, "Nearly five weeks of siege had left both the besieged and the besiegers not only hungry and sick but bored and anxious; many found it difficult to decide which was harder to bear, the acute physical suffering or the more subtle emotional strain."[43] James Henry McBride of the Seventy-Fourth Ohio noted in his diary that rations were very bad and he hoped people at home understood their sacrifice. "This Army has been on very slim rations some days the men had to go without any things to eat, people at home have no idea what the men here have to endure but we were willing to bear even more for the sake of holding Chattanooga," McBride wrote.[44] Because both armies were unhappy with their lack of supplies, soldiers sought relief in making a choice to fraternize. Frederick Hess of the 104th Illinois wrote about his hunger, patriotism, and fraternization at Chattanooga. In a letter to his wife, Hess wrote, "We didn't get quite two crackers yesterday morning and a piece of pork it wasn't any more than enough for breakfast and it is all we get until the teams can cross but that is nothing it is all in a soldiers life and it is for the union."[45] While he awaited Grant's "cracker line," Hess felt the effects of the siege but continued to remain committed. However, in addition to writing about his hunger, he also wrote about instances where he fraternized with Confederates. In one instance Hess noted, "The rebels keep quiet around here and the pickets exchange papers every day."[46] Privation and anxiety during sieges caused men to reach across the lines for comfort and commodities. This behavior, however, was not limited to besieged soldiers in western armies.

The siege at Petersburg saw rampant fraternization due to the lack of material supplies, particularly for the Confederates. Access to food, clothing, water, and shelter stood as a determinant of morale. "Patriotism is like some other sensation dependent a great deal upon the condition of the larder, and a hungry stomach," admitted Confederate soldier John West Haley.[47] Because the Army of the Potomac surrounded Petersburg, food could not be transported to Confederate soldiers inside the city. Union soldiers were well aware of the Confederate privations and showed compassion to their enemy while on picket duty. According to a private in the Ninth Louisiana, "A starving soldier crawled out between the lines one day after a sympathetic Yankee held up a large chunk of meat and offered it to him. He was rewarded with meat, hardtack, bread, and coffee, which he brought back to his appreciative comrades."⁴⁸ Aside from food, the second most necessary material good was clothing and the protection it provided from the elements. "I think that we will have more suffering in the Army this winter than we have ever had before because of the greater exposure and the scarcity of wood," wrote confederate James Jones.⁴⁹ Although the Confederate Army faced uniform shortages from the onset of the war, the lack of Southern manufacturing ability took a toll on Confederate soldiers during the winter in Petersburg. A Maine soldier, while on picket duty, described a Confederate as, "The most forlorn picture of humanity was a Confederate deserter trudging along in the pouring rain. These emaciated, filthy men, clothed in tattered scraps, many barefooted or with their feet bound in rags, old carpets or quilts covering their shoulders."⁵⁰ Inadequate food and exposure to the elements tested the wills of even the most steadfast soldiers.

The men who previously traded across the Rappahannock spent the remainder of the war in trenches. Soldiers took it upon themselves to gain supplies that were not readily available and used what they had to barter with their enemy. After fraternizing with North Carolinians, Charles Wellington Reed wrote, "They are very affable with our boys during the last two days exchanging papers, tobacco, and their soft bread for our coffee and hardtack."⁵¹ Instead of constructing toy boats, men now snuck into the "neutral zone" between the lines under the cover of darkness. Marion Hill Fitzpatrick explained, "Our boys give them tobacco and cornbread for crackers and knives, soap, pockette books, etc. I gave one of them the other day a plug of tobacco for a pockette knife and six crackers."⁵² By the fall of 1864, it was evident Confederate troops lacked full rations because deserters fled to Union lines to relieve starvation. "Deserters were so plenty in our lines," wrote Federal John West Haley, "as many as 20 sometimes coming in one evening. They complained that the food was mighty scarce over there."⁵³ However, some Confederate soldiers saw fraternization as a way to receive commodities without deserting. And Union soldiers, after being fired upon, continued to help them. Haley wrote, "On picket, the rebs threw a few shells at us but no one was hit. After this we went out and carried on a little trading with our friends from the South. We gave them pork, hard tack and coffee for tobacco, the supply of which seemed to be without limit."[54] Perhaps Haley was able to differentiate between the Confederate artillery who shelled them and the infantry in their immediate front. Or, by the end of the war, men became hardened to constant fire. Either way, Haley's experience verified soldiers' propensity to speedily transition from fighting to fraternizing.

Like in Tennessee, when men in Virginia did not have food to trade, they also bartered any type of regalia or trinket they had available. The trade of these items demonstrated that the ritual of exchange sometimes signified more than just the need for a quick fix of highly coveted coffee or tobacco. Francis Bayol wrote, "Ned Pareture and myself with several others, meet two of the Yankee pickets and chatted a while and exchanged buttons and different little tricks. One gave me an envelope with his address on it. I sent it home yesterday in a letter."[55] Unlike other forms of resistance that soldiers tended to keep secret from comrades and friends, soldiers openly sent these items home. Union soldiers gave Confederates their overcoats, and Southerners gave their enemy letters to mail north. Private Truehart noted, "Some 4 or 5 of our boys have actually traded horses with the pickets theirs being government, and ours private horses—we giving a mean old poor horse for a fine fat one—the yanks saying that all he wanted was a rebel horse. We then frequently exchange buttons, or any other little thing we happen to have, just as a memento."[56] Because soldiers sent these items home or kept them throughout their service, these keepsakes served as a memory of their encounter with the enemy. "About sunset I went out in front of my post and had an interview with a Johnny Reb. He advanced half way and I the other half. He wanted something that belonged to the Yankees but what should I have? I suggested to him that I should swap hats with him and so he let me have it," mentioned John West Haley.[57] But keeping goods, such as a Confederate hat, which could be detected during inspection, was a risk. The exchange of trinkets materialized fraternization, suggesting that soldiers viewed it as a worthwhile experience. John L. Smith noted, "We sat there for a good while, and went 7 times yesterday and traded with them when we parted we shook hands and said good bye Johnny and take care of yourself and he said good bye Yank and do the same. I got the Johnny to give me a ring, he said a little girl gave it to him. Send your letter with this stamp, the Reb gave me it."[58] The items Smith alluded to in his letter provided no tangible benefit for a soldier, but possibly an intrinsic value. The excitement over the trade of seemingly insignificant novelties suggests these young men were curious and intrigued about men on the other side. "Our boys give them tobacco and cornbread for crackers and knives, soap, pockette books, etc. I gave one of them the other day a plug of tobacco for a pockette knife and six crackers. . . . I swapped my old knife yesterday to one of our sharpshooters for a neat little knife that he got from a yank. It has a crosshandle with U.S. on it," wrote Virginian Marion Hill Fitzpatrick in a letter to his wife.[59] When taken at face value, these interactions appeared simply as a method to break up the boredom of camp, but in actuality they symbolized how fraternization created some semblance of normalcy in a chaotic environment. Subconsciously, those tokens represented a soldier's choice, something he rarely had as an enlisted man.

Officers on both sides saw these exchanges as counterproductive and continued to issue orders against fraternization. Because this was an unforeseen consequence of warfare, the more men fraternized, the more the high command enforced measures to stop it. When the picket lines were close together, the commanding generals passed special orders against intercourse between enemies. When a unit came to the front lines for picket duty, officers would read these orders and continuously send "officers of the day" to the front to deter men from fraternizing. Nevertheless, it kept happening, and men were caught. Officers punished soldiers in front of their units, and when it became unclear whether the officer on the post had allowed the fraternization or not, their cases went to the court-martial. At Port Royal, South Carolina, in January 1863, Union soldiers crossed the Coosaw River by boat to converse and trade items with Confederate pickets. When they were caught, Corporal Albert C. Berry was reduced in rank, and Private Albert D. W. Emerson was ordered to solitary confinement for seven days with only bread and water along with a forfeiture of two months' pay.[60] Similarly, James Wait of the Sixty-Seventh Ohio swam across the river between Folly Island and Morris Island, South Carolina. He stayed within Confederate lines for five minutes and traded. Wait was found guilty of violating the 57th article of war and was sentenced to two months hard labor.[61] Others were also sentenced to hard labor for fraternizing. Private John H. Longbottom of the 126th Ohio was found guilty for trading with the enemy at Petersburg and sentenced to three months hard labor with a ten-dollar fine per month.[62] Some men were punished by public humiliation in order to deter others from fraternizing. For trading on the Rapidan River with the enemy, Second Lieutenant Charles Roberts's sentence was read aloud in the General Orders, and Cavalryman Marshall St. Germaine had to stand on a barrel for four hours per day for two days in front of his regimental headquarters.[63] Despite these crackdowns, more men got away with fraternizing than were caught. If commanders themselves did not want to be on the front lines and sent their men instead to guard the army's main body, they would not be able to fully regulate it.

Undoubtedly, men who traded and went into enemy lines were caught. Private G. F. Baum went to the Confederate lines at Petersburg to trade. The officer of the day, Sergeant William Fisher, caught him returning to his post. Despite being found guilty, the court only docked Baum one month's pay.[64] On the other hand, Private Paul Frank was caught by Confederate officers while trading within their lines. Frank was thus tried for desertion and sentenced to death. His mother wrote General Meade asking to spare his life, which he did, and Frank spent the remainder of the war in hard labor at Fort Delaware and was released on November 11, 1865.[65] Frank's sentence was one of the strictest issued for fraternizing, demonstrating officers' growing angst over the behavior late in the war. It also illustrated the risk associated with these choices. On the other hand, some men walked free. On August 29, 1864, Private John O'Dell went in between the lines, exchanged coffee for tobacco with a Confederate soldier, and was caught by his officer upon returning to the lines. O'Dell claimed, "I did not know of any order contrary to holding communication with the enemy for I had received no such orders," and had he known it was wrong, he never would have gone out. The court acquitted O'Dell.[66] In October 1864 two privates of the Twentieth Indiana, McDonough Harmes and Charles Homan, were tried for allowing a Confederate to come into their lines and visit their picket pit. A witness from their regiment claimed he was on picket at the time and never saw a rebel. The statement proved to be enough evidence, as both Harmes and Homan were acquitted.[67] The inconsistency of the rulings, based upon hearsay and witness testimony rather than physical evidence, further demonstrates the difficulties the high command had in both understanding and controlling soldier fraternization. It also represented a way common soldiers, when called as witnesses, protected both their fellow comrades in the rank and file and the trade networks they had established with the enemy.

Despite these crackdowns against fraternization, soldiers did not oblige and developed new methods to circumnavigate officer control. "Among the tricks resorted to by the enemy to hold communication was this: they would write anything they desired to communicate upon a small piece of paper and roll it around a Minnie and throw it across the line," wrote a Confederate private. "One of these missiles brought over read: 'Johnny—will you trade papers with us? We have all about the capture of the Alabama, the raid on Harpers Ferry, etc. Meet me half way; you need not be afraid of our shooting you. We can have a friendly game of euchre and wind up with whiskey."[68] Because soldiers carried out fraternization for their own purposes, they sought ways to maintain this system. James Beard described, "In the night we talk to them, trade papers, we can write on a piece of paper what we want to trade, roll

FIG. 5. Union and Confederate soldiers come out from their earthworks and meet between the lines to barter items and discuss the war. Edwin Forbes, *Pickets Trading between the Lines*. Library of Congress Prints and Photographs Division. Morgan collection of Civil War drawings, LC-USZ62-6210.

it around a cartridge and toss it into their pits and they will do the same with us."[69] Beard's experience represented the actions soldiers took in order to uphold these mutual trade agreements. In a letter to his mother, John Smith wrote, "There is a ravine we go down that the rebs come up it and our officers cant see us and there officers cant see them, so we trade there and set down and have a chat there were 7 rebs there when I went down the last time and 4 of our feller. I sat there for over an hour and a half talking with them."[70] Smith continued, "Did you get the paper I sent you a Reb paper, I was on picket yesterday and I traded papers here is the note they stuck on a stick in between the 2 picket lines—I went out and got it, take care of it."[71] Interestingly enough, Smith not only sent his mother the paper but asked her to preserve it. The extent to which men protected and documented their ability to fraternize proved the value these exchanges held for them.

80   TRADE

Regardless of the place—picket duty, on the march, in trenches—swapping goods fostered very meaningful conversations between enemies. The content went beyond the banter and wit that opened the lines of communication. Before the war, fraternal spaces allowed men to "vent their hostilities."[72] When men carved out these spaces to trade with their enemy, they could openly discuss their thoughts and frustrations. "We met just half ways so while we were trading two more of the rebs came and we had a good talk together about the war," wrote William Winkleman after his experience fraternizing in the neutral zone.[73] These conversations grew substantially in depth and frankness. "I was on Picket the other day Down by the River the Rebs and our boys visited back and forth thay crass in a boat," wrote George H. Ewing. "Thay are as sick of the war is eny of us thay said that if we Privets had it to we would do it in a short time."[74] Fraternization taught men they were not alone in their feelings of alienation. According to historian Tony Ashworth, "The enemy now was not just a trading partner nor was the relationship with him merely one of self-interest. The enemy was not only a person with whom one exchanged services but someone for whom one also had fellow-feelings."[75] For the first time, men heard their enemy's opinions, not from political propaganda, but directly from them. Antagonists were in agreement that because they did the fighting, they earned the right to end it. "A party of the enemy pickets crossed the river yesterday, and mingled in a friendly manner with our troops. They expressed themselves as heartily sick of the war, and proposed as a means of amicable settlement that the rebel army should hang Yancey, and that we should do the same for Horace Greeley, and then 'shake hands and call it square,'" described a Union soldier. "Another proposition was that the soldiers of both armies bring their officers up to the front, and let them fight it out among themselves."[76]

When soldiers had discussions with men on the opposite side, the war's end and home were at the forefront of these conversations. Both Union and Confederate men blamed the leadership for their state of affairs. A crucial factor they had in common was distrust in the politicians and lack of identification with their commanders. Talks of, and hopes for, peace between soldiers marked the realization that their enemy too felt expendable. "The rebels came over with boats and would trade tobacco for coffee with us some of them had on our clothes and very well wish that the war would close," shared a Massachusetts infantryman with his wife.[77] In talking with men on the opposite side, soldiers came to realize their enemy experienced the same privation, fear, and loss as did they. One Mississippian claimed, "The Yankees express the desire that President Davis and Lincoln will soon give us peace," while another offered, "For coffee, our pickets trade tobacco. We have become friendly with Yankee pickets. We all agree that we've had enough of the war and are ready to go home."[78] By bringing to light the enemy's shared plight, fraternization furthered soldiers' suspicions that they were pulled into the war for the advancement of a few. "The artillery men then asked the question, 'if he (john reb) would be willing to take a drink and settle this war' 'yes' was the answer 'and would be damn glad to settle it without a drink,'" documented a New Yorker.[79] These expressions demonstrate the class division that resonated throughout the entirety of the war. One Michigan sergeant stated, "A perfect feeling exists between the privates of both of the two armies. They are quite as sick of this inhumane, wholesale manslaughter as we are. If a vote of those composing the rank and file of both armies could settle this, there would be no more battles."[80] Fraternization allowed some soldiers to conclude that if it were left up to them, they could quickly settle their differences.

The "talks of peace" during fraternization also showed that men grew to respect their enemy's endurance. As seasoned veterans, men felt comfortable enough to let their guard down and empathize, as equals. For example, John West Haley wrote, "Our men generally treated the Johnnies to a cup of coffee and a few sutler's cakes. One would hardly have thought there were two hostile armies facing each other and practicing defiant strategy. There seemed to be an entire absence of malice between the two armies and we feel positive that if the rebel leaders had been out of the war, we could have had peace in twenty four hours."[81] When soldiers met in person they realized that, like themselves, their enemy was just as fed up and as anxious to be done with the war.[82] Joseph Banks Lyle stated, "I exchanged papers with a Yankee Marylander—said he was heartily tired of the war and that fighting could not end it."[83] Soldiers used the Marylander's phrase "tired of the war" repeatedly during fraternization. Men admitted their fatigue and hopes for peace to their enemy without fear of looking weak or cowardly. In October 1864, John L. Smith noted, "One time in front of Petersburg I was trading with a Reb Sargent and he said he had $300 in our money and I asked him where he got it and he said he got it in the wilderness from the dead. He said he was going to keep it in case he got taken prisoner. We got up and parted, we shook hands, wished each other well, and hope to meet you when this war is over and then I will treat you and used to get the best of them."[84] The sharing of "well wishes" and "talks of peace" proved soldiers came to understand their enemy's bravery and fortitude.

What was missing from these "talks of peace" during fraternization was the discussion of the terms. Union men never wrote if they would be willing to recognize Southern independence. Confederate soldiers did not articulate whether they would recognize any type of emancipation, gradual or immediate, nor sectional reunification. A significant part of fraternal spaces for men, before the war and during the war in soldiers' own camps, was the discussion of political matters, even if it became heated. Why then would enemy soldiers hesitate to discuss what they would be willing to settle upon? One explanation was that enemies may not have thought that far in advance or cared. An end to the war to them was simply that—an end to the bloodshed and the return home. On the other hand, these talks may have been less about negotiating peace or even an end to the war but more about finding common ground. Rather than focusing on the issues that divided them, men highlighted shared frustrations and sacrifices. Men poked fun at their leaders and complained about the war because that was what soldiers did with men on their own side. But, perhaps, they bypassed these topics on purpose. The agreement of peace, rather than an argument of the causes, was a much preferred, respectable parting when the trade ended. Men were sensitive to these issues. War, the world in which they were living, was the result of disagreement. Thus, fraternization marked a departure from prewar debates over slavery. Fraternalism during the war represented the first steps in the restoration of white male solidarity. In order to make this happen, out of respect, causation and consequences were not discussed in that space. These fraternizers, therefore, set a precedent: when white men came together, they applauded what unified them and avoided the issue of race.

Information

4

Not only were articles of food exchanged, such as coffee and bacon for tobacco, but also the latest newspapers, so that many important designs, which should be covered by the veil of secrecy from the enemy, reach them through trafficking and the imprudence of editors that published unwarranted details.

—Captain JOHN DOOLEY, First Virginia Volunteer Infantry

On the night of February 20, 1863, Private Milton Barrett of the Eighteenth Georgia Infantry and his regiment held a twenty-four hour picket post along the bank of the Rappahannock River. Upon returning to camp the following day, Private Barrett wrote home to his brother and sister, "Our regiment has just come off picket. We stood close together and could talk to each other, then when the officers were not present we exchanged papers. . . . We managed this is with a small boat. Some of our boys went over and stayed awhile. The Yankees would let us know when to come back. This correspondence has to be kept secret from the officers."[1] On the opposite bank, approximately 150 yards, stood Union soldiers holding their picket line in Falmouth, Virginia. After his turn on picket duty, Private John Martin Steffan of the Seventy-First Pennsylvania Infantry wrote a letter to his friend enclosed with an enemy paper he received. "This paper was floated across the river to me by one of the secesh pickets, and while reading on the bank of the river, he asked me how I liked the paper. This paper I should have delivered at Brigade Head Quarters, according to orders, but thinking that I might as well send it home," wrote Steffan.² Aside from coffee and tobacco, the most frequently traded item between enemies was newspapers. Both Barrett and Steffan openly admitted exchanging papers was against orders but, according to their records, upheld the truces and did not report the incidents. A primary reason the high command prohibited fraternization was because it risked spreading military secrets to the enemy. "Of course this intercourse is contrary to orders," Private Wilbur Fisk noted, when he offered his enemy a Sunday Morning *Chronicle* in exchange for a Southern paper. When the commanders broke up the exchange, a corporal went over the next morning with a *New York Herald, Boston Post*, and *Windsor Journal*.³ Soldiers who were bored on picket duty and wanted new reading material welcomed the exchange of papers. "While I was on the [picket] lines last night one of our men and theirs met each other half way and shook hands when they met, exchanged papers, and then shook hands when they parted," wrote G. J. Huntley.⁴ In the same way, Roland E. Bowen of the Fifteenth Massachusetts wrote, "Our pickets are on one side and the secesh on the other. We agree to have no shooting and some of the boys go out half on to the lot and the rebs come the other half way and exchange papers. One day by noon we had a Richmond morning paper, the name was the Richmond Whig."⁵ Although these instances appeared similar to the coffee and tobacco trade, soldiers exchanged newspapers because it was beneficial to them for different reasons.

Fraternization allowed men to access information from the other side. Other than hearsay and camp rumors, newspapers were the only method soldiers had to learn of current events. For a private, these vital links to the outside world allowed him to understand his role within the broader schemes at play. Enemy papers contained information that aided a soldier's awareness of several important topics, first of all, details on his own army and the one he opposed. The high command gave men in the ranks very little information about campaign strategy. Men were often left to guess at their unit's next move based on the latest buzz around camp. Enemy papers,

FIG. 6. Union soldier lying on ground reading a newspaper. Edwin Forbes, *News from Home*, September 30, 1863, Culpepper, Virginia. Library of Congress Prints and Photographs Division. Morgan collection of Civil War drawings, LC-USZ62-1843.

however, allowed them to understand major happenings such as changes in leadership or army maneuvers. Second, enemy newspapers provided information about developments in other theaters. Soldiers constantly wondered how, and sometimes even if, other armies in the field aided their current situation. Especially during sieges, men hoped that other armies were getting the job done. This made their sacrifice more tolerable and worthwhile. It also gave soldiers an indication of what future sacrifices had to be made. Third, papers provided political context. Men looked for developments, and hopefully setbacks, in the enemy's government as well as the enemy's perception of their own administration. A private's fate was contingent upon major events such as Lincoln's Emancipation Proclamation, prisoner exchanges, and the presidential election of 1864. Men were able to understand their current position more easily if they could link it to broader political aims. Last, soldiers saw updates in papers on how the enemy's home front perceived the war. Both Northern and Southern men wanted their sacrifice, and that of those they lost, to be worth it. Difficulties on the enemy's home front validated their efforts. Unfortunately, some of the news they read intensified frustrations. Nevertheless, it was through the exchange of papers that soldiers seized authority and made sense of their position in the ranks.

The first point in the war when there was a significant exchange of papers, like that of coffee and tobacco, was during the winter on the Rappahannock. For the Army of the Potomac and Army of Northern Virginia, there were two major topics of discussion in early 1863—the Emancipation Proclamation and General Burnside's replacement. Beginning with emancipation, the Union soldier reaction varied considerably between individuals. Many soldiers applauded it. "I regard it as wise politic, and beneficial. A year ago today it could not have been made," wrote a New Yorker. "Now it is almost gladly welcomed and at the worse excites but little opposition as far as my observation exceeds."[6] Private Poor's sentiment reiterates James McPherson's argument, which claims, "The Emancipation Proclamation had given a sharper edge to the controversy. Soldiers who had advocated an anti-slavery war from the beginning naturally welcomed the Proclamation."[7] Some understood the broader implications. Men realized the Emancipation Proclamation hurt the capacity of the Confederacy to wage war. Private Burrage Rice wrote, "The proclamation of freedom has now gone into effect and full force and that will tend in the course of time to weaken the rebels by taking from them a large portion of their bone and sinew, yet it will take many of the negroes a long time to escape from bondage and many never will—but as an institution in this country I believe the fate of slavery is sealed."[8] Although some men reacted positively to emancipation, it redirected the aims of the Union war effort, and for some men that was not part of the ideology for which they had signed up to fight. Union men had mixed emotions about abolition, and some viewed it as a threat to their own mastery and white supremacy. In relation to rumors of enlisting freedmen, a Union soldier retorted, "I see that some amalgamating senator has introduced a bill to have n—— enlisted in the army. If such a thing is ever done, I can only say 'my occupation's gone' my worst wish for the officious senator is that he may be a private in the some company where a sable son of Ethiopia is orderly sergeant, that's all."[9] Some men felt betrayed because, initially, President Lincoln promised the war was meant to save the Union and not to free the slaves.[10] "The emancipation proclamation of 'honest abe' has created more dissatisfaction and more 'croaking' than the affair at Fredericksburg did," a Union soldier admitted to his parents.[11]

Across campfires and in their letters home, soldiers debated what the next move would be and who would lead them. General George B. McClellan was reluctant to attack and harshly criticized by the Lincoln administration, while General Ambrose E. Burnside commenced a quick attack that led to criticism of the slaughter. Many soldiers remained loyal to General McClellan and felt no other general could live up to his command. The bloodshed and loss at the Battle of Fredericksburg aggravated the fragile relationship between soldiers and their officers. Men in the ranks felt the commanders seemed to be more concerned about competing with one another than with soldiers' well-being. "As long as military and political jealousy is allowed, full sway of the rebellion will never be put down. Never! Not one of our generals that have begun to make themselves popular and shown that they were men of the times," exclaimed a Union soldier.[12] Particularly in the wake of the disaster at Fredericksburg, soldiers felt extreme detachment and an overall lack of trust in their officers. The final straw for General Burnside was the fateful "Mud March." When Burnside led his men on a maneuver on January 20, 1863, they failed because intense rain caused the whole army to become stuck in mud.[13] General Burnside was relieved of command on January 25, 1863, and replaced by General Joseph Hooker.[14]

Confederate soldiers were eager to hear about emancipation and the Army of the Potomac's new leader from the Northern perspective. A Georgian told his mother, "I sent over some later Richmond papers & they readily exchanged the New Herald, Bal. Sun, & in fact all of the latest Northern papers. Got old Abe's message. They had many questions to ask about the war."[15] From procuring their

FIG. 7. On the back of this sketch, Lumley wrote: "One of the rebel Pickets (11th Ala) crossed over on rocks to the union pickets to Exchange Tobacco and a Richmond paper for the N.Y. Herald there is a mutual understanding among the pickets of both sides that the[y] will not be arrested [crossed out] captured, for the[y] trust the honor of the enemy in such case." Arthur Lumley, *An Incident of the War*, September 1862. Library of Congress Prints and Photographs Division. LC-USZ62-14886.

enemy's papers, soldiers could learn about the latest happenings and the reactions on the home front. In order to obtain these papers, men used the same makeshift boats they used for tobacco and coffee. For example, Egbert M. Rogers of the U.S. Signal Corps wrote in a letter, "There was a 'packet' I found to be loaded with mail. 'On deck', we found a Charleston paper, The Richmond Examiner, and a couple of other papers, all neatly folded and in perfect condition; accompanied with the request 'Please send us the latest you have.' Accordingly a N.Y. Herald, a Philadelphia Enquirer, and a Harper's Weekly, and another paper were duly folded and placed on board and the packet's sail trimmed and turned for 'Secessia' again."[16] In some cases, soldiers crossed the river themselves. "Two men out of our company took a little boat, went across the river and exchanged newspapers with them," said a Union infantryman to his wife.[17] The exchange of papers symbolized soldiers' efforts to go beyond the realm of what little information their officers told them, which was made possible only through the participation of their foes.

Enemies even aligned against their own commanders in order to keep their reciprocal system intact. When a Union officer captured Tally Simpson's boat, Simpson wrote about the Union men, "They told us they would be back in two or three days and would bring us plenty of papers and that as soon as they returned to camp they intended to put that damned stricter of an officer up as a target and have a shooting match at him."[18] Although the Union soldiers embellished their plot to shoot the officer, their suggestion shows their frustration with his intrusion and the hope to restore trade. Soldiers kept papers and, even more important, mail, hidden from their officers. In one instance, a Union soldier obtained a letter from a Confederate to mail to his sweetheart in the North, and the soldier kept the letter hidden from his commander.[19] The Federal soldier understood the importance of maintaining communication with a loved one and empathized with his enemy, rather than follow his own army's regulation. Soon, the practice of sending enemies' letters took hold. "They furnished us with the Richmond papers every day, and sometimes brought over letters to be sent to their friends in the North. These letters were not sealed and our officers requested to inspect them," documented a Union soldier. "We sent letters over there—those that had friends in the south—which they promised to forward them, and without doubt they will do as they have agreed."[20] Common soldiers understood the critical value of mail and contact with the home front; they maintained these connections for the enemy. Despite their efforts to circumnavigate the regulations against fraternization, some men were caught.

Of the approximately thirty Union court-martial cases for fraternization, over half of them dealt with the exchange of newspa-

MEETING OF UNION AND REBEL PICKETS IN THE RAPPAHANNOCK.—[SKETCHED BY MR. OERTEL.]

FIG. 8. Union and Confederate cavalry meet in the river and exchange papers. Mr. Oertel, *Meeting of Union and Rebel Pickets in the Rappahannock River*, 1863. Library of Congress Prints and Photographs Division. LC-USZ62-100583.

pers. More than any other commodity, the high command feared news about strategy sneaking through the lines the most. General Hooker feared that newspapers contained details on public opinion and the state of the army, which were best kept out of enemy hands.[21] Private George Vanderpool of the Fourth U.S. Infantry was charged with "Disobedience of Orders" because he reportedly swam across the Rappahannock River while on picket duty, which was in violation of the Fifth Army Corps General Orders No. 3. Vanderpool pled guilty and made a statement to the court claiming he did not know he was in violation of orders. "I had seen exchanges made daily by pickets," said Vanderpool. "I took it upon myself having a paper then to exchange. Not being acquainted with the customs of military proceedings I was innocent in doing so, not intending to communicate in any way with the enemy having only joined my regiment last December and not knowing the consequences of doing so."²² Vanderpool's attempt to claim ignorance, like that of many soldiers, fell short. He was found guilty and was docked five dollars of his monthly pay for three months. The court-martial also ordered a public reprimand by the commanding officer in the presence of the entire regiment. Despite the prevalence of cases pertaining to the exchange of newspapers, the court-martial acquitted a handful of soldiers who were brought up on these charges. Acquittals were usually due to lack of evidence or men being caught only with the intent to trade. Sergeant B. Belzonne and Private Frederick Meyer, both of the Seventh New York Infantry, were charged with "Disobedience of Orders." The two men were said to have received a boat or float sent from the enemy's side of the river, near Fredericksburg, containing newspapers printed in enemy territory and retained them in their possession. A witness for the prosecution claimed he never saw them trade or hold any papers, and both men were acquitted.²³ Similarly, two brothers, Privates Samuel and Parley Post of the Sixth New York Calvary, were charged with "Disobedience of Orders." While posted at a vedette upon the banks of the Rappahannock they held communication with the rebel pickets opposite them by answering them and calling over to them. Because of lack of evidence, the men were found not guilty.²⁴ Because the number of court-martials pale in comparison to the number of instances documented in soldiers' accounts, this may suggest that lower-ranking officers on picket duty turned a blind eye to fraternization. Yet officers viewed the effects of fraternization as a threat to order and structure, not to mention a stain on their own record of control of their subordinates. Evidence suggests soldiers were overwhelmingly successful in conducting these exchange operations without detection.

In the western theater, soldiers benefitted from obtaining enemy papers to learn of command changes and army maneuvers. For the Union armies, the first series of these major changes happened after the Confederate victory at Chickamauga. On October 28, 1863, George H. Alverson of the Tenth Wisconsin wrote, "A great change has been made in our army since I wrote to you last. Brigade and

Division have been consolidated. General Roseycrans has gone to Washington. Our army and the army of the Mississippi are joined together and General Grant in command here."[25] After Chickamauga, the Lincoln administration relieved Rosecrans from command and promoted General Grant to commander of all western armies. The War Department also placed General George Thomas in command of the Army of the Cumberland. That army would be joined with the Army of the Tennessee, veterans of Vicksburg, now led by General William Tecumseh Sherman. President Lincoln also sent two corps from the Army of the Potomac, the Eleventh and Twelfth, under command of General Joseph Hooker, to assist in Tennessee.[26] Grant's first order of business was to feed his troops. He quickly drew up plans to build his supply line, or the "cracker line" as it became known, fearing an assault from Bragg's Army. However, General Bragg dealt with internal factions of his own.

Despite the recent victory at Chickamauga, Bragg had difficulty leading his subordinates; this volatility trickled down to the troops. In terms of the distrust in leadership, while camped on Lookout Mountain, William Montgomery wrote, "I am sorry to inform you that I am not in good spirits, I would like to be for I assure you I am tired of General Bragg and am very anxious to be in old Virginia under my favorite General the best man of the age."[27] General Bragg, thus, focused his energies on unifying his subordinates rather than drawing up a plan to attack the Union Army surrounding them at Chattanooga. Bragg reorganized brigades from Tennessee and Kentucky, some of which were led by his most outspoken critics.[28] Additionally, Bragg sent Longstreet's Corps to Knoxville on November 4. For Confederate soldiers, this wariness about leadership, coupled with a lack of food, lice infestation, and having only poor clothing, led to a rise in desertions. Georgian John Kennerly Farris wrote, "All around me seems darkness, and before me trouble, like mountains rise to my view."[29] Farris's anxiety about the future reflected the fact that the army had gained little at Chickamauga because Union armies continued to reinforce themselves. "Food and clothing are pretty scarce with the army now and I fear we shall suffer more before very long," acknowledged Farris.[30] Since all these factors kept compounding for Confederate troops, when Sherman's Army of the Tennessee arrived, many fled to Union picket lines at night. Bragg instituted stricter crackdowns on inspections, which he thought would alleviate the problem of desertion, when in actuality it only made matters worse. Henry Welch of the 123rd New York talked with Confederate deserters, and when he asked why so many of their men desert, one responded, "We know that our cause is hopeless and our families starving to death. We do not want to make this war last any longer and cause our families and ourselves to suffer any more."[31] Others turned to alcohol. "It takes a man of courage and firmness to resist the contagions. Get drunk every chance seems to be the motto of a good many," Henry Gilliam admitted to his wife.[32] The major victory at Chickamauga was not enough to revitalize Bragg's demoralized army. Alabamian Edward Norphlet Brown summed up the carnage: "Yankees and Rebels lie dead together, some on their faces, some on their backs, some on their all-fours, some with bowels torn out, some with heads shot off, some with limbs torn away, and all seem to have been struggling for the mastery when they died. But I cannot describe the terror of a battle and the horror of a battlefield when the strife is over. I have seen the fields where three great battles were fought and I pray God that I may be spared the sight of a fourth."[33] As the Confederates held the heights surrounding the city of Chattanooga, their plight equaled that of the besieged Federal troops. For the troops that remained loyal to their unit, a sure method to cope with the difficult conditions and fear of the future was fraternization.

As a means to understand what might be their army's next move or for updated insight about the leadership changes, men attempted to gain enemy papers. "The regiment went on picket today. A yankee came to our lines to exchange newspapers. We let him go back to yankeedom without paroling him. He said he belonged to the 6th Kentucky," penned Joseph Miller Rand.[34] One of the primary ways soldiers could rationalize their conditions, alleviate worry, and make sense of the larger war aims was through enemy newspapers. Jason Phillips, in *Diehard Rebels*, argues, "Combatants seldom grasped the battles they fought, let alone comprehended the developments of entire campaigns."[35] The exchange of newspapers gave men hints as to when Grant might attack. On November 20 Frank Phelps of the Tenth Wisconsin went on picket duty where only a few yards and a little creek stood between him and his enemy. "The rebs were very friendly, coming down on the bank to trade papers, canteens or anything they could get," wrote Phelps. "I had a *New York Tribune*, which I exchanged for an Augusta paper. The next day, I exchanged a Wis. *State Journal* for the *Richmond News*."[36] Men sought knowledge beyond the swirling camp rumors, hoping it would help quell the anxiety of the unknown.

Due to lack of records, we cannot determine if Confederate soldiers were court-martialed for trading papers. But, similar to other places where fraternization happened frequently, at Chattanooga Union men were arrested for allegedly trading papers with the enemy. On October 23, 1863, Henry Eich of the Second Missouri Infantry, Army of the Cumberland, was brought in front of a court-martial. His first charge was "Disobedience of Orders," with the accusation that he laid down his arms, left his post, and exchanged papers while posted as a sentinel on picket station No. 1 near Chattanooga on October 2, 1863. He was also charged with "Intercourse with the Enemy" for leaving his post, going beyond the picket line, and exchanging papers with the enemy. Eich admitted that he did it, but in his defense stated that the officers on the picket line told him to do so. His witnesses corroborated his account, but when the prosecution questioned the officers, they stated that they told him no. Eich was found guilty and sentenced to two months hard labor and six months without pay.[37] Eich's sentence was one of the harshest handed out to a soldier found guilty for fraternization. It was also an instance where the word of a private, versus his officers, did not hold up in front of the court-martial. Although most cases in the fall of 1863 dealt with mutiny, disorderly conduct, and desertion, the high command hoped to stop fraternization as well.

The trade of newspapers, however, abruptly ended when General Grant took the initiative and did the unthinkable—attacked the Confederates on their heavily entrenched position. After six weeks of siege, on November 23, General Grant ordered General Thomas's corps to take a ridge in front of Missionary Ridge called Orchard Knob.[38] When General Bragg secured his line on Missionary Ridge, Grant ordered Sherman's men to attack on the northern end, Tunnel Hill, and Hooker's men to attack on the south at Lookout Mountain and later Rossville Gap.[39] Grant kept Thomas at Orchard Knob in order to keep Bragg distracted and prohibit his ability to shift troops to reinforce his flanks. However, because Sherman had difficulty at Tunnel Hill on November 25, Grant changed his plan and ordered Thomas's men to launch a frontal assault on Missionary Ridge.[40] This improvisation at Missionary Ridge demonstrated Grant's ability to "find a way to get the job done."[41] Artillerist John T. Cheney watched from his position and wrote, "General Thomas must pass through the valley or into it to be ready to scale the hill at the proper time. It might as well be called the dark valley of the shadow of death. Soon four columns of infantry could be seen marching up a hill, led by a hero with the stars and stripes floating in the breeze."[42] Thomas's Army of the Cumberland ascended the heights and made it to the Confederate rifle pits. Thomas's assault, which would become known as "The Miracle," astounded Union and Confederate troops who watched, but for the men who ascended Missionary Ridge, the heart of the Confederate line awaited them at the crest. "Our brigade lay in such a position that we could witness the whole affair and the grandest sight of all was the assault and taking of Missionary Ridge by Thomas' men. The best part of it was that we lost so few men the rebel prisoners said our men walked over them like as if they were chickens," recorded James Henry McBride.[43] While Thomas's men fought, Hooker's assault at Rossville Gap rolled up the Confederate right flank, and, during the night of November 25, Bragg began his retreat south into Georgia. The Army of Tennessee referred to their defeat at Chattanooga as "the death knell of the Confederacy."[44] Historian Peter Cozzens argues, "The night of November

25, 1863, was the saddest to date in the largely depressing history of the Army of Tennessee."[45] Joseph E. Johnston replaced Braxton Bragg and took over the Army of Tennessee. Although the majority of Confederate soldiers applauded this move, the removal of Bragg disappointed some. Edward Norphlet Brown wrote, "I am afraid we have lost more by the change in commanders than we have at the hands of the enemy. I am a great admirer of General Bragg and I regret excessively that he has thought it best to leave the Army. It is my deliberate judgment that Braxton Bragg is the greatest General of this revolution."[46] Most haunting for these men in the ranks when the year 1864 began was the ample time they had to wonder what future sacrifices would have to be made.

When the campaigning began in spring 1864, William Tecumseh Sherman now commanded all armies in the West. His goal was to take the Armies of the Cumberland, Ohio, and Tennessee and push toward Atlanta. For veterans of Vicksburg in the Army of the Tennessee, this style of combat resembled their push toward Vicksburg a year earlier. However, for those in Army of the Cumberland, like Thomas Bell, who did not fight at Vicksburg, the continual fighting caused a new set of frustrations. At Dallas, Bell wrote, "A private has but little chance of knowing what movements are or what they are for. They are calculated to know enough to do what they are ordered to and no more."[47] This lack of control and fear of the unknown could be placated through information in newspapers. For example, after he heard some places along the line traded with the enemy, Harvey Reid went to the picket line to investigate these "amicable proceedings." Reid wrote, "The opposite bank was heavily wooded, so that we could not see the rebel pickets, except in one place where there was a log house and a small clearing, the house being about 80 rods from our line. One of the boys was waving a newspaper in his hand. Three rebs started down the hill with papers in their hands. Three of our boys also started with their papers."[48] Reid's observations confirmed that even when conditions did not allow, soldiers found ways to exchange papers. Reading the latest reports allowed soldiers to understand how their daily efforts fit into the larger campaign aims and goals. Volunteer soldier of the Nineteenth Michigan Infantry, Union Army of Tennessee, Sergeant Hamlin Alexander Coe followed William Tecumseh Sherman on the advance toward the Confederate city of Atlanta. "This morning some of our boys had quite a time exchanging paper with the Rebs, and they seemed to have a good time between themselves," wrote Coe. "It commenced by our boys asking the Rebs to exchange papers, when both parties started with a paper waving over their heads and without arms."[49] Papers also provided knowledge about the movements of other armies, particularly Lee's and Grant's push through Virginia, and the political happenings leading up to the presidential primary that summer.

An interesting situation occurred in mid-June over an exchange of papers. Both a brigadier general and a private in his division documented their perspectives on these interactions. New Yorker Henry Welch exchanged papers and talked with Confederate soldiers while on picket duty. Welch wrote, "Our picket line is in speaking distance of the rebel pickets. We exchanged papers with them every day. They think or did think that Lee was whipping Grant badly. They say that they are going to drive us out of Georgia. They say that Hooker's men fight differently than western troops do. They wanted to know if Hooker's men were not mostly regular soldiers."[50] The Confederate soldiers respectfully paid a compliment to their enemy's fighting style. Welch's unit, 123rd New York, was part of Hooker's Twentieth Corps, now under the Army of the Cumberland. His divisional commander, Brigadier General Alpheus S. Williams, observed his men that day and wrote about it in a letter to his daughter. "For the last few days our pickets completely fraternized. They have been exchanging papers, coffee, tobacco, and the like." General Williams continued, "The next day I found them actually sitting together on the banks of a small stream, a branch of the Allatoona Creek. I was obliged to stop fraternal intercourse. Isn't it strange that men in mortal strife one hour are on affectionate terms the next! And apparently fast friends. Strange are the commingled events and incidents of war!"[51] An officer who had not endured the hardships of a private could not fathom how enemies came together. He noted the quick shift between fighting and fraternizing. But his reaction validated his inability to understand fraternization, further confirming the disconnect between common soldiers and the men who led them.

While Sherman's and Johnston's men fought their way to the gates of Atlanta, Lee's and Grant's armies were doing the same. Soldiers in these armies survived the bloodiest battles in the war but had yet to experience continuous warfare. "The sheer volume of killing, the numbers of lives lost, shocked even the hardest veteran and drove many men to psychological collapse."[52] Because both the Lincoln and Davis administrations put such weight on the upcoming 1864 elections, the politicians and generals asked their men to fight out the summer in the trenches surrounding Petersburg.[53] President Lincoln knew that the Democratic Party in the North called for a peaceful end to the war through proposing recognition of Southern independence. Therefore, Lincoln was fully aware that winning reelection in November, and ultimately saving the Union, was contingent upon what happened in the battlefield.[54] In 1864 all Confederate armies had the same plan: survive until November with the hope that President Lincoln would lose reelection. President Jefferson Davis and the Confederate government were aware that Northern Copperheads and Peace Democrats promised to honor Southern legitimacy if voted into the White House. Casualty lists from the Overland Campaign, particularly from Cold Harbor, fueled Peace Democrat propaganda and caused many civilians to question whether or not the cost was worth victory.[55] Even though Grant crossed the James River, sieges took months to play out.[56] Because time was of the essence, the War Department ordered Union forces to press the Confederate lines. Historian of the campaign Richard Sommers describes the conditions thus: "Heavy casualties, exhaustion, and debilitating climate all helped transform the mobile war of spring into the grinding, monotonous attrition of summer."[57] The soldiers who pushed south and suffered loss of comrades along the way: Union men had to

FIG. 9. An off-duty Union soldier reads the news. Edwin Forbes, *Reading the News*, March 12, 1864. Library of Congress Prints and Photographs Division. Morgan collection of Civil War drawings, LC-USZ62-9274.

win battles to secure votes, and Confederate men had to survive. Thus, soldiers were left to make sense of how their daily miseries were dependent upon several moving parts.

Soldiers spent time reading papers, contemplating their next move, and circulating "camp rumors,"[58] activities not limited strictly to men on their own sides. Enemy papers provided insight and allowed men to further speculate what might transpire during the summer of 1864. Private Randolph Valentine said, "The pickets conversed with each other freely and exchanged papers," and Private Julius Whitney wrote, "Laid in the breast works all day. There wasn't much firing in the front. Some of the men exchanged papers with the rebels."[59] Soldiers on both sides waited in the trenches and became vigilant about securing information. Men speculated about the ramifications of the election of 1864, Sherman's presence in Atlanta, and the battle over the Shenandoah Valley. Soldiers needed to know how these developments determined their fate, and they fraternized to gather clues. "Last Monday I was on picket of course it rained as it does always when I am out all night. The arrangements the two picket lines have established are, they can talk and exchange papers etc etc etc from six am till six pm. I tried to exchange papers with Johnnie Reb. I went passed our vedettes nearly half way over to their lines in full shot view. I waved my Herald all the time till I nearly got half way over then I called to them, 'If you meet me half way over, I will change papers with you,'" stated New Yorker Killian van Rensselaer.[60] Soldiers like van Rensselaer took risks to get information. However, the high command made numerous attempts to stop it and caught dozens of men.

After the Battle of Cold Harbor, on June 9, 1864, commanding general of the Army of the Potomac George Gordon Meade issued Special Order No. 154. It read:

> No communication will be held with the enemy unless specially authorized from these or superior Head Quarters, or except so far as may be necessary to properly receive a flag of truce coming from the enemy's lines.

All other communication is strictly prohibited, whether by means of conversation, signals or otherwise, or by interchange of newspapers or commodities. Corps Commanders will see that the unauthorized intercourse with the enemy, which it is known from time to time to take place, notwithstanding the reiterated orders upon the subject, is no longer tolerated.[61]

The following month, on July 18, 1864, General Robert E. Lee issued Special Order No. 167, with the headline "In regard to intercourse between our pickets and skirmishers, and those of the enemy. It shall not be allowed. Instructions given, should a flag of truce be sent by the enemy." In the letter, addressed to the First Army Corps Commander, Lieutenant General R. H. Anderson, Lee ordered:

The practice of permitting communication between our pickets and skirmishers and those of the enemy, is highly injurious to the service and subversive of discipline.

It is enjoined upon all officers to prohibit it strictly.

The enemy must be kept within his lines, and whenever any of his men attempt to approach ours, except under a regularly authorize flag of truce, or show themselves within range, they will in all cases be fired upon and driven back.

No intercourse or conversation with the enemy shall be allowed, and no officers or man will be permitted to go outside of our picket lines except by authority of the Corps commander or officer commanding detached troops.

Should a Flag of Truce be sent by the enemy, it will not be received until the fact has been reported to the Corps commander or officer commanding detached troops, who will designate the person by whom it shall be met.

The enforcement of this order is enjoined upon the Corps and other commanding officers.

By command of General R. E. Lee (Major Taylor)[62]

These orders, made by both commanding generals, prove the exchange of newspapers became quite frequent at Petersburg. Despite the crackdown against fraternization, men did not listen. During the last year of the war it became more necessary and beneficial than ever before.

Between June 1864 and February 1865, fifteen Union soldiers were arrested and brought in front of a court-martial for exchanging papers with the enemy. Petersburg had the highest number of fraternization court-martial cases during the war, and the exchange of papers was the most frequent charge. In seven of the cases, the court found the men not guilty. For privates accused, they often pled ignorance. Isaac Brown said, "I heard no orders against exchanging papers. Everybody was doing it and I supposed it was permitted," and he was acquitted.[63] Officers accused of letting men go out in front of the lines to get papers claimed it was unbeknownst to them. Lieutenant Loring Farr stated, "I had no idea that they were there," and was subsequently acquitted.[64] Lieutenant Presley Cannon claimed, "I understood that it was common practice to trade on the line—tobacco, papers, etc. I did not think it right and without receiving any orders to do so, I ordered it to be stopped."[65] However, some men were not so lucky. Men who were honest more often than not were found guilty. Private John Vaughn went outside the lines to exchange papers at Bermuda Hundred in September 1864. During his trial, "He said he knew it was against orders but they had always been in the habit of exchanging papers and thought there would be no harm in it."[66] The court found Vaughn guilty and sentenced him to be confined under guard for thirty days of hard labor. Officers and men passed the blame off on one another, turning most cases into one man's word against another's. Private I. L. G. Crandall of the Ninety-Eighth New York pled his company officer notified him of a rebel picket nearby and asked him to go exchange papers, but he was found guilty and sentenced to two months hard labor without pay.[67] Conversely, in the trial of Lieutenant Charles Goldenburgh, one of his men stated, "I had orders to go out and trade papers by Lieutenant Goldenburgh. He told me to go out and get a Richmond Enquirer and he would send them a New York Herald in the afternoon." Goldenburgh was found guilty and dismissed from the U.S. service with the "loss of all pay and allowances," one of the harshest sentences for fraternization.⁶⁸ In one case, three officers—Major Lyman Knapp of the Seventeenth Vermont, Second Lieutenant John Andrews of the 179th New York, and Sergeant John Vandermark of the 179th New York—were all charged with "Disobedience of Orders" for allowing their men to fraternize. The question in this case was at what point in the chain of command was the order against fraternization not given. Vandermark argued that he witnessed the exchange of papers so often he assumed the orders against intercourse with the enemy were revoked. Knapp and Andrews were acquitted, while Vandermark was found guilty of violating Special Order No. 157, demoted, and reduced to the ranks.⁶⁹ Although Andrews and Vandermark were of the same unit, the lowest ranking of the three was the only man found guilty. Proceedings, thus, became ambiguous, lacked precedent, and the decisions were made on a case-by-case basis. Nonetheless, the charges for fraternization demonstrate not only the high command's efforts to halt the trade of newspapers, but its regularity during the siege.

One particularly interesting situation occurred at the siege at Petersburg in November 1864, while Captain O. Dudley of the Eleventh New Hampshire Infantry was in charge of his men. The Union Army outside the city of Petersburg positioned units, including the Eleventh New Hampshire, in earthworks roughly one hundred yards opposite the Confederate lines. "I have the honor to report that Private Roger A. Pryor, Third Virginia Cavalry, was captured in front of our picket-line, near Doctor Boisseau's house, under the following circumstances: Lieutenant Durgin, Thirty-Second Maine Volunteers, who was on the right of the line, noticed this man several times between the lines waving papers and importuning our men to come out and exchange," Dudley wrote. "The lieutenant sent to the left of the line for me, and when I came up this man (Pryor) came out front their lines and, waving his papers, beckoned me to come out and meet him. I immediately went out to meet him, and shook hands with him, telling him at the same time that he might consider himself my prisoner."[70] Word of Pryor's capture made its way up the Confederate Army of Northern Virginia's chain of command. Divisional commander Major General Cadmus Wilcox sent a letter to Union headquarters asking for Pryor's release. Commander of the Union Army of the Potomac George Gordon Meade responded to Wilcox's request. General Meade wrote:

> Your letter of the 28th instant has been referred to me by Lieut. Gen. U. S. Grant, with directions to reply to it. I regret extremely it is not in my power to accede to your request by returning to your lines Private R. A. Pryor, Third Virginia Cavalry. The same considerations which prevented you from applying to your commanding general preclude me from sanctioning this irregular intercourse between the opposing pickets, which is in direct violation of my orders, and for violating which and thus permitting himself to be captured in a similar manner. Private Pryor will have to suffer the consequences of his imprudence. He will be held as a prisoner of war.[71]

General Meade's response to his enemy regarding Pryor's capture demonstrated both the severity of the infraction and the illegality of any contact with the enemy. When the war began, the leadership did not anticipate soldiers would interact with one another so frequently. Thus, officers constantly enacted measures to prevent the flow of goods and information between the lines. These restrictions, however, did not seem to deter men from fraternizing. Men continued to exchange papers to learn as much as they could about other armies, the political administrations, and, most importantly, morale on the home front.

Soldiers on both sides felt their relationship with the home front strain during the last year of the war. Inevitably, soldiers read opinions, most likely written by those who were wealthy enough to pay for substitutes to fight in their place, that disapproved of their efforts on the battlefield. Obtaining enemy papers was a double-edged sword. Southern newspapers detailed "talks of peace" from Northern Democrats, which insulted soldiers' efforts on the front lines. Soldiers vehemently opposed politicians who criticized their sacrifice and efforts on the battlefield. Historian Jennifer L. Weber argues, "Given the privations, disease, and discomfort they suffered, not to mention the peril that battle presented, bluecoats deeply resented any lack of support for their efforts."[72] Copperheads and Peace Democrats not only threatened the state of the Union but reinforced class divisions in the North. John Price Kepner stated in a letter to his parents, "The Vallandigham party has gone too far that the masses see this and are fired thoroughly with a revengeful indignation is indeed cheering news to the soldiers. But to the young man I say come, 'tis no disgrace to shoulder a musket in your country's defense. Gold lace and epaulets do not make a man."[73] Soldiers like Kepner felt that if George McClellan and the Peace Democrats won the presidency, their efforts over the past three years would be negated and the men who perished would have died in vain. Yet, for the first time ever, soldiers in the field were allowed to vote. "We had a regular election here in the army. Our regiment went from 130 majority for Lincoln. Some companies did not cast a vote for Mac," wrote Private Henry Matrau.[74] Although Copperhead propaganda influenced the home front, soldiers wrote home and urged their male family and friends to vote for Lincoln over McClellan.[75] George P. McClelland wrote to his family, "Tell him to vote for Lincoln and not for the tool of unprincipled anti-Republican-liberty men. Three-fourths of the Army will vote for Uncle Abe."[76] Similarly, in a letter to his parents, Zerah Coston Monks stated, "The army is loyal, sensible, I might say, of the vast events that are transpiring and we want the war ended once and forever. To do this the present administration must be heartily sustained and President Lincoln reelected. Then we will feel confident that our peace can be brought about and the confederate yield to our terms or yield to our bayonets."[77] Union soldiers felt that acquiring peace on their own terms was only possible through the election of Lincoln. These men viewed Copperheadism as slanderous to their service and caused them to question whether those who stayed at home were even aware of what they were enduring on the battlefield.

Conversely, for the Army of Northern Virginia, news on antiwar advocates in the North bolstered Southern morale. The trade of newspapers allowed Confederate soldiers to know if their hunger and hardship would play out in their favor. "While we were out yesterday Sunday July 3rd, one of the Johnnies stood up on their works and shook a paper at us—and sung out to exchange. One of the boys from the regiment advanced from the breastworks, half way across the field with a paper in his hand," detailed Samuel Pierce. "As Paul had a paper, he went half way across. He neared the johnnie with whom he exchanged papers. The paper Paul gave him was Harpers Weekly containing a portrait of General Lee. The paper Paul received from the reb was the Petersburg Daily."[78] Unfortunately, Northern papers also carried very troubling news for Southern soldiers. When Confederate soldiers read about Union Army movements and success across the South in Northern papers, it added fuel to the fire of disillusionment and explains why desertion peaked during the last year of the war. Reading these accounts prompted even the most loyal veterans to question their reasons for remaining in ranks. When they read about General Sherman's encroaching Federal troops or food shortages, many Confederates felt coerced to choose between home and country. For example, James F. Jones wrote to his mother, "I trouble myself about my relatives and friends because I know they cannot be comfortably provided for—in these days of desperation where the 'powers that be' lay in hands upon supplies of every kind—without any regard to consequences on the grounds of military necessity. Our poor people must suffer without relief."[79] If Confederate soldiers knew their loved ones suffered, then they felt they had failed at their duty.[80] Georgian John Everett wrote to his wife, "It is hard for us to stay in Virginia and fight and the yanks all over Georgia is not right for the Georgia soldier to stay here. You stated in your letter than you was now willing for me to desert and go home."[81] Although Union armies had been in the South since 1861, with General Sherman's "hard war" policy during the Petersburg siege, the situation became desperate. For soldiers who deserted their trenches at Petersburg, the reason was not so much cowardice but rather the realization that they were not fulfilling their primary duty—to protect their families. Mark Weitz, a scholar on desertions among Georgia troops, argues, "The Union desertion program did not attract cowards because the weak-hearted had left long before 1864. They returned home only after the situation in Georgia became unbearable and when they realized that their sacrifice had not been matched by other Georgians, particularly the wealthy and slaveholder classes, who stood to benefit most from the war and contributed the least to it."[82] When Southern men read Northern papers they obtained while fraternizing, it was not always the news they hoped to hear. Thousands deserted when the desolation in the trenches and their families in despair outweighed the risk of being captured or labeled a coward.

By January 1865 General Grant, well aware of peaks in Confederate desertion, issued an ordinance that not only exempted Confederate deserters from capture or front-line duty but issued them free transportation to anywhere in the North and, if they swore allegiance to the United States, gave them employment with the army quartermaster. In addition, if they deserted with any type of arms, property, or horses, they received compensation for their goods.[83] While on picket duty, Union men would go in between the lines and post circulars of this ordinance for Southern soldiers to read. Rhode Islander Elisha Hunt Rhodes noted in his diary, "We have some circulars printed offering to pay each Rebel deserter for his musket and equipment and to give him a free passage to the North. We send men out in the night and place these circulars on the stumps of trees, and the Rebels find them and so distribute them to their men."[84] Men on picket duty enticed hungry Confederates with these circulars and food. The Seventeenth Maine received at least fifty deserters one night while on picket duty and welcomed the Confederates with gallons of coffee and meat pies.[85] Franklin Boyts wrote, "You would hardly believe what a large number of rebel deserters come in daily. Yesterday, 300 were brought in from Grant's Army. Every day over a hundred are brought into the city. Lee's Army is in deplorable condition. These poor beings present a miserable appearance; some almost entirely naked, and dirty beyond description—while hunger is another severe enemy."[86] Some were sick of fighting, many were starving, and others claimed they lost hope. "They are losing a great many men every day from desertion. I talked with many and they all tell pretty near the same story. There is great destitution in the South. Scarcely anything to eat or to wear. There is also great dissatisfaction with the Jeff Davis Administration," said Wesley Gould.[87] Lee reported 1,094 desertions between February 15 and 25, 779 during the next ten days, and 1,061 between March 9 and 18.[88] Captain Charles Blackford described the disillusionment at Petersburg thus: "There have been more desertions of late than ever before. I hear that even some Virginians have deserted to the enemy. The hard lives they lead and a certain degree of hopelessness which is stealing over the conviction of the best and braves will have some effect in inducing demoralization hitherto unknown."[89] Desertions in the spring of 1865 indicated an inevitable collapse of the strongest Confederate army. But for the diehards who remained until the bitter end, they continued to work with the enemy in arguably the most beneficial way—to limit meaningless bloodshed and survive.

5

Ceasefires

We have a trench outside five feet deep that the artillery fired at all night. The Johns made an agreement with our pickets not to fire at one another they are so close there and if either party should have orders to advance they fire their first shots in the air to let them know the agreement was broke.

—Corporal JOHN L. SMITH, 118th Pennsylvania Infantry

When officers ordered men on picket duty to keep up constant fire, soldiers took it upon themselves to arrange ceasefires. Through fraternization, soldiers used their environment to reduce danger and, according to historian Tony Ashworth, developed a system of "live and let live." In his research on World War I soldiers, Ashworth maintains that men mitigated the horrors of trench warfare through observing one another and arranging ceasefires to lessen hostilities.[1] With the development of earthworks and trenches during the Civil War, soldiers gained some protection against the accuracy of rifles and range of artillery.[2] However, trench and siege tactics drastically blurred the line between camp and battlefield, which had previously been very definitive during the first half of the war. Within their positions, soldiers dealt with continuous enemy fire and exposure to the elements, and worked tenaciously to protect themselves from both. Soldiers found it exhausting to be vigilant all the time. In an attempt to stay alive, men warned their enemy about impending attacks and hoped the gesture would be returned. James McBeth wrote, "I am writing this letter to you on picket and in speaking distance from the enemy's line when we came out here first off they would shoot whenever we would see a head above the corn field but since we have came to an understanding and not a shot is exchanged and we are talking to each other just as if we were best friends in the world they are on one side of the cornfield and we are on the other."[3] Ceasefires, as described by McBeth, allowed soldiers to control their conditions on picket duty, particularly when they learned there was little to be gained from constant fire. New York soldier George Bryan of the 125th New York wrote, "Yesterday we came out on picket duty. Our picket line is about half a mile from the enemy's line. We can see them all of the time. They are quite friendly now. They do not fire at pickets on either side now so there is no danger unless we attempt to cross their lines."[4] The negotiation of ceasefires made life on picket duty easier, while at the same time creating the most beneficial result of fraternization: lessening the carnage. As previously noted, the sharing of conversation, coffee and tobacco, and newspapers all served significant purposes, but the ability to increase one's chances of survival was the most useful purpose for fraternization.

The first soldiers to suggest armistices were those of the Army of the Tennessee and the Department of the Mississippi while at Vicksburg. This was most likely due to characteristics of siege warfare, which included being under constant fire and in proximity to one another. Confederate soldier John Guilford Earnest described his experience: "During this time we endured as much as mortals ever endured in an army—every day from daylight until late in the night—sometimes all night, we were in the midst of hissing shells and balls of every character that were ever manufactured."[5] On the opposite side from Private Earnest, Richmond V. Black of the 114th Illinois experienced similar circumstances. In a letter to his wife, Black wrote, "The day we got here was the 19th the battle has been raging hot and strong from that time to the present and will continue from day to day until the rebs surrender. We have 100 cannon besides our gunboats playing on them all the time. I am writing under rather peculiar circumstances the bullets are whistling over our heads all the time but we have got used to the sound of bullets, solid shot, and the shriek of shells."[6] Both men's descriptions highlight the exceptional nature of siege warfare. The constant artillery fire and sharpshooting affected their understanding of battle. No longer was there a time and space for combat and then a separate time and space for other soldiering duties such as labor, logistics, and rest. Everything, during a siege, coalesced into one space without a lull in hostilities. Isaac Jackson wrote, "Our men are working and digging at the fort now. The only thing that separated them is the bank of the fort. It is only 3 miles to Vicksburg and we have to get there under great difficulties, such as shells and Minnie balls and hand shells."[7] When Grant's army got closer to the rebel line, the Confederates replaced artillery fire with infantry-thrown "hand shells." William Stone described the "hand shells" as "cotton balls dipped in turpentine and set on fire over our heads, which dropped a few feet in our rear and kept up a light so that they could see us in case we made an attempt to leave our place."[8] These conditions forced soldiers to constantly be on guard while keeping up very tedious work. No amount of drilling could prepare soldiers for the type of warfare they faced at Vicksburg. Therefore, soldiers had to alter their perception of what it meant to be a "good soldier" to include the concept of combat endurance.

When commanders issued a "white flag" for burial duty, it was the first time soldiers could breathe a sigh of relief and walk about freely. But, there was no reason to celebrate. On May 25 the stench of the decaying bodies left in between the lines became so awful that General Pemberton called a truce. "Our dead was the most sickening sight I ever beheld, most of them had fallen in the charge of Friday last and lying exposed of the scorching rays of the sun is a sufficient description of their appearance. The stench was intolerable," wrote Iowan Alfred Rigby.[9] Also in reference to the slain, William Pitt Chambers described, "On the afternoon of Monday, May 25th, a truce of two or three hours was arranged in order to bury the dead who lay between lines. These bodies had become so offensive that our troops could hardly remain in the trenches along those points where the slaughter had been the greatest. Hence our men gladly assisted to burial of their fallen foes. And among them were found living men, who had fallen, perhaps on Wednesday and certainly not later than Friday before, who had lain there without a drop of water or particle of shade."[10] Given this scene, illustrated by Rigby and Chambers, one would think such a gruesome sight would polarize enemies even further. But, rather than blaming the enemy for the loss of comrades, soldiers distanced themselves from that emotion and saw the break in action as an opportunity to fraternize.

Soldiers capitalized on the officer-led burial truces and modified them for their own purposes of trade and fraternity. "There was a cessation of hostilities for a couple of hours the other day to enable each party to bury their dead. . . . The rebs were quite friendly to us while the white flag was up. They came out of their entrenchments and we went out of ours and met them down in the ravine which separates their breastworks from ours. We had a long talk over matters and things in general," James Newtown told his mother. "They agreed with us perfectly on one thing. If the settlement of this war was left to the enlisted men of both sides we would soon go home. I think they were right, don't you?"[11] Newton documented the opinion, heard time and time again, that if it were left up to the men in the ranks, the war would come to a speedy end. Alfred Rigby wrote, "The greatest familiarity seems to exist between soldiers of both sides."[12] Alabamian W. D. Willet reported, "Then occurred a good scene in war after the flag of truce went out, the confederates and federals were 300 yards apart, left their arms, and met midway, and commenced friendly conversations, talked about home, exchanged tobacco for canteens, papers, etc. for a moment (against orders) they met mingled talked and seemed like friends, when the flag disappeared, both parties got to their places of safety, and all enemies again. Strange Sight! I had a view of two miles on the line and the same appeared everywhere."[13] Private Willet described this instance as "a good scene in war" amid the continuous fighting and bloodshed. Similarly, Ohioan George Pardee wrote, "When the flag came out I approached the works to within ten feet, had some conversation with the rebs, gave them a newspaper, etc."[14]

Also during these armistices, soldiers looked for friends and relatives on the opposing side and, astoundingly, found them. Iowan soldier George Burmeister wrote, "About 5 pm the rebels sent out a flag of truce to request an armistice for several hours to bury their dead which was granted. As soon as it was known that an armistice existed, the rebels and our soldiers came out onto their works, some friends met just half way between the rebel works and ours, glad to see each other."[15] After recognizing a childhood friend, Burmeister wrote, "I saw my old chum, the friend from my boyhood, the best friend I ever had, coming from the rebel works, his name is J.V. Smith, adjt. of the 2nd Mo. I had a long talk with him."[16] Other men used this opportunity to do the same. "When the gruesome task was completed, we, the common soldiers of both armies, met on halfway ground and had a friendly chat. Old acquaintances were hunted up, and the broken ties of friendship and consanguinity were reunited," illustrated William Chambers. "When the bugles gave the signal that the truce was ended, I saw *two* pairs of brothers clasp hands in farewell and go in opposite directions. After such a meeting it was with seeming reluctance that the firing was resumed, and even next day it seemed less vicious than before."[17] Chambers noted that it was the "common soldiers" who met and that acquaintances, and even siblings, found one another. His account also revealed that, after meeting the enemy, the fighting seemed less hostile. Even though the leadership ordered these armistices, men in the ranks saw what benefits they brought, especially during a siege. Beginning in the fall of 1863, soldiers in the armies that converged in Tennessee realized they could call their own ceasefires.

Fraternization and the development of ceasefires both evolved throughout the war. Instead of waiting for their commanders to issue a truce, men initiated cessations in hostilities on their own. On September 3, 1863, Charles Edwin Cort of the Ninety-Second Illinois, part of General George H. Thomas's Fourteenth Corps, was set to cross the Tennessee River. While on picket at the river,

Cort and his unit encountered Confederate skirmishers and fired a few shots. "We began to talk to each other and agreed with the post opposite not to shoot at each other but some below us kept cracking away. Collins, Willie, and I striped off and went in a swimming. When they saw we were not afraid of them they quit shooting and we were soon on good terms and talking across the river to each other. Willie swam to the middle to an old treetop and met one of them and had a good talk," Cort wrote his friends.[18] Because this was a soldier-orchestrated ceasefire, trust developed between antagonists. "The next morning," continued Cort, "they made the same agreement and four of our boys swam across the river and stayed a couple hours. You would have laughed to have seen two or three naked men perched on the old tree top in the middle of the river reb and union both."[19] Another member of the Ninety-Second Illinois, John King, explained what happened when both armies agreed not to fire on one another when they went for a swim. "Collins Willey of Co. H swam out to a shallow spot in the middle of the river and met a Johnny Reb and there the two boys, as naked as the day they were born, visited and chatted like two old women at a gossiping tea party. It was a novel visit under peculiar circumstance, and they both enjoyed the novelty and cracked many pleasant jokes, and each laughed as gaily as a school girl just emerging from a school room," wrote King.[20] This "swimming party," which included both Union and Confederates, represented a jovial occasion created by and for soldiers of the rank and file. However, like so many times before, men knew these were short-lived and parted ways. The bloodshed at Chickamauga soon eclipsed this lighthearted moment in time.

Following the Battle of Chickamauga, while the high command sorted out their strategic issues, the men of both armies attempted to cope with the slaughter they witnessed. Some men helped the enemy's wounded. Georgian soldier Benjamin Abbott walked along the battlefield and showed amnesty to his enemy on two occasions. First, Abbott came across mortally wounded Union Captain Barnett and agreed to communicate to his wife of his death. In an even more significant instance, Abbott saw a suffering Union soldier and asked him if he could do anything to help. The Union soldier asked to be buried decently, and Abbott agreed. "I took from my pocket a small vial of morphia and gave him about a half of grain and he was relieved very soon of pain and died easily and rationally. I had carried this little vial during all my service, fearing I might be wounded and left suffering on the field. It had never served me, but it was now to relieve an enemy," wrote Abbott. "In my own heart before the battle I felt very bitter against these men who had invaded our soil, as I believed against every principle of right, and yet in the hour of victory we soldiers were touched with pity for these wounded and dying enemies. It was not the place to discuss right and wrong: it was simply a question of humanity."[21] It was with these words that Abbott expressed the inherent difficulty surrounding civil war. Despite his aversion to the enemy, emotions caused from experiencing such carnage often eclipsed victory and vindication. In this moment Abbott realized the fate of his foe could have just as easily been his own. The empathy he felt stemmed from soldiers' ability to identify with one another. Death that surrounded them connected soldiers in ways that often surpassed the causes that divided them.

Because the Army of the Cumberland retreated so hastily to Chattanooga, General Rosecrans sent troops back to Chickamauga Creek to retrieve the wounded and dead. Subsequently, a very unique type of burial truce took place. Usually, troops would meet in between lines to collect their dead, but, due to the length of Rosecrans's retreat, the Army of Tennessee controlled what remained of the Union line at Missionary Ridge. Therefore, ambulances could only go as far as Confederate picket lines, and then Confederates collected the Union wounded and brought them back to the drivers.[22] While the drivers waited, pickets on both sides did not fire at one another. Chesley A. Mosman of the Fifty-Ninth Illinois wrote, "Three rebels pickets out in plain sight but we don't shoot. Seems wrong to murder a fellow not doing anything offensive. Instead of shooting at them we talk to them and ask them to come over to our side of the creek for a chat and a game of euchre."[23] Mosman's interaction with the Confederates revealed that, in the wake of such death, men preferred a friendly chat and a card game rather than more killing. On the second day of the burial detail, Mosman wrote, "Pickets on both sides come right out in the open in full view of each other. The rebel pickets are from Company G of the 6th South Carolina infantry and are fine, handsome, stout lot of fellows, better dressed than we are, their uniforms being apparently new. I went down among them. Some trading of tobacco for coffee going on. Two boys of the 74th Illinois join the johnnies in a game of cards."[24] Mosman's thoughts and interactions, taken at face value, demonstrated a sense of curiosity. However, placed in the context of both the battle that happened a week earlier and the mutilated, dying comrades being pulled off the field, these occurrences represented something more. Instead of essentially hating their enemy for their present circumstances, soldiers sought comfort in mutual fraternal and congenial gestures. Soldiers fraternized because it was an escape from reality and, in an incomprehensible situation, it made sense to them.

Because they had experienced the benefits of ceasefires in Mississippi and Tennessee in 1863, soldiers integrated them into their 1864 campaigning in Georgia and Virginia. Soldier-coordinated armistices peaked during the last year of the war. Men on both sides, although committed to finishing the job, grew tired of meaningless, continuous picket firing. For the armies in the western theater, the most frequent scenes of ceasefire occurred during the continuous and costly fighting from May through September, occurring at Kennesaw Mountain, along the Chattahoochee River, and during the Siege of Atlanta. Before General Sherman's army besieged the Army of Tennessee at Atlanta, however, these armies fought for three months along a line that began at Dalton, Georgia. Men did not have ample time to recover the wounded and resupply but experienced a constant pattern of quick strikes and continual marching south. At Dallas, Chester H. Southworth wrote, "If we are not relieved soon I think that I will not be worth a damn if there should be any fighting as this makes the 5th day of our being in the entrenchments without any sleep to speak of."[25] Men were constantly on picket duty but not to rest and prevent a general engagement like in earlier campaigns, but to maintain contact with the enemy and dig breastworks. Taylor Lester Dewitt wrote, "Last night our men attempted to get still nearer, by rolling barrels, casks, and boxes, filled with sand before them. They would then with spades build good works. And this is the way it is carried out on this campaign we have to chafe and dig them out, they contesting every foot of ground."[26] While units used the pick and shovel to construct new lines, there was almost always constant fire. "As soon as it got light enough we could see their picket line less than 100 yards from us and saluted each other good morning. We spent the remainder of the evening shooting at the yanks and they at us, at every opportunity," recorded J. P. Cannon.[27] It was under these conditions that men saw the opportunity to negotiate ceasefires. In June Hamlin Alexander Coe wrote, "The Rebs were eager to exchange tobacco for coffee. Among other agreements was one to discontinue firing upon pickets."[28] Thus, rank-and-file soldiers slowed down the pace, called truces, and stopped firing.

Although General Joseph E. Johnston's Confederate troops and Sherman's Union troops craftily constructed the means to fraternize during the fast-paced campaign, after Kennesaw Mountain the opportunity presented itself more than at any other point on the road to Atlanta. For Sherman's army, the Battle at Kennesaw Mountain was a disaster. Johnston's Army of Tennessee fortified their position atop Kennesaw Mountain from June 19 to July 3. Due to impassible roads, Sherman could not continue the tradition of attacking Johnston's left flank. Instead, Sherman assumed that, because Johnston's line stretched for seven miles, it was thin in the middle.[29] On June 27 at 8:00 a.m., the Fifteenth and Fourteenth Corps began the attack on Kennesaw Mountain. Midwesterners who climbed the steep, rocky terrain were met with infantry and artillery fire. Not only were these men repulsed by Johnston's Confederates but abatis in front of the fortifications caught fire, which severely threatened the Union wounded. The Fourteenth Corps that attacked at

Cheatham's Hill was also repulsed but was able to remain close to the Confederate line and fortified their position. June 27 ended with a decisive victory for Johnston's army as it sustained less than one thousand casualties, whereas Sherman lost roughly three thousand.[30] For the next few days sharpshooting continued while Johnston and Sherman contemplated their next moves. Amid the firing, men on both sides deemed it useless and arranged their own armistices. For example, William C. Buchanan of the Thirty-Sixth Illinois wrote, "Things are very quiet on the skirmish line today according to agreement between our boys and the rebels they are not firing at all, but are talking and trading back and forth."[31]

On June 29 a white flag signified a burial truce, and soldiers made the most of it. Due to the sight and stench of swollen, decaying bodies in between the lines, from 9:00 a.m. to 1:00 p.m. details from both sides gathered their dead.[32] "The enemy sent in a flag of truce for our division to go over and bury their dead. The smell was getting so offensive that they could not stand it," wrote John Hill Ferguson.[33] Similar to the scene at Vicksburg a year earlier, it would not be unreasonable to assume that when soldiers saw their comrades in such condition, the flood of emotions would radicalize them even further against their enemy. Yet, just as at Vicksburg, enemies saw burial detail as an opportunity to fraternize. Mosman noted, "Boys made a compromise and swapped papers and coffee for tobacco with the rebels," and Ferguson admitted, "I talked with some of the rebs. They were very friendly and anxious to trade tobacco or something with us in order to get come coffee."[34] Soldiers chose to spend that time talking and trading with each other regardless of the circumstances behind the truce. Upson wrote, "When the gun was fired that announced that the truce ended we parted with expressions of good will such as 'I hope to miss you, Yank, if I happen to shoot in your direction' and 'May I never hit you Johnny if we fight again.'"[35] Upson's account illustrates that these fraternal moments, however brief they were, transcended sectional animosity. Of course these parting sentiments could have just been cordial yet empty words to end the encounter. But some men elaborated on what these expressions meant. Alabamian J. P. Cannon further described this "respect" when he fraternized during the burial truce on June 29. Cannon wrote, "Johnny and Yank met on the most friendly terms. We had quite a sociable time, for there are no bad feelings as individuals. Brave men respect each other, no matter how much they differ in opinion."[36] Fraternization proves that, as the war entered its fourth year, soldiers valued and respected grit and sacrifice, even if it came from their foe. This mutual recognition of bravery separated soldiers from those at home. Historian Reid Mitchell suggests, "The gulf between stay-at-home and the soldier sometimes seemed greater than that which separated the Confederate and Union soldiers."[37] This respect was also why, in some instances, veteran soldiers loathed cowards on their own side more than the enemy.

The fraternization on June 29 was significant but short-lived. Johnston could either hold the Kennesaw line or move south to protect his railroad line. Sherman, who was fully aware that another assault on Kennesaw was out of the question, also knew he could not wait. On July 2 Sherman ordered the Army of the Tennessee, now under command of General James McPherson, south past Johnston's left flank and toward the Chattahoochee River.[38] Johnston set up his last line of defense before the city of Atlanta on the Chattahoochee. After slogging it out opposite one another for two months, almost like clockwork, soldiers continued to converse across the river. Like the Rappahannock River, the Chattahoochee River served as a permeable space soldiers deemed a "neutral zone." Richard T. Van Wyck wrote, "We remain encamped much the same as at Kelly's Ford, VA. The advance link is along the Chattahoochee River, only one hundred yards in width. The exchanging of tobacco, etc. with the rebs goes on to a greater extent than ever before and besides this, much talk and sentiment."[39] However, unlike the fraternization at earlier points of the war, the exchanges on the Chattahoochee were not about coffee or newspapers but out of a dire need to diminish danger.

In mid-July fraternization along the Chattahoochee River was one of the most frequently documented by soldiers in the western armies. Unlike incidents on the Rappahannock, accounts by soldiers outside of Atlanta depicted constant "heavy fire" and "bullets flying thick." Thus, soldiers took matters into their own hands. Van Wyck wrote, "A mutual understanding seems to exist between two parties as to firing, and when Johnny Reb thinks it is his duty to fire he intimates to Yankee to 'lie low' and vice versa."[40] As veteran soldiers, men in the rank and file deemed continual picket fire worth little gain. "Without consulting the officers we have agreed upon an armistice. All firing between pickets has ceased and consequently we have had a very quiet day, with the exception of the artillery, who is not included in the truce," described Cannon. This armistice signified a unity among infantry in creating a space on their own terms. Cannon went on to write, "Johnnies and Yanks have become quite friendly, exchanging many articles, such as tobacco for coffee canteens, but it has to be done in sly to keep the officers from finding out as they would hardly sanction so much familiarity."[41] This disconnect between infantrymen and their officers was even further exemplified when Cannon stated, "No doubt the officers are wondering why everything is so silent on the picket line. Of course, we do not propose to volunteer any information for we are enjoying the respite, and they might have so little regard for our feelings as to break up the truce."[42] Once officers learned of these truces and units rotated, the situation fluctuated throughout the day. "They will talk a while, and then shoot a while," noted Ferguson.[43] Officers even moved pickets back from the river bank because they were becoming "too intimate" or, as Coe deduced, "They were becoming friendly, proving to me clearly that if the privates of both armies were turned loose they would settle this war in a hurry."[44] Ceasefires sealed trust between enemies, limited threats, and allowed the flow of information and goods across the lines to continue.

Most notable on the Chattahoochee were the swimming parties. In the hot Georgia summer, enemy soldiers swam together in the river. "Everything is very quiet on both sides here this morning and the rebs and our skirmishers are having a social swim in the river, both sides agreeing not to fire on the other for so long a time. So they swim from one side to the other and have a friendly chat over matters and things," Simeon McCord described to his sister.[45] Swimming parties represented a peaceful moment where men escaped the continuous fighting. "In the evening yanks and rebs have a social swim where their pontoon used to be. Our men swam over to the rebs and traded coffee for tobacco," Illinoisan George Dalton told his wife.[46] Crossing the river for the usual commodities often progressed into acts of friendship. Harvey Reid wrote, "In out front the infantry pickets do not fire at all. The pickets often talk across the river and occasionally a good swimmer will cross for the purpose of trading coffee for tobacco. A few days ago 'Johnny Reb' invited one of the 85th Indiana boys over and wrote a letter to his sweetheart in Kingston, Georgia and sent it by him."[47]

General Alpheus Williams, who witnessed and grappled with the fraternization on the Allatoona Creek, also commented on the ceasefires on the Chattahoochee. "Our 'boys' have got up an armistice and they bathe on the opposite banks of the river and meet on a neutral log in the center of the stream and joke one another like old friends, making trades in tobacco, coffee, and the like, exchanging newspapers," observed Williams. He used the phrase "old friends" like so many soldiers did when describing fraternization. Williams continued, "Those in my division have not fired a shot for several days but are on the most quiet and joking terms with the opposite Johnnies."[48] He went on to explain that he was pleased when picket-firing stopped as it had "no effect upon the results of war" and is a "useless kind of murder." Williams's view of continuous fire mirrored that of the masses on the front lines. Because he too saw no use in picket fire, he turned a blind eye to fraternization within his division, allowing it to happen without consequence. Not all commanders did the same, however. Like so many times before, the peaceful pleasantries on the Chattahoochee ended as enemies moved in preparation to fight for the city.

When Sherman sent his forces toward Atlanta, this merriment ended almost as quickly as it began. Sherman designed the besiegement of Atlanta to inflict consistent pressure on all enemy fronts, which, as a result, made fraternization difficult at times. Like the Army of the Tennessee did at Vicksburg, Union skirmishers pushed their line closer to the Confederate main line, all under constant firing. Thus, the bulk of Confederates, now under the command of John Bell Hood, remained behind walls that made up a line extending from the west side of Atlanta to East Point.[49] Confederate soldiers felt the full effect of the siege. On August 8 Georgian James W. Watkins wrote, "We are seeing hard times. We are on duty every day or night we have been in the ditches 18 days and we have to eat and sleep right in the ditches all the time it rained so hard that everything that we had got wet. There is a grate many of ours men running a way every nite and a grate many is sick in the hospital."[50] Other Confederates also characterized their experience at Atlanta by the filthy, disease-ridden trenches they lived in.[51] For example, George S. Lea wrote, "We have to lie in the wet ditches till all of us look as a dog just out of a rabbit hole. Instead of being white we are all red."[52] Lea was also at Vicksburg but described Atlanta as, "The hardest times now that we have ever seen. Men being killed and wounded every day. I would give a great deal for the campaign to stop much less the war. Oh it is a terrible time with us and I am afraid the worse has not come yet."[53] Lea, a three-year veteran, indicated the difficulties and anxieties soldiers faced during the campaign. "We cant raise our heads above the works without being shot at and while back at the main line we have to lie in ditches owing to the heavy shelling every day," described Lea.[54] Because of their continual susceptibility to enemy fire, the men made arrangements with the enemy to limit the danger. When Hood's men rotated for picket duty, it placed them outside the fortification, and, again, they generated a space to arrange ceasefires and trade.

A few soldiers wrote about their truces with the enemy while stationed in the trenches at Atlanta, and these instances prove to be some of the most significant in the western theater. On August 22, 1864, Chester Southworth wrote, "The boys got trading papers for tobacco with them, but this was put a stop to by General Claibourne giving orders to shoot the next Yank that came beyond the skirmish

FIG. 10. General Sherman's troops in their constructed earthworks around the city of Atlanta. George N. Barnard, *Atlanta, Georgia (Vicinity). Federal Pickets before the City*, 1864. Library of Congress Prints and Photographs Division. LC-DIG-cwpb-03385.

line. One of our boys went out and the Rebel Major in command of the picket told him what orders he had and he proposed we cease firing altogether which we acceded to."[55] Southworth's account represented a key instance in which a soldier, lodged in the middle of a siege, reached his limit. Soldiers were no longer surprised at these interactions: at this point in the war, they pushed for them. Similarly, a very steadfast soldier from the Tenth Illinois wrote about his dedication and obligation as a soldier during the Atlanta campaign. Thomas Bell wrote, "His only duty is to receive orders and obey them. It is natural for the human race to complain and be dissatisfied with their lot in life whether it be high or low. But the true soldier endures his trials and hardship in silence knowing that it is all for that dear old flag."[56] Two weeks after Bell wrote such patriotic words, he fraternized. On August 12, 1864, Bell wrote, "There was an armistice between the two lines today. And a very little firing ensued. Our boys trade coffee with the rebs for tobacco. And both parties seemed well pleased with their bargain."[57] Bell's experience indicates men fraternized because they felt empowered constructing moments of safety in a world they otherwise had very little control over.

John Hill Ferguson, one of Bell's fellow Tenth Illinois comrades, also documented the fraternization that transpired on August 12. Ferguson noted that for days they and the enemy pickets had been firing upon one another continuously, both day and night. But on the twelfth, both sides starting "hollering" at one another, and "the two parties for the first time at this place, quit shooting and entered into conversation. They agreed to quit shooting and be more friendly." Not only did the shooting cease but now both parties were able to sit atop their rifle pits, which were only fifty yards apart. Then, they agreed to meet. "Soon privates were comeing from both parties shakeing hands and rejoiceing at their meeting as if they were old friends and had been absent for a long time," wrote Ferguson. "Both parties sit down in the brush to have a general chat and when another of our boys would go over, the Rebs would all get up and each one shake hands with the knew comer in the most friendly terms." Ferguson and his men would do the same, greeting the incoming Confederates with "How do you do, Johney?" As expected, while the men conversed, they traded coffee and tobacco. The details of his account depict a sense of excitement and relief. Shortly thereafter, the Tenth Illinois was relieved from their post on the picket line and returned to camp. On the fourteenth Ferguson mentioned the lasting success of the ceasefire. "Our lines are very quiet today, but little firing has been dun on the picket line since our regiment was on picket on the 12th," stated Ferguson. On the seventeenth he went back out on picket and noted the Rebs would not talk to them as it was strictly prohibited by their officers. Ferguson wrote, "3 or 4 of our boys have went over near their pits, without arms and holding up a newspaper, but they Rebs would signal for them to go back but would not speak."[58] Even a Confederate lieutenant stood up on the works and told them to go away. Ferguson emanated a sense of frustration when the system he and his comrades developed ended. The officers' attempts to stop it, however, do show the frequency with which these ceasefires materialized among privates on the front lines.

When General Hood fled the city on September 1, 1864, the entire country felt the impact surrounding the fall of Atlanta. The men in the Army of Tennessee moved north while Hood devised a campaign to draw Sherman back into the mountains northwest of Atlanta. General Thomas pursued and opposed Hood in what became known as the Franklin-Nashville Campaign.[59] Meanwhile, Sherman led his Army of the Tennessee through the heartland of Georgia toward Savannah, commonly known as the "March to the Sea." Most importantly, the Northern home front attributed Lincoln's eventual reelection to the fall of Atlanta. Thus, the Confederate strategy to hold out until the November election was no longer feasible as their hope for independence could only be achieved on the battlefield. Just as Sherman attacked the Army of Tennessee's left flank through Georgia in the early summer, General Grant simultaneously pursued General Lee's army south through Virginia. When Sherman and Hood met in Atlanta, Grant had already besieged Lee at Petersburg, Virginia. Therefore, aside from the survival of Hood's battered army in Tennessee, the hope for Southern independence now rested in the hands of the Army of Northern Virginia at Petersburg.

In the summer of 1864, the tactical nature of siege warfare forced soldiers to reconfigure how they fought. Historian Kenneth Noe argues, "As the summer passed, all soldiers . . . experienced a new kind of war. It was unrelenting, marked by constant fighting, daily advances and retreats, the constant physical labor involving the construction and repair of earthworks, and unremitting bloodletting."[60] Instead of the outdated open-field Napoleonic tactics these men experienced at Antietam, Fredericksburg, and Gettysburg, trench warfare allowed soldiers some protection against the accuracy of the rifles and range of artillery.[61] But, that protection came with its own set of challenges. About the siege at Petersburg, Joseph Glatthaar contends, "The longer they remained in one location the worse vermin, sanitation, and illness problems became. . . . Enemy lines were so near that Lee's troops could not move back out of range to relax, and soldiers found it very difficult to sleep in the trenches."[62] Soldiers had to be on guard all the time and became both physically and mentally exhausted. "'Courage,' 'honor,' 'self-sacrifice,' 'heroism' now belonged to those distant, 'unreal' worlds outside of the trench system," asserts historian Eric Leed.[63] "If any man thinks soldiering is a holiday affair let him come to the 'trenches' and he will be enlightened I think. We have to bring wood on our shoulders over half a mile, cook, wash, drill, and picket, not to say anything about an occasional drill in close 'bayonet exercise' and the ball manual," described James Thomas Perry.[64] Instead of there being a clear spatial difference in what constituted a battlefield and camp, like at Vicksburg, at Petersburg the soldiers' camp *was* the battlefield. Joseph Banks Lyle wrote, "With the enemy sharpshooters 200 yards from our works—we have to stick to our trenches—no chance to get out by the right, the left, or the rear—but stay in the most cramped, disgusting, and confined place I have ever been in."[65] The implications of siege warfare in Virginia brought about new conceptions of labor and combat for men in these armies.

If soldiers were left to fight it out in the earthworks, eventually the lid on the pressure cooker had to come off. Like at Vicksburg, Kennesaw Mountain, and Atlanta, in order to alleviate the seemingly unremitting sense of danger, soldiers arbitrated ceasefires to reduce the continuous death. Soldiers warned their enemy about impending attacks. For example, Major Abner R. Small wrote, "When a battery was about to open fire, some friendly skirmisher would shout 'Down, Yank!' or 'Down, Reb!'"[66] Similarly, a Confederate soldier wrote, "We were out in front of the breastworks on picket a few nights ago. Pretty soon the yankee relief came and they called out to our boys 'rats to your holes' and fired their guns in the air."[67] These "warnings" indicated that soldiers understood their susceptibility to being caught off guard and the anxiety it caused. "Occa-

FIG. 11. Soldiers constructed trenches like these for protection from continuous fire. Each side's first line of trenches was within close range of the other's. *Petersburg, Virginia. Earthworks in Front of Petersburg.* Petersburg, Virginia, 1865. Library of Congress Prints and Photographs Division. LC-DIG-cwpb-03624.

sionally, a Reb would show himself and shout some good natured badinage at us 'yanks our time will be in three days—we are then coming over to see you' which we responded in a strain pitched to the same time," documented Samuel Pierce.[68] His account reveals that by offering a "warning," soldiers shared their orders with the enemy. Illinoisan soldier Valentine C. Randolph wrote, "The men on both sides became careless and left the ditches without any fear whatever. Suddenly a voice from the rebel lines warned us that hostilities were to commence in a few minutes—'get into your pits, we are going to open fire.'"[69] Through this agreement to warn one another, soldiers were able to let their guard down during their strenuous twenty-four-hour picket-duty shift. A significant example of the tendency to warn the enemy took place during Confederate general John B. Gordon's assault on Fort Stedman in March 1865. General Gordon came to the picket line to ensure that his men would not alert Federal artillerists of their attack. A Union picket called out, "'What are you doing over there Johnny?' and the Confederate private from the Sixth Louisiana replied, 'Never mind, Yank. Lie down and go to sleep. We are just gathering a little corn, you know our rations are short over here.' The Union picket responded, 'All right, Johnny—go ahead and get your corn. I'll not shoot at you while you are drawing your rations.' As Gordon repeated the order to fire the shot, the rifleman called out, 'Hello yank! Wake up. We are going to shell the woods. Look out, we are coming!'"[70] The private's inclination to warn the Union soldier represented a reciprocal understanding between enemies on the front lines.

Even more effective than warnings, soldiers honored their own armistices to placate the fear and anxiety brought about by continuous fire. Captain Joseph Banks Lyle noted how both sides' "pickets agree to stop sharpshooting."[71] By this point in the war, soldiers in the eastern armies also felt sharpshooting accomplished nothing. Reaching out to the enemy to halt the firing was practical. "We hold a line in close proximity to the enemy but an arrangement existed preventing firing by either part upon the other," explained a Confederate private.[72] As men sat in the trenches grappling with the physical and emotional difficulties, these arrangements allowed men to feel in control. "Made peace with the Yankees for a while," wrote a Mississippian. "Talked with them about a ½ hour."[73] Soldiers' descriptions of peacefulness and relief during the ceasefires demonstrated their efficacy. Charles Wellington Reed described, "The day before yesterday our pickets and the reb pickets erected an armistice early in the morning and agreed not to fire on one another, which suited us 'to a T' as more than half of their infernal bullets come flying, buzzing, and skipping all around us, which is exceedingly annoying especially when a fellow wants to get a canteen of water or do a little cooking."[74] The ceasefire carried considerable weight for Reed and his comrades because it allowed them to eat, rest, and let their guard down. A week later, after the Battle on the Jerusalem Plank Road, Reed wrote, "The second morning our pickets and the rebs got tired of their murderous work agreed not to fire on one another and from that time to this we have enjoyed the utmost tranquility and having the best rest since crossing the Rapidan."[75] Reed's noting of "tranquility" and "rest" as a result of these ceasefires proves why exhausted soldiers arranged them. "It hardly seems we were so close to a large army of the enemy. Everything is so quiet. We have no firing between pickets. But there exists on both sides the most friendly relations on that part of the line where the opposing parties are closest," expressed Joseph Ward in his diary.[76] Soldiers realized that by establishing a ceasefire, they could recreate the camp they grew accustomed to, one that was absent of immediate peril.

Ceasefires allowed enemies to continue the trade network the established two years prior. Private John West Haley described, "No firing during the day. Our men have been out all day trading and playing cards with the Johnnies. There was a big tree about half way between our line and theirs, and thither we and they resorted for the purposes above named."[77] The tree Haley alluded to was both in the "neutral zone" and inconspicuous to the high command. William Ray described how soldiers honored these truces: "A man from each side sallied forth with a paper and someone in our brigade to the right of us fired. At that they ran back to the works and the boys in the brigade hollowed 'kill that fellow that shot.' Most everybody seems to think he deserved death for shooting on such an occasion."[78] Ray continued, "But in two or three minutes they sallied out again and this time they met, shook hands, and exchanged papers."[79] In this instance, Ray's account shows that both Union and Confederate soldiers considered that the man who fired was breaking a fragile trust between enemies. "Sometimes we meet enemy pickets who are cutting wood just as we are. As enemies we are supposed to try to capture or kill each other. Humanity requires that we be cautious but kind. So regardless of our orders, we cut wood, exchange papers or coffee and tobacco, and go on our way," admitted Mississippian Franklin Lafayette Riley.[80] As Riley illustrates, Northern and Southern men needed firewood to keep warm and did not see the purpose in using aggression against each other. Through these arrangements men came together in the space they created, as equals, as a means of self-preservation. Whether they knew it or not, soldiers' actions and the fraternal spaces they created were a rehearsal for Reconstruction.

Relations between black troops and their enemy provided another major test for conditions in postwar society. The siege at Petersburg involved a significant number of African American troops, approximately twenty thousand. United States Colored Troops (USCTs) fought, in segregated units, at the Second Battle of Petersburg, the Battle of the Crater, and the New Market Heights in Richmond. For Northern men, their sentiments about fighting alongside black men ranged from anger to appreciation.[81] For Southern men, in 1865 the Davis administration contemplated, but never issued, an ordinance that would enlist Southern blacks with the promise of emancipation in exchange for their service to the Confederacy. Confederate soldier Lavender Ray asked, "Why not make the negro useful to us in achieving our independence? We can put 100,000 in service and discipline them so they will do good fighting. I have seen white men who were made to fight by the dread of their officers. If white men can be frightened into battle and made to do good service why cannot Negroes be thus frightened?"[82] Ray's statement represented the Southern tradition of using black men for the personal gain of whites. The notion of arming black soldiers to fight for the South showed the drastic measures the Confederacy considered in order to survive. Although some Confederates considered using black troops, most feared overturning the long-established "slave code" that prohibited men of color from using weapons. Southerners, outnumbered by the slave population in most places, feared slave rebellion. So, when Confederate soldiers saw former slaves in uniform, they absolutely could not come to terms with fighting against black men. Confederate soldiers admitted both their surprise and abhorrence in fighting USCTs for the first time. "On picket at 5pm. Negro pickets in our front for the first time. Opened on the yankee pickets—negroes—all along our division line suddenly at 9:00am. Got my first view of a 'cuffee' as a soldier on the Yankee picket line, in full view not 200 yards from me. It may have been only fancy but they really seemed the blackest of all black animals I ever beheld. They were pretty imprudent, flaunting their newspapers in our faces for exchange!" stated James Thomas Perry. Those whom Confederates viewed as chattel, and thereby absent of any degree of masculinity, were now armed, in uniform, and competing for equal social status. Perry continued, "Strict orders were issued against firing else several of them would have gone to keep John Brown company in the 'Happy Land of Canaan' where his active spirit is supposed to be still 'marching along.' Heard the negroes across the way singing songs tonight that reminded me of the good old 'husking' days in the happy past."[83] Private Perry's emotions of contempt and nostalgia demonstrated the blow that arming African American men struck to the Southern psyche.

Just as black Union soldiers fought alongside their white comrades, they too took their turn on picket duty. However, white Union soldiers could tell when the USCTs were on picket duty because the Confederates did not honor the neutral zone and never ceased fire. Private Haley noted, "No fighting, but picket firing in front of the 18th Corps where there are n——. In front of these, the Rebs keep up a continual firing and the 'gentlemen of African descent' have to lay low, their heads not being impervious to bullets if they are black."[84] Similarly, Union soldier George McClelland wrote, "Both sides are peaceably inclined [on picket duty] and walk about with impunity—but just on our immediate right the firing is kept up incessantly by 'Burnside's N——:' the Rebs seem to have a spite at them."[85] Therefore, Southern soldiers who knew of the benefits to ceasefire gave no such amnesty to USCTs. "Although the rebel pickets and ours are in plain sight all the time, at our part of the line, we do not fire at each other. But they are firing constantly night and day at each other about a quarter of a mile to the right of us. Negro regiments of Burnside's Corps," expressed Samuel Pierce.[86] Whereas Confederates attempted to lessen the sharpshooting with their white counterparts, they gave no such amnesty to Union men of color. Marion Hill Fitzpatrick wrote, "Also since I left here the sharpshooters have had some brisk skirmishing with negro troops that were put in our front on the yankee skirmish line. Our boys could not stand for negro troops to be so near them and pitched into them and drove them off."[87] Southerners' reactions to seeing black men in uniform proved fraternization was solely for white men.

When Confederates saw their former slaves as soldiers it threatened the Southern racial caste system. According to historian A. Wilson Greene, "The Confederates' rage stemmed their belief that the use of slave soldiers violated every social, moral, and ethical principle they held dear."[88] The sight of Confederate soldiers fraternizing with white Union troops and firing relentlessly on black Union troops confirmed the power of the Southern racial hierarchy. "For after a while we came on these lines our pickets and the Yankees were quite friendly, they talked and traded with each other every day, but the Yankees a people who are so fond of changing could not be content with white men out front, so they concluded they would try their sable colored troops in front of our pickets," wrote Edmund Fitzgerald Stone. "It so enraged our boys that the officers could hardly keep them from firing on them as soon as they discovered negroes in their front. The next morning at eight o clock an order came in a few minutes every man was at his post with gun in hand and thumb on hammer and finger on trigger ready to fire a deadly volley into the ranks of the unsuspecting blacks who were at the time standing in groups at each pit."[89] This deep-seated hatred expressed by Private Stone demonstrates the absolutism of white supremacy in the Southern consciousness. When Southern soldiers saw white Union men on picket duty, they felt emotions of humanity and empathy. For black soldiers, it was quite the opposite. When Confederates saw soldiers of color up close, it served as a reminder of slavery's soon-to-be fate and evoked rage. USCTs felt deadly hostility not only from Confederate soldiers but also faced animosity from Southern noncombatants. After the Battle of the Crater, General A. P. Hill put the 1,500 Union prisoners on parade in the city of Petersburg. Hill ordered the integration of white officers and soldiers with USCT prisoners. As the prisoners paraded around town, civilians taunted both white and black soldiers incessantly. Civilians shouted, "See the white and n—— equality soldiers. Yanks and n—— sleep in the same bed."[90] Southerners unleashed their anger at white Union officers for leading their slaves against the Confederacy. This confrontation between Southern civilians and Northern soldiers illustrated the social dynamics set to play out in the postwar era. Northerners had to make a choice: freedmen or Southerners. And, wartime fraternization foreshadowed that decision. White men, although enemies, chose to reunite at the expense of people of color.

On the morning of April 2, 1865, the Union Sixth Corps, after nearly a week of persistent fighting, broke through the Confederate defensive at the Boydton Plank Road. General Grant's Army met with Sheridan's forces and pursued Lee's army north to Richmond, where the city evacuated and fell to Northern control. Even as the Federal troops moved into Petersburg and Richmond, fraternization continued. Enos Bennage of the Ninety-Ninth Pennsylvania wrote, "I took a walk down to the capital square with two rebels and had a long talk with them and they seemed to be very nice men."[91] Just as they did while fraternizing during combat, soldiers took strides to honor one another's courage and ignore the political differences. Men on both sides were glad the war was over and viewed their comrades as fellow veterans who not only experienced the same horrors but survived. After Confederate armies surrendered and veteran soldiers returned home, the nation now faced the mammoth task of sectional reunification. The devastated nation needed to bury the dead, readmit Confederate states, protect freedmen, and rehabilitate the Southern landscape. But, it was not a watershed moment in American history. The focus on amnesty and shared sacrifices between the picket lines indicated how the postwar period would play out and who it would leave out. Fraternization was a litmus test for Reconstruction.

6

Memory

The two armies that stood facing each other, were beginning to entertain a decided respect for each other.

—Thomas Mann, Eighteenth Massachusetts Volunteer Infantry

In 1917 Isaac Van Houten, veteran of the Twenty-Fifth New Jersey Infantry, gave a speech at the Fifty-fifth Anniversary of the Battle of Fredericksburg. During his address Van Houten stated, "Picketing along the shores of the Rappahannock soon became our daily avocation, after our evacuation, with the enemy doing like duty opposite. The retorts and chaffing between Blue and Gray were events some of which outlived the shock of battle, and culminated in the formation of friendships that still live."[1] Van Houten's depiction of fraternization closely resembles the accounts documented in 1863. At face value, he may have chosen to speak about fraternization simply because it was a significant part of his campaign on the Rappahannock. Or, he may have mentioned it for a different purpose. Van Houten spoke these words a few months after America's entry into World War I. Perhaps he used the example of fraternization to advocate for shedding any residual sectional animosity in order to unite as a nation at war. But the use of wartime fraternization for political purposes did not begin in 1917. After Congress passed the Compromise of 1877 and declared Reconstruction over, fraternalism between former enemies emerged as a dominant theme. It was within this political culture that Southerners constructed a narrative, commonly known as the "Lost Cause," which promoted the honor, sacrifice, and courage of men on both sides rather than the causes and consequences of the war.[2] Those who sought to push this agenda applauded accounts of friendliness among soldiers to prove that, if enemies got along amid the bloodshed, they could most certainly get along during peacetime. Champions of the Lost Cause embellished, and even fabricated, accounts of fraternization to use as propaganda for a postwar society that elevated white supremacy at the expense of African American equality. This makes interpreting postwar accounts of fraternization a difficult and cautionary process. In order to assess the correlation between memory and fraternization, veterans' agency is key. Historian James Marten argues that, in order to understand memory and the process of reunion, the role of veterans is essential.[3] Although soldiers' letters and most diaries stopped at the end of the war, these men continued to process their experiences.[4] Thousands of soldiers went back to the battlefields to find closure and to get the facts straight. Ex-soldiers felt that, once their generation passed, witnesses would no longer be able to accurately interpret these locations. When veterans wrote memoirs, they proved to be an essential coping mechanism and allowed them to control the memory of their service. Postwar political culture did influence veterans, but they did not simply tow the reconciliationist line. Soldiers had already formed fraternal bonds with the enemy during the war. They did not need others to convince them to do it. In staking their claim over the record, veterans documented their experiences of fraternizing and shaped Civil War memory. Postwar accounts of fraternization demonstrate that being an influencer of memory and being influenced by it were not mutually exclusive.

This chapter provides evidence from several different types of accounts: first from soldiers' memoirs, both published and unpublished, then through periodicals, beginning with those written by and for the former high command and then followed by those read by a popular audience, including veterans. The differences in these portrayals of fraternization are striking. Both the intended audiences and the authors' and publishers' motivations explain the differences. The accounts of fraternization in periodicals tend to be much more embellished. With an extensive readership and a very public platform, periodicals inflated wartime fraternization by forcing these connections and perpetuating themes of chivalry, honor, and civility. As wartime accounts of fraternization illustrate, these connections did not need to be forced, they were already there. But reconciliationists embraced these moments of war and tailored them to fit their political agenda. On the other hand, the majority of veterans' recollections did not exaggerate fraternization. Their memoirs were personal, more private, and written for themselves and their families. The evidence in their memoirs suggests that veterans who wrote about fraternization did so because they deemed it a significant part of their service. Fraternization was a ritual only those in the rank and file understood. Historians of the postwar era agree that not only were the men who returned from war different but the world they returned to could not fully comprehend what they had seen and experienced.[5] The separation men felt from noncombatants during the war resonated in the postwar years as soldiers gained sympathy, rather than empathy, from their families. In addition to their former comrades who joined Grand Army of the Republic and United Confederate Veterans chapters alongside them, their former enemies also understood this disconnect. At Blue-Gray reunions, suggests historian Caroline Janney, "veterans agreed not to discuss the causes of the war but rather commiserate the severity of camp life and commend each other on their bravery."[6] This tendency was not exceptional to the postwar era. During the war, fraternization occurred because of a mutual recognition of sufferings and sacrifices. Fraternizing soldiers had avoided both discussion of the causes of the war and the terms of their "peace agreements." These fraternal bonds did not begin at the turn of the twentieth century. Veterans demonstrated their role as both political actors and purveyors of sectional reunification well before they became old and gray.

FIG. 12. Civil War veterans William H. Calvert of Co. C, Seventy-Seventh Pennsylvania Infantry Regiment, with ladder badge and crutches, and William G. DeLashmutt of Co. D, First Maryland Cavalry Battalion, with United Confederate Veterans medal, shaking hands at the Gettysburg reunion. Gettysburg, Pennsylvania, United States, 1913. International News Service, Copyright Claimant. Library of Congress Prints and Photographs Division. Liljenquist family collection of Civil War Photographs, LC-DIG-ppmsca-58172.

Veterans wanted to showcase the innovative ways they created a fraternal relationship with the enemy and survived the war. Their memoirs contain descriptions of friendly conversations with their enemy in wartime sites where the previous chapters of this book have shown fraternization was most common. In reference to the winter on the Rappahannock, Daniel Emerson Hurd wrote, "We had religious services Sundays, drilled some, went down opposite the city on picket duty and chatted with the rebel pickets on the other side of the river, 'Hello, Reb,' 'Hello, Yank,' etc."[7] After the Battle of Chickamauga John Beatty wrote, "The pickets of the two armies are growing quite intimate, sitting about on logs together, talking over the great battle, and exchanging views as to the results of a future engagement."[8] Beatty's account was comparable to those who wrote about fraternization on picket duty in front of Lookout Mountain. On the Chattahoochee River before Atlanta, William Burge recalled, "We helped mine the fort, dig ditches, and build breastworks up so close to the Johnnies that we could converse with them. I was on the firing line every day from that to the 22nd of July 1864. One time when I was on picket duty in front of Mt. Kennesaw we had a line established close enough to the rebel line that we could communicate with them. Their guards agreed to cease firing while we would go across to visit and exchange coffee for tobacco."[9] Burge's recollection is in line with fraternization accounts from mid-July after Kennesaw Mountain and before the Army of the Cumberland pushed forward to Atlanta. At Petersburg, George Darby recalled, "We sat on top of our rifle pits reading aloud from our Northern newspapers for Johnnies edification, and Johnnie would reciprocate in kind, by reading aloud to us the papers of his section."[10] Again, Darby's vignette of sharing papers compares to wartime depictions of fraternization at Petersburg. On the Rapidan River, William Seymour characterized fraternization as: "Our pickets held one bank while the enemy's were on the other; there was no firing between them and they got to be on quite intimate terms with each other—exchanging friendly salutations and courtesies, and oftentimes swimming the river to hold sociable confabs."[11] Seymour then continued with a description of an occurrence in which one of his comrades was a Northerner by birth and discovered that men from his native town of Albany, New York, were on picket post across the river. "The yankee captain and his men used their utmost powers of persuasion to induce their visitor to desert from the confederate army, promising him a safe conduct to his parents in Albany and that he should never be called to do duty in the federal army; at the same time reminding him of his tattered clothing, scanty and indifferent food," Seymour noted.[12] Similar to how other soldiers who fraternized shunned desertion, Seymour recalled that the Confederate "spurned the dishonorable offer" and said "he would not desert his colors for all the gold that the federal government could command."[13] Seymour's incident confirmed that veteran soldiers who vehemently opposed desertion did not view fraternization as a similar offense and, in this case, fraternized themselves.

Veterans wrote about the trade agreements with the enemy in their memoirs. These depictions also fell closely in line with wartime accounts in terms of accuracy. "When night would come on, and the firing slacken, it was not an uncommon thing to hear the boys talking to the 'reb' boys in the most friendly manner. These conversations would generally end in the 'rebs' asking the yankee if he had any coffee to trade for confederate script when an armistice would be agreed on, and the boys would meet between the lines, make their trades, and have a friendly chat," stated Ira Blanchard.[14] This account accurately documents the wartime evolution of trade through a mutually beneficial system. James Merrill recalled, "Frequent interchanges would occur. Questions asked and answered. Quite often during the day a small package of tobacco would be tied up with a stone and thrown over which was invariably followed by a good mess of coffee."[15] Merrill depicted the coffee for tobacco trade seen so many times throughout the war. Pennsylvanian Frank M. Smith recollected, "At the time there was generally a truce during the day. Often one of the boys would load up with coffee and meet some reb between the lines and trade for tobacco and make a frequent trade of buttons and other things to send home for souvenirs."[16] Similar to how Smith alluded to the exchange of souvenirs that many wrote about in their wartime accounts, others recalled the trade of newspapers. Ohioan John Calvin Hartzell wrote, "You will notice some of the boys are reading old newspapers. You see when the pickets are good and friendly they often meet half way and trade things, sometimes newspapers; and when we get a Charleston, Richmond, or new Orleans paper we gather in groups to hear it read."[17] Hartzell continued, "A lull during the day gave me a chance to go down to Chattanooga Creek, and I got up a parley. We soon struck a trade, and I gave an old, dog-eared deck of cards for this little sack of kinikinick tobacco and this Richmond newspaper."[18] Veterans recollections of trade agreements emanate similar purposes—acquiring commodities and information that made daily life tolerable.

Comparable to how soldiers noted the agreement of ceasefires, veterans described their efforts to limit incessant firing. Former soldiers acknowledged the toll frontline combat took on their morale and how they attempted to alleviate that anxiety. J. H. Jones described the difficulty during the siege of Vicksburg that "created a mental strain," and he noted that "who's next? Was on every man's lips. Here were men, one minute engaged in deadly strife, and the next meeting as friends. Here was bloody tragedy changed to laughing comedy in an instant."[19] Now with the advantage of hindsight, former soldiers applauded their efforts to cut back on the hostilities during picket duty. At Fredericksburg, "I was sent up the river in command of pickets, and upon reaching there, some of the men came up to me and told me that the Federal commander across the river wanted to talk to me," recalled George A. Clark. "I went down the bank of the river and he shouted across that he saw no necessity for picket firing and would like to make arrangements with them, that if any movement was contemplated by his force he would notify us in time to get cover, if I would agree to do the same."[20] Clark agreed to do the same and went on to say the "winter passed pleasantly" as a result of their compromise. "At Petersburg, upon each picket pit a white cloth floated with the understanding that while it was there no shots would be fired," admitted James Flint Merrill.[21] Veterans highlighted these ceasefires as examples of how they controlled certain circumstances of their day-to-day lives. Don Wickman wrote, "After the sounds of battle subsided and men stopped shooting, it was not unusual to see peace reign on the picket lines. The men in the 9th fully endorsed such action and officers subtly condone the verbal agreement."[22] The officers Wickman referred to were lower-ranking unit or company commanders who participated in fraternization while on the front lines.

Veterans' accounts of fraternization documented their attempts to push back against the high command as a unique form of resistance. In his recollections J. H. Jones describes this feeling as: "The chord became too tense and had to be relaxed, or else it would break and relief was sought in enforced amusement when the shadows of night permitted."[23] Jones's statement proved the leadership's control over soldiers became so stifling at times that men needed ways to escape. Veterans documented ways they resisted by disregarding rules against fraternization. Clark noted, "Several amusing incidents occurred between us but no especial harm was done. Our boys now and then would swim across the river and get things from the Yankees, and they in turn would get things from us. All this of course was done while the officers were not watching."[24] Ex-soldiers noted how they and their enemy worked together to conduct the exchanges. "To facilitate these exchanges, one or the other tossed a stone with a twine attached across the river, thus enabling a rope ferry," recalled Thomas Mann about the Rappahannock. "Foggy weather along the river banks was the rule, and a conversation was easiest carried on when a fog shut down so thick as to hide one bank from the other."[25] Also stationed along the Rappahannock, George Clark stated, "Our boys made boats that could sail directly up and across the river, and give the Federals directions how to set the boat to come back to us. On one occasion one of my men was captured and taken into custody as a prisoner, but the next day he was released and brought back to us by way of Fredericksburg."²⁶ Veterans openly admitted their behavior was against orders and a punishable offense. Sergeant George W. Darby wrote, "This arrangement was made between the men without consent or knowledge of the officers. We finally became upon such good terms with each other that traffic sprang up between us. The barter was usually coffee and tobacco. The conditions of the trade were favorable, and under this treaty we became quite neighborly."²⁷ Darby's recognition that soldiers purposefully broke orders to fraternize proved that veterans continued to feature these moments, just as they had during the war.

Even more than in accounts written during the war, veteran soldiers wrote about the methods they developed to go about fraternizing with the enemy undetected. With time to reflect and no longer under officer scrutiny, veterans provided more detail and analysis to their postwar accounts. For example, "At times quite a brisk traffic was carried on between the opposing lines; logs were dug out and converted into miniature boats, to which ingeniously contrived sails were fitted; these little crafts were filled with tobacco and Richmond newspapers—the only articles of traffic that our poor fellows possessed.... The Yankees would send return cargoes of many acceptable articles, but the most eagerly sought after highly prized were coffee and sugar," described William Seymour.²⁸ This depiction of trade, articulated by Seymour, revealed the lengths soldiers went to in order to receive commodities of such importance. Howard Malcolm Walthall recalled, "On our extreme right there was a splendid spring of good water, about half way between the lines. Often a daring soldier would steal to that hidden spot and meet one from the other side, and they would exchange tobacco for coffee, sugar and newspapers."²⁹ Surprisingly, Walthall went on to admit something not seen in wartime accounts of fraternization. Walthall stated, "This familiarity led to bad consequences, because there were many dissatisfied men on our side who preferred prison on the other side to continual hardships on their own, and often they would go away with their newly chosen friends."³⁰ During the war, officers cracked down on fraternization for this very reason.

Soldiers noted the frequency of deserters but did not state outright the correlation between fraternization and desertion. In hindsight, Walthall either correlated the effect fraternization had on demoralized men or possibly made a false assumption.

Writing about displays of amnesty was another way former soldiers controlled how their service would be remembered. Veterans wanted to draw attention to their bravery, especially when it was compassionate. These depictions, sometimes, were questionable in terms of complete accuracy. For example, about the works at Vicksburg, J. H. Jones later wrote, "On the right of my regiment the federal lines were about one hundred yards down the hill, and every night 'johnnie' and 'yank' would call a truce and meet between the lines in friendly intercourse, and thus the 38th Mississippi and the 17th Illinois became good friends."[31] Soldiers documented this scene several times at Vicksburg, but then, Jones continued by recalling, "Our friends of the 17th Illinois fraternized with the 38th and aided us greatly by the many acts of kindness. They would go out to their sutler's tent with the greenbacks we had borrowed from their dead comrades and purchased food for us, and doubtless many a starving reb felt his life was thus saved."[32] Several wartime accounts depicted Union men sharing rations with Southerners, but not to the extent that they purchased food for them. When veterans embellished accounts, it was usually to inflate their own image, but in this case, Jones gives all the credit to his Northern counterparts, so perhaps this event actually did happen. In his postwar memoir, John Oliver Andrews recollected a point when he was returning from guard duty and saw a wounded Union soldier. Andrews then described, "I readily saw the situation, so I told him to give me the cup that was tied to his belt and he could go his way. He never said a word and handed me the cup. I said 'farewell yank' and he said 'Good bye Johnnie.'"[33] This anecdote could have also been true, but Andrews also could have used his memoir as an opportunity to fabricate his benevolence. If men felt guilt or regret about their wartime experiences, their memoirs were ways to reconstruct that narrative.

Lower-ranking officers asserted more authority in their later memoirs than in their wartime letters. These men had been less likely to verbalize their allowance of and participation in fraternization while under scrutiny of their superiors. However, after the war, these men embraced opportunities to speak freely. For instance, Captain William J. Seymour wrote, "The hostile lines did not fire upon each other, there being a mutual understanding that the armies maintained their present positions."[34] Similarly, Captain Henry Newton Comey recalled, "On one occasion at Kennesaw, by mutual understanding, firing had ceased when a rebel officer came along and ordered his pickets to keep the firing, but the pickets yelled across to our pickets 'yanks lay low, we have got orders to fire,' whereupon all took cover. That's what I call honorable."[35] It is unclear whether Seymour's and Comey's roles on the front lines were to prevent such negotiations, but they most likely took part in these agreements or, at the very least, turned a blind eye to them. Sergeant Darby wrote, "The opposing lines were in such close proximity on some parts of the field, that a conversation with the enemy could be carried on in an ordinary tone of voice, and we finally arranged a truce, the conditions of which were, that in case either side received orders to reopen hostilities, a signal shot must be fired in the air, as a fair warning to the other side. And to the honor of both parties, be it said this stipulation was faithfully carried out."[36] Although it was against orders during the war, Darby wanted to describe the practicality in making these truces. On another occasion, Darby was apparently very close to an enemy vidette and prepared to shoot a Confederate soldier lying in the open. He wrote, however, "It occurred to me that it would be too much akin to deliberate murder. I could not pull the trigger. I have often thought that if 'somebody's darling' had realized how near he was to deaths door that evening, it would have caused the chills to chase each other up his spinal marrow in rapid succession."[37] This particular example questions the accuracy of veterans' postwar accounts. Darby's thought process surrounding his act of amnesty appears to be contrived. After years of reflection, some veterans added or omitted details to paint themselves in the best light.

In some veterans' accounts, remembrances of fraternization contain varying degrees of presentism and romanticization. Rivalries between different states on the same side in the war affected the accuracy of memoirs. David Blight argues that early memoirists wanted to "set the record straight," and, in many cases, veterans were not in a contest with their former enemy but with themselves.[38] Veterans' narratives commonly place themselves and their regiments at the "hottest spots" on the battlefield and usually find units from other states to be at fault. Although there are many instances of this in soldiers' memoirs, for the purpose of this study, those that deal with fraternization are of particular interest. While on picket at Chattanooga, J. B. Polley noted,

> A truce along the picket lines in front of the Texans was arranged; that is, there was no more shooting at each other's picket. But the South Carolinians, whose picket line began at our left, their first rifle-pit being within fifty feet of the last one of the First Texas, could make no terms whatsoever. The Federals charge them with being the instigators and beginners of war and always exclude them from the benefit of truces between the pickets. It is certainly an odd spectacle to see the Carolinians hiding in their rifle pits and not daring to show their heads while not 50 feet away, the Texans sit on the ground playing poker, in plain view and within a hundred yards of the Yankees.[39]

In this case, the Texan wanted to argue that men from his state were welcomed in negotiated ceasefires but not the South Carolinians, because they were to blame for the war.

Nativism, inherent to Progressive Era society, also appeared in veterans' recollections of fraternization. After the Battle of Nashville, M. A. Ryan described that he was wounded and was unable to move. A drunk soldier "who was a Russian" would have wounded him had it not been for a Federal officer who shoved his soldier away from Ryan. "While lying there two young men, Illinois soldiers, approached me and asked me what regiment I belonged. I told them the 14th Mississippi," said Ryan. They said, "You were at Fort Donaldson. We were there too. You fought bravely."[40] In this instance, Ryan demonstrated how a "foreign" soldier was hostile, and "the foreigner's" own commander, who showed Ryan amnesty, stopped him. Additionally, this recollection reveals how his enemy commended Ryan's bravery at Fort Donelson. Another example of nativism appearing in postwar fraternization accounts was in J. H. Jones's memoir. Jones explained that enemies would spend evenings on picket duties entertaining one another with jokes. One joke Jones recalled: "Why are greenbacks like the Jews? Oh course the 'yanks' had to 'give it up.' The answer was 'Because they have Abraham for their father and no redeemer.'"[41] This very well could have been said during the war, but in the wartime accounts I surveyed for previous chapters, I found no documented anti-Semitic jokes shared between enemies. The division between native-born Civil War veterans, regardless of side, and the new Europeans migrants arriving in the early twentieth century found its way into these veterans' memoirs.

Another characteristic of veterans' postwar narratives was the romanticization of fraternization. Some men fabricated depictions of fraternization to the extent they seemed highly unlikely. One in particular is the memoir of Mississippi private David Holt, where he described two scenes of fraternization. The first took place during the Battle of Spotsylvania in May 1864. Holt saw a Federal sharpshooter approach him under cover, and his comrade, named Tommy, shot the man. The wounded Union man cried for help, and Tommy asked his captain if he could go out to assist him. The captain obliged, and Tommy went out to assist the dying man. Because they were only thirty paces away, Holt heard the conversation and wrote:

> "What can I do for you?" Tommy said in a low voice.
>
> "Put your hand into the breast pocket of my jacket and get out the daguerreotype of my wife and child and hold it before my eyes," answered the Yank in a weak low voice.
>
> We plainly heard the yank sob, "My darlings, Oh my darlings! It's hard to leave you." Then he said to Tommy, "My sight is failing and I am dying. I want you to promise me man to man that you will send this picture back to her. The address is on some letters that you can take off

my body, and I give you all my belongings and money. Tell her that I died gazing fondly on her dear face, and her name was on my lips."[42]

Tommy came back and "cried like a baby," while Holt admitted to having tears in his eyes. Holt wrote, "After all, we were all Americans and brothers. Underneath all the sectional hatred and political strife was the broad foundation of blood relation."[43] Tommy carried around the man's items for a few weeks until an exchange of coffee and tobacco took place at Petersburg. Holt stated that during fraternization, "Tommy got in touch with the yank's command and sent back everything the Yank had, to every cent of his money."[44] Holt likely felt guilty about this incident and through writing his memoir gained some degree of closure. The episode demonstrated that all men, regardless of which side they fought on, valued their families above all else and were under constant fear of never seeing them again. Tommy's guilt over taking a man away from his loved ones no doubt spurred his quest to return the man's belongings to his family. Although Holt was not the shooter, as a witness to this incident, it may have weighed heavy on his mind.

The second instance described by Holt also exuded characteristics of prolonged emotions that needed to be put to rest. While on the skirmish lines at the South Anna River, Holt and a Union sharpshooter fired upon each other. The man dropped his weapon, fled, and Holt took the gun, inscribed "J.B. Starr, 48th Michigan." Later at Petersburg, Holt fraternized with Union troops and traded coffee for tobacco. The Union men Holt traded with were coincidently part of the Forty-Eighth Michigan and knew Starr. Holt said, "Tell J.B. Starr that I am the man that got his gun at the South Anna River, and he can have it back if he is man enough to take it."[45] The man asked to see Holt's hat and looked at the blue patch in the crown. "Well," he exclaimed, "I will be dad-blamed if that hat done bear out with what Starr told us. When up the hill came a little devil about as thick as a match, with a thin hatchet face, and a bright blue patch in the top of his hat."[46] The Union man explained that his comrade was healing from the flesh wound Holt inflicted upon him. First, it should be noted that not only was there not a Forty-Eighth Michigan in the Army of the Potomac but that regiment did not exist at all in the Civil War.[47] In addition to factual inaccuracies, Holt's second account in particular seems fabricated because of the slim chance he would meet someone who knew "J.B. Starr." There was no doubt Holt wanted to show his bravery, but why did he embellish these interactions with the enemy? Perhaps Holt wanted to assure himself that he did not kill the man. Unlike the majority of unpublished and published memoirs, Holt's account goes beyond the typical reminiscences of fraternization by romanticizing these occurrences to a much higher degree. Holt's account demonstrates that some veterans were unable to separate their wartime experiences from the present political culture, one that whitewashed causation, promoted shared sacrifice, and reinforced sectional reconciliation. Widely read periodicals, on the other hand, endorsed this narrative much more frequently than individual soldiers' memoirs.

Higher-ranking officers and elites wrote editorials published in two postwar journals titled *Battles and Leaders of the Civil War* and *Southern Historical Society Papers*. Rather than argue the causes and consequences of the war, these accounts featured battlefield leadership, decision-making, and tactical maneuvers from the officers' viewpoint. Caroline Janney notes that commercial presses realized they could benefit from writing about both the North and South, but, in order to do that, the presses needed to eliminate discussion of the causes of war to prevent offsetting the fragile sectional balance.[48] David Blight similarly claims some forms of sectional bipartisanship were "staged as a means of cementing commercial ties between Northern money and Southern economic development."[49] These assertions explain why instances of fraternization would be of particular interest to those promoting sectional reunification. When these periodicals presented anything on the common soldier, former officers wrote on behalf of their troops. Therefore, those who previously enacted measures to prevent soldier fraternization were now writing about it. Why then did former commanders recollect moments when they essentially did not maintain control of their subordinates? Former officers, who held positions of political and economic power, wanted to use stories of fraternization to aid in their present agenda. Blight concludes, "We reminisce not merely to render the past retrievable, but to serve present interests and needs."[50] Aside from reunions, memorials, and common experiences, during which they championed valor, courage, and duty, officers saw recounting moments of amnesty and fraternalism during the war as a powerful way to shed remnants of sectional bitterness. The former officers and politicians used scenes of fraternization as a model for postwar social relations. Fraternalism promoted masculinity, respectability, and, most importantly, white superiority.

In *Battles and Leaders of the Civil War*, only a few instances of fraternization were depicted. One account, written by Colonel John S. Mosby, was accurate in terms of its comparison to common soldier accounts. Under the heading "A Bit of Partisan Service," Mosby wrote, "When the year 1863 arrived Fredericksburg had been fought, and the two armies, in winter quarters, were confronting each other on the Rappahannock. Both sides sought rest; the pickets on the opposite banks of the river had ceased firing and gone to swapping coffee and tobacco."[51] Mosby's account acknowledged the most common scene of fraternization, the exchange of coffee and tobacco at Fredericksburg. On the other hand, an account of fraternization under the heading "Fighting for Petersburg" went into greater detail. Thomas R. Roche recalled, "Under such perfect discipline did Mahone have his men that had we been suddenly attacked he could place us almost instantly in position without confusion. Fortunately, during our stay of over three months everything was quiet on that part of the line, the enemy in our front being peaceable, gentlemanly, and obliging."[52] Aside from pointing out the excellence of his commander, Roche explained that the friendly relations with his enemy went on for over three months. In wartime accounts, ceasefires and trade networks would take place, but then soldiers would return to shooting. Roche continued that, while his unit was cutting wood during the cold winter months, "An unarmed squad of Federals appeared, who greeted us with 'Hello, Johnnies, are you after wood?' In a few minutes Yanks and rebs were on the best of terms. Strange sight, but nevertheless true. The Federals tendered us the use of their sharp axes, which was readily accepted. Some of the Federals were so anxious to show their kind feelings for us that they actually helped us cut our wood! This neighborly feeling existed as long as we remained there."[53] In wartime accounts, soldiers at Petersburg wrote that when they ventured outside the picket line for wood and if they saw the enemy doing the same, antagonists would not fire upon one another. However, there was no evidence that soldiers cut wood for each other in these spaces. The extent of Roche's fabrication showed when he described that the Federals invited him to their picket post for dinner. Roche stayed for over an hour because "they assured him on their honor as soldiers" he would be safe and they would make sure he returned to his lines. At this point, to quell any doubt by the readers, Roche concluded, "These facts seem strange and improbable to the reader who did not participate in the late unpleasantness, but there are thousands today who cherish the remembrance of many such incidents."[54] Aside from Roche's use of the Southern-constructed postwar term for the Civil War, he discretely asks readers to follow the soldiers' lead and exhibit trans-sectional kindness.

Even more than *Battles and Leaders*, the *Southern Historical Society Papers* contain significant reminiscences of fraternization, most of which were written by former officers. One of the most widely known legends constructed in the postwar period was about Sergeant Richard Kirkland at Fredericksburg. Brigadier General Joseph Kershaw, Kirkland's brigade commander, recalled the actions of the "Angel of Marye's Heights" during the battle. After Burnside's frontal assault on the Confederate line at Marye's Heights, the wounded and dying Union soldiers remained pinned on the ground for three days. Kershaw recalled, "Kirkland came up and said 'General! I cant stand this. All night and all day I have heard those poor people crying for water, and I can stand it no longer. I come to ask permission to go and give them water."[55] Kershaw explained that he warned Kirkland of the risks and denied permission to show a white flag of truce. Kirkland went over the wall and gave water to the Union soldiers. "He laid him tenderly down, placed his knapsack under his head, straightened out his broken limb, spread his overcoat over him, replaced his empty canteen with a full one, and turned to another sufferer," wrote Kershaw.[56] As accounts discussed in previous chapters have indicated, soldiers did show one another amnesty, but whether it was to the degree that Kershaw describes remains up for interpretation. Kershaw's purpose in documenting Kirkland's actions was to promote "an example which dignifies our common humanity," or, in other words, white male unity.[57] In the wartime accounts of Fredericksburg there was no mention of this instance. However, a large statue was erected to Richard Kirkland on the Fredericksburg Battlefield in 1965, during the height of the civil rights movement. The idea and funding for the monument came from a South Carolinian, Dr. Richard Nunn Lanier, who was director of the Fredericksburg Centennial Commission.[58]

Another instance of fraternization described in the *Southern Historical Society Papers* came from General John B. Gordon. Interestingly, as noted previously, soldiers in Gordon's division wrote about warning the Union troops after Gordon came down to the picket line, ordering his men to fire. In his editorial, titled "They Would Mix on the Picket Line. Anecdote of the War by General Gordon," Gordon recollected a point when Lee ordered him to break up fraternization on the Rapidan River. His troops along the river claimed nothing was going on, but Gordon moved some bushes and found a Union soldier. Gordon told the man he was to be taken prisoner, but the man pleaded that he would rather be shot than taken prisoner. After Gordon threatened to take him to Libby Prison, the Confederate soldiers objected, "General, don't be too hard on him, he's a pretty good fellow! He didn't mean any harm he just wanted to talk with us."[59] Gordon admitted that he did not plan to arrest the man and let him go back to his side. In front of their commanding officer these men had asked for leniency toward their enemy, and, in return, Gordon allegedly showed it.

There were a few editorials by former common soldiers published in the *Southern Historical Society Papers*. An account of fraternization was published under the headline "Brilliant Page in History of War." At Petersburg, when a flag of truce for burial detail came up, John C. Featherston recalled, "When this work was commenced I witnessed one of the grandest sights I ever saw. Where not a man could be seen a few minutes before, the two armies arose up out of the ground, and the face of the earth was peopled with men. Both sides came over their works, and, meeting in the center, mingled, chatted, and exchanged courtesies, as though they had not sought in desperate effort to take each other's lives but an hour before."[60] Featherston's account runs very close to descriptions of fraternization during burial detail mentioned in wartime accounts. In an article written by the Association of the Defenders of Port Hudson entitled "Another Flag of Truce," the description of fraternization was also similar to the wartime reports. "An informal kind of truce was arranged between the men of both sides on our extreme right on the 16th, which lasted about a week, during which both sides stopped sharpshooting," the authors state. "In some cases soldiers would meet each other half way between the hostile lines and make exchanges, in which the Federals showed much liberality, making presents of tobacco, coffee, and newspapers, at times getting small quantities of sugar and molasses in return."[61] The ceasefire, meetings, and trading of commodities represented the standard characteristics of fraternization. M. J. Smith, president of the association, then recalled, "Our men working during the day in full view of the enemy. The men who were working would occasionally exchange words with each other regarding their respective avocations as amicably and jovially as if the siege was only a joke and the contending parties were the best of friends."[62] This conclusion that combatant soldiers seemed like friends rather than enemies was a continuous theme among many common soldier wartime accounts. Thus, former members of the high command, who served on the editorial board for the publication, were willing to admit moments when their men acted out of order, a mark against their control, for the larger aim of sectional harmony.

Despite coming from a bottom-up perspective, some of these accounts perpetuated elitist intentions. A key aspect embedded in common soldier anecdotes, articulated in the *Southern Historical Society Papers*, was fraternalism. Soldiers used romantic language, particularly in describing moments of brotherhood and fraternity, in order to highlight connections that remained intact through the war. For example, J. G. Law wrote about a long line of Union prisoners passing his cavalry. One of his comrades recognized his brother and he gave him plenty of rations. From this instance, Law reflected, "One of the sad features of this bloody war is that it is a fratricidal strife. It was quite affecting to witness the meeting between the two brothers, one a ragged, war-torn, and half-starved confederate, and the other a well-dressed and well-fed federal. Yesterday they were enemies and would have shot each other down in the heat of battle. Today they are friends and the Confederate ministers to the bodily comfort of his federal brother."[63] Law's statement supported the postwar notion that veterans completely shed their hatred of the enemy and now lived in peaceful harmony with their former antagonists. Law also promoted part of the "Lost Cause" narrative in which the Union won because they had more well-equipped men, while Southerners lacked the supplies and troops needed to continue the war. In an entry titled "Combatants Fraternizing," M. J. Smith recollected, "Soldiers swarmed from their places of concealment on either side and met each other in the most cordial and fraternal spirit." This description appeared similar to the wartime accounts of fraternization during burial truces. But, he then wrote: "Not a single case occurred in which the enemy, either officers or privates, exhibited a disposition to exult over their victory, but on the contrary, whenever the subject came up in conversation, it elicited from them only compliments upon the skill and bravery of the defense."[64] During wartime fraternization men did joke with one another about victories and defeats quite often. Smith's recollection, however, had an ulterior motive. He wanted to send a message to society that, when discussing the war, only mention veterans' shared bravery and sacrifice; avoid causes and consequences, ignore victories and defeats.

The most far-fetched example found in the *Southern Historical Society Papers* was entitled "Phi Gamma in War—Instances of Restoration of Good Will and Fraternity." Upon secession, the Masonic and fraternal lodges active before the war did not dissolve; in fact, as chapter 1 shows, prewar fraternities established the precedent that brought enemies together. However, the unknown author of "Phi Gamma" fabricated the magnitude of these bonds. For instance, this article describes that, during the Battle of Bull Run, a Confederate approached a wounded Union soldier. After the Confederate offered him water, the Union soldier "looked up and smiled, and received a pitying, kindly smile in return, accompanied by more water. On the breast of the Federal was the pin of Phi Gam."[65] After realizing they were both Phi Gammas, the "Confederate placed beneath the Federal's head a carefully-folded blanket, gave him another drink of water from his own canteen, placed a well-filled canteen of water within easy reach of him, looked wistfully and lovingly into his pallid face, touched the pin, pressed his hands again, said: 'God be with you Phi Gam,' turned away and disappeared."[66] Then, at the Battle of Chantilly, Virginia, a wounded Confederate asked a Union soldier for water as he was about to die. The Federal covered him with his blanket and sat beside him. In the morning the Confederate uttered family members' names and a quote from Horace. The Federal asked him, "'When did you read Horace?' and he said, 'When I was first a Phi Gam.' 'I am a Phi Gam,' said the Federal, with choking voice. When he died the 'Federal scooped out a grave, kissed the forehead and the hair of his brother Phi Gam, lowered his body into the grave, and tenderly covered it with the soil of Virginia.'"[67] Next, at Lookout Mountain, a wounded Confederate asked a Federal officer, "Please, sir, my left leg is shot and broken, and I need some water. I am so thirsty, sir; can you give me some water?" The Federal gave water to the wounded Confederate and after the battle helped him to the foot of the mountain and sought a surgeon for him. The surgeon's lantern "fell upon a Phi Gamma pin fastened to the breast of his coat."[68] The Confederate asked if he was a Phi Gam because both he and his father were. The Federal replied to the surgeon, "Doctor, this is my brother; as you value my friendship, deal gently and uprightly with him. Give him your best attention, your best skill."[69] It does not stop there. The story became even more unlikely when it continued thirty years later.

In January 1895 the same Federal officer was at Lookout Mountain. A Confederate listening, with one leg, on crutches, came up to him and said:

> I believe I know you, sir. I know your face and your voice. God grant me that I am not mistaken, sir. As your forces charged along the side of Lookout, a Federal officer gave a wounded Confederate a canteen of water, told him to drink, put a knapsack under his head, and then rushed on with his men. That evening he came back to the wounded confederate, called a surgeon, pleaded him to care for and treat the Confederate and then went back to his men. Do you know anything about that officer sir? Trembling with emotion that he could not conceal the Federal said: "I am that Federal, and you ——." They hugged and wept and then joined hands and sang "Long may our land be bright, with freedom's holy light Great God, our King."[70]

This saga of the unknown Northern and Southern Phi Gammas is a classic exemplar of the Lost Cause. The *Southern Historical Society*, composed of ex-Confederate leadership and some of the most ardent secessionists, used the "Phi Gamma" story to promote fraternal traditions of Southern masculinity and civility while ignoring questions over slavery, secession, and surrender.

Two Southern-based magazines, *Confederate Veteran* and the *Southern Bivouac*, and two Northern-based magazines, the *National Tribune* and *Blue and Gray*, also championed soldier sacrifice through depictions of battle and daily life. Like *Battles and Leaders* and *Southern Historical Society Papers*, these magazines also lessened notions of causation and ideological differences as the editors and companies sought to provide their audiences with themes of mutual sacrifice, manliness, and honor. In fact, former Confederate general Jubal Early criticized the *Southern Bivouac* because it "printed too many articles by low-ranking officers and enlisted men."[71] Perhaps

Early feared their accounts were too accurate and would expose parts of the war that were incompatible to the "Lost Cause" narrative. Nevertheless, because of editorial oversight and apparent criticism, veteran magazines, rather than debating the issues that caused such carnage, emphasized similarities in the common soldier experience. These publications contained vivid descriptions of meetings in the neutral zone, ceasefires, and trade networks reminiscent of the fraternization described by soldiers in their wartime accounts. For example, in an article featured in the *Confederate Veteran*, W. A. Day of the Forty-Ninth North Carolina recalled, "Our boys walked over and busily helped the Federal boys eat their rations. The boy in my front, Horace G. Soloman was in Co. D of the 7th Indiana Regiment. He went in bathing and wallowed in the water at my feet. He said he hoped we would live through the war and meet in Indiana over a big bottle of brandy."[72] Though accounts of fraternization during the war documented swimming parties and trading, the degree to which Day elaborates on this occurrence demonstrates his need to promote notions of friendliness and fraternity. In an April 1918 issue of the *Confederate Veteran*, A. C. Jones wrote about his experience fraternizing in a section titled "Inaugurating the Picket Exchange." Jones started by relating the present conflict in Europe to the Civil War and hoped to provide an anecdote on the lighter side of war. Jones recalled that, while at Fredericksburg, on the Rappahannock, he spotted a Yankee sentinel straight across from him. After they called out to one another, Jones said, "'I want to know if it is peace or war.' Promptly came the reply, 'If you wont shoot, I wont.' I then said: I wish to make a bargain with you. I intend to place a line of pickets on this side of the river. If you will not fire upon them, we will agree to keep the peace.' 'Alright,' he answered, 'and thank you.'"[73] Jones's interaction with the Federal soldier describes a ceasefire, but, according to all the wartime accounts, ceasefires were not needed on the Rappahannock. The *Southern Bivouac* published a similar account with the title "Why the Pickets Ceased Firing at Each Other." According to the article, pickets continuously fired at one another until a

Confederate soldier called out to the Union line across from him asking for an agreement to cease fire. The Union men agreed, and the Confederate called out, "'Say, Yank, tell the man on your left not to shoot; would just as lief be shot hy you as by him.' So the word passed from man to man till not a gun was fired on the picket-line."[74] Although this account did not note the location, it accurately represents how truces formed. Accounts of fraternization in Southern periodicals showcased soldiers' capacity for restraint and respect while simultaneously avoiding questions surrounding the Confederate defeat.

Northern periodicals like the *National Tribune*, based out of Washington DC, contained comparable vignettes on fraternization. In an editorial titled "Military Memoirs," a veteran in the Fourteenth Corps noted his experience during the Battle of Atlanta. The veteran recollected that after tedious skirmishing and monotony in camp life, "In the same way a very kind sort of feeling sprang up between the pickets of the opposing armies. It resulted from the habit of trading along the picket lines between the men. The Confederates had excellent tobacco, and more than they wanted."[75] This account denoted the mutual sentiment among men on both sides. In a piece titled "Recitals and Reminiscences—Stories Eminently Worth Telling of Experiences and Adventures in the Great National Struggle," a veteran gave his thoughts on fraternization at Malvern Hill. The veteran wrote, "Fraternization was going on all that day. They smoked our tobacco, ate our hardtack, and exchanged jokes until we wondered if there was really a bloody war going on in the land between Americans."[76] This example suggests that Southern men needed their Northern brethren and, as in the Southern periodicals, these articles advocated for these moments to be the takeaways of the war. About a visit between United Confederate Veterans and Grand Army of the Republic members, an article stated, "So far from reviving sectional feeling, this friendly personal intercourse between the survivors of the Union and confederate armies appears to have had the effect of obliterating all differences of opinion in regard to the issues of the war and of bringing about a sentiment of mutual respect and esteem. Yank and Johnny Reb find that they can talk over their old campaigns without overstepping the bounds of friendly discussion, and are thus coming to look upon each other as brothers once more in the best and broadest sense of the term."[77] This testimony argued that it was not until 1884 that men were able to make these connections. It also suggested that only through much-needed time and permission from the leadership were men able to meet on common ground. This account negates soldier agency in forming fraternal bonds during the war.

Aside from the *National Tribune*, the other leading veteran periodical based in the North (Philadelphia) was titled *Blue and Gray; The Patriotic American Magazine*. Walker Y. Page wrote a compelling, and most likely fabricated, account of amnesty and empathy in a piece titled "The Old Log Cabin on the Rapidan." Just as soldiers loathed the Copperheads and elite politicians who brought about the war but stayed home and criticized the soldiers' sacrifice, veterans continued to detest these men in the postwar era. Page prefaced his vignette on fraternization by stating, "It is only those—the stay at homes—to whose delicate nostrils the smell of powder would be an offence and the clash of contending arms a vulgar horror, who are willing to stir up stride and send soldiers to the field of battle, while they themselves occupy the soft and safe and lucrative places far out of reach of shot and shell."[78] Clearly, from these words, Page wanted to voice his discontent with those who stayed home, and he argued that soldiers, regardless of which side, were quite the opposite of the stay at homes. Page then admitted, "I want to emphasize what I said about the soldier and their feelings toward the war and toward each other (I mean, of course, the soldiers of both sections), and, by way of illustration, let me narrate one of the many little incidents of the war bearing upon the subject of our conversation, all of which I saw, et quorum pars fui, and I mention to show that as between the soldier of the 'blue' and the soldier of the 'gray' no bitterness existed, even while duty called upon them to cut each other's throats in battle."[79] More than most accounts on fraternization, Page laid out his intentions in recounting moments between antagonists. In a sense, Page's reasoning shows that ordinary soldiers' hatred toward one another was a construction by the stay at homes in order to raise support for the war and allow their personal gains to come to fruition. Like so many soldiers lamented during the war, if it were left up to them, the war would be settled. During the winter of 1863–64, Page was on the picket line and witnessed a group of Confederates go into an abandoned slave cabin in the neutral zone. Upon reaching the cabin, Page heard them praying, dropped his arms, and entered the cabin. After exchanging greetings with the men and mingling, Page went back to his commanding officer and asked that the Confederate sanctuary be respected by other units guarding that area. The officer issued the order: "To every officer in charge of that portion of the line, the rebs should remain undisturbed while holding religious services in said log cabin."[80] The reason for *Blue and Gray*'s use of accounts of fraternization is clear: to promote commonalities, in this case piety, among former enemies, rather than sectional differences.

Another scene of fraternization depicted in *Blue and Gray* also emphasized mutual amnesty between antagonists. An anecdote entitled "Fraternity along the Rappahannock" centers on the mutual importance of family. A Union soldier on the banks of the river heard a Confederate approach their lines. His comrade asked the man what he needed, and the Confederate responded, "I have a sister living in Illinois, and I have written a letter to her, telling all about our mother's death, and mother's last message to her, and I want you to forward the letter to her; I have it here, unsealed, and you can read it if you wish, to see that it is all right."[81] The Union soldier's "heart was touched," and he allowed the Confederate to come ashore. "The two enemies thus strangely brought together were having an interesting chat over war matters," the veteran wrote. "When the corporal of the picket came along and could do no less than take both of them into custody, as the picket had disobeyed orders."[82] Although the Union soldier pleaded both their innocence, the general scolded the soldier for "allowing his sympathies" to get the best of him. However, the general assured the letter would be sent to Illinois, allowed the Union man to return to his post, and most significantly, let the Confederate return to his side. The Union veteran concluded, "The picket had the satisfaction of having performed a kind deed to a foeman, of seeing his new friend recross the river, and of witnessing the cordial welcome which he received from his own comrades when he arrived there."[83] Thus, all were affected positively from this act of benevolence. Speaking to the nation as a whole, this article intended to show that everyone benefitted when the two sides came together. Because Northern-based publications chose to inflate these moments of the war, they downplayed Union victory, failed to question if the promises of freedom were carried out, and, ultimately, allowed the Southern version of Civil War memory to prevail.

This evidence of fraternization in postwar accounts sheds light on how veterans shaped Civil War memory. In documenting their experience, former soldiers had the power of choice in what they included, exaggerated, or left out. Because veterans wrote about fraternization, they wanted their families, friends, and future generations to remember a humane side of war, a side that highlighted American male fraternity, civility, and respectability. Documenting fraternization served a number of purposes. First, occurrences of fraternization made facing the memory of their service more palatable. Just as these moments were an escape from fear, loss, and privation throughout the war, remembering occasions of fraternization served as an oasis from more haunting memories. Second, fraternization demonstrated antagonists' mutual efforts for survival. Veteran reminiscences contained anecdotes of how they withstood hardships, overcame loss, and exemplified bravery. What veterans rarely admitted in their memoirs was their role in shirking, deserting, or defying their duty. Thus, soldiers saw fraternization as an act of dissent, practicality, and autonomy that should be celebrated rather than forgotten. Comparable to how personal gain from fraternization outweighed its risks during the war, memorializing these occurrences outweighed any stigma of weakness through the postwar era. Most important, recollections of fraternization verified that veterans were both influenced by and creators of Civil War memory. Those who wrote postwar accounts of friendliness between enemies did so in the context of Southern redemption and Jim Crow. And, for those who sought to keep the racial hierarchy intact, instances of fraternization became powerful evidence for the endorsement of sectional reunification and white male supremacy. These fraternal bonds, however, did not begin after the guns fell silent in 1865. Veterans wrote about fraternization in their memoirs to prove they had clasped hands across the bloody chasm—on the Rappahannock and the Chattahoochee, at Vicksburg and Petersburg—long before the Blue-Gray reunions.

Conclusion

Because it was a more palatable side of the Civil War, modern portrayals of soldier fraternization perpetuate the brother versus brother narrative. The efforts of popular and public historians, according to Civil War historian Gary Gallagher, "shape and reflect Americans' understanding of the war."[1] Ken Burns's *The Civil War* (1990) documentary series begins and ends with footage of veteran soldiers shaking hands at reunions. Broadsides and battlefield museum exhibits titled *Friendly Enemies* and *Fraternization* present these images to the general public.[2] In his painting *My Friend, the Enemy*, artist Mort Kunstler illustrates a Confederate with a cup of coffee and a Union soldier with a tobacco pipe standing together on the icy Rappahannock River. Two popular Hollywood interpretations of the Civil War, *Gettysburg* (1993) and *Gods and Generals* (2003), both portray scenes of fraternization. Interestingly, during the fraternization scene in *Gettysburg*, the soldiers ask one another "Why are you fighting this war?" In the wartime accounts of soldier fraternization, there was not a single instance in which this happened. Based on the evidence in this book, soldiers avoided discussing causation with their enemy. Thus, historians' rationales behind interpreting these instances vary. It could be to highlight a seemingly strange, yet lighter side of war, to represent sectional reunification, or perhaps to exemplify the exceptionalism of the Civil War in relation to other American wars that followed during the twentieth century. Regardless of how society chooses to interpret fraternization, one thing is certain. The fraternity that existed between enemies was not a postwar construction. The hundreds of soldiers' accounts in this study prove fraternization was not a romanticized projection of how Americans prefer to remember the war but a practice of great value to the men who partook in it.

The American Civil War was not the only conflict in recent history where fraternization occurred between common soldiers. The development of trench warfare in the mid-nineteenth century continued to serve as the primary tactical approach to combat in the early twentieth century. Because men needed to protect themselves against technologically advanced weaponry, the trench network along the western front in World War I forced men into a difficult set of conditions and circumstances. World War I soldiers documented experiences of fraternization that closely resembled those during the Civil War. A British soldier of the Royal Fusiliers wrote, "The Germans made an organized effort to obtain a truce, which lasted about two hours. Later they began to sing and to shout remarks to the 1/2nd Londons and to the Leinsers . . . who returned the compliment with interest. . . . It was amusing to see the heads of Germans popping up and down like marionettes, behind their trenches, to the accompaniment of loud laughter."[3] This depiction of a ceasefire, arranged by men who spoke different languages, indicated the efforts of soldiers to alleviate the rigors of trench life. "They're quiet fellows, the Saxons, they don't want to fight any more than we do, so there's a kind of understanding between us. Don't fire at us and we'll not fire at you," a British soldier explained to new recruits.[4] The threat of continuous fire not only kept soldiers on guard but also seemed meaningless. "Items of news, more or less mendacious, were exchanged when the trenches were near enough to permit of vocal intercourse. Curious conventions grew up, and at certain hours of the day and, less commonly, of the night, there was a kind of informal armistice," noted British soldier J. H. Morgan. "In one section of the hour of 8 to 9 a.m. was regarded as consecrated 'private business,' and certain places indicated by a flag were regarded as out of bounds by the snipers on both sides."⁵ Although these men fought with different ideological motivations than Civil War soldiers and fifty years later, continuity existed in their attempts to alleviate the hardships of trench warfare through relations with their enemy.

Although the exchange of fellow feelings on the western front mirrored those shared between the Blue and the Gray at Vicksburg and Petersburg, it must be cautioned that fraternization was not an inherent consequence of all warfare. The ability for soldiers to meet with one another was dependent upon three major factors. First, armies had to be positioned close to one another. Particularly in siege warfare, as seen in these chapters, there was a demarcation between a soldier's trench and that of his enemy's. Commanders ordered soldiers to trench lines and picket bunkers within yards of one another. But as weaponry and technology changed throughout the twentieth century, so too did the battle spaces, and the likelihood of a definitive neutral zone decreased. Second, there needed to be a unambiguous understanding of who the enemy was, whether it be by their uniform, formation, or insignia. In nonconventional or irregular warfare, by Western standards, enemies, civilians, and insurgents created new challenges for those who fought. Although the military responded by developing new technologies, doctrinal changes, and counterinsurgency, in modern warfare it is often unclear as to who the enemy may be.⁶ Last, both visible and deepseated racial, ethnic, and cultural differences have made the bonds of fraternalism less likely to form as they did in 1861 and 1914. Having similar phenotypes and shared traditions, history, and religion allowed men to empathize more easily with their enemies than with enemies from unfamiliar backgrounds. Thus, the confluence of particular military and cultural factors produced fraternization between enemies during the Civil War and the First World War.

Fraternization can be used as a lens to understand common Civil War soldiers; it verifies the complexities and nuances of their service. A thorough investigation of these occurrences sheds light on not only how soldiers fraternized but, more importantly, why they did. Fraternization proves factors beyond victory and defeat effected soldiers. After a battle, both the victor and the vanquished fraternized. After Fredericksburg, the victorious Army of Northern Virginia fraternized, just as the victorious Army of the Tennessee did after Vicksburg. The besieged Department of the Mississippi fraternized at Vicksburg, just as the Army of the Cumberland did after Chickamauga. The effects of battle, rather than the outcome, oftentimes resonated more deeply among men in the ranks. Victory did not promise full rations, a break from drill, or a removal of an untrusted officer. Yet, the Civil War soldier was expected to withstand whatever came his way. A soldier's duty was to do as the commander ordered him while simultaneously shedding anxiety and frustration. What those who sent these men to war failed to recognize was that their justification for war countered the very nature of warfare itself. In order to rally an entire generation for war, politicians told men their independence was in danger and threatened by the opposing section. Because citizen soldiers viewed their service as a means to both protect and amplify their individuality, the reality of war drastically deterred this vision. Thereby, in order for men to do what was expected of them, they took action. To survive and ensure their basic needs were met, soldiers crafted methods to shape their day-to-day life. Rooted in prewar traditions of fraternity and resistance, men used their enemy and environment to improve their conditions and cope with warfare, without regard to authority. The trade of newspapers, swimming parties, and barter of goods all restored their sense of control and made soldiering doable. Soldiers' joint efforts to cease fire demonstrated how fraternization became a method of self-preservation. Out of these interactions came mutual respect for one another's courage and tenacity. Fraternal bonds allowed men to envision peace, reunion, and a restoration of white male solidarity. Fraternization was beneficial, practical, and empowering. It indicated how the Civil War soldier fought to remain independent, to survive, and to prove he was never just a cog in the proverbial machine.

Notes

Abbreviations

ADAH	Alabama Department of Archives and History, Montgomery, Alabama
CWMC	Civil War Miscellaneous Collection, U.S. Army Military History Institute, Carlisle, Pennsylvania
FSNMP	Fredericksburg and Spotsylvania National Military Park, Fredericksburg, Virginia
HSPA	Historical Society of Pennsylvania, Philadelphia
LOC	Library of Congress, Washington DC
MARBL	Manuscripts and Rare Book Library, Emory University, Atlanta, Georgia
MDAH	Mississippi Department of Archives and History, Jackson, Mississippi
MHM	Missouri History Museum Library and Research Center, St. Louis, Missouri
NA	National Archives, Washington DC
NYHS	New York Historical Society, New York City
NYPL	New York Public Library, New York City
SAF	State Archives of Florida, Tallahassee, Florida
USAMHI	U.S. Army Military History Institute, Carlisle Barracks, Pennsylvania
USM	University of Southern Mississippi Special Collections, Hattiesburg, Mississippi
VHS	Virginia Historical Society, Richmond, Virginia

Introduction

1. Morris Brown Jr. to mother, Oct. 5, 1863, in Mahood, *Fight All Day, March all Night*, 83–84. Please note that, within all quotations from primary sources, here and throughout, misspellings and errors in the original texts have been retained.

2. William Harris Clayton to Father, June 25, 1862, William Harris Clayton Papers, VHS.

3. Mark Lyons to Amelia, Feb. 21, 1861, Mark Lyons Letters, ADAH.

4. Mark Lyons to Amelia, Mar. 14, 1862, Mark Lyons Letters, ADAH.

5. George Sinclair to wife, May 22, 1863, CWMC.

6. William B. Kidd, diary entry, Dec. 25, 1861, William Kidd Diary, VHS.

7. Wiley, *Life of Johnny Reb*, 15–17; McPherson, *For Cause and Comrades*, 104–16; Robertson, *Soldiers Blue and Gray*, 3–17. For specifically Confederate soldiers, see Faust, *Creation of Confederate Nationalism*, 6–7; McCurry, *Masters of Small Worlds*, 304, and *Confederate Reckoning*, 21; Sheehan-Dean, *Why Confederates Fought*, 1–3; Berry, *All That Makes a Man*, 10–13. For Union soldiers, see Gallagher, *The Union War*, 6; Foner, *Free Soil, Free Labor, Free Men*, 17; For religion, see Miller, Stout, and Wilson, *Religion and the American Civil War*, 4–18; Rable, *God's Almost Chosen Peoples*, 1–9.

8. Sheehan-Dean, *View from the Ground*, 3.

9. Phillips, *Diehard Rebels*, 2.

10. Glatthaar, *General Lee's Army*, xv.

11. Hess, *Union Soldier in Battle*, 126.

12. Manning, *What This Cruel War Was Over*, 5–7.

13. Foote, *Gentlemen and the Roughs*, 3–6.

14. Carmichael, *War for the Common Soldier*, 6–11.

15. Of the eleven Confederate states, I did not find any soldiers who fraternized from Arkansas. For Union states (other than California and Oregon), I did not find any soldiers who fraternized from Kansas, Maryland, or West Virginia. With the exception of Maryland, I was unable to access soldiers' manuscripts from these states mostly due to the small proportion of soldiers who served.

16. Army Command Policy, "Army Regulation 600–20," Headquarters, Department of the Army, Washington DC.

17. McPherson, *For Cause and Comrades*, 12.

18. Ruegmer, *Slave Law and the Politics of Resistance in the Early Atlantic World*.

19. McCurry, *Masters of Small Worlds*, 56–61; Pflugrad-Jackisch, *Brothers of Vow*.

20. Johnson, *Soul by Soul* and *River of Dark Dreams*; Berry, *The Price for Their Pound of Flesh*.

21. For punishment and torture, see Baptist, *The Half Has Never Been Told*, 139–41; for slave resistance, see Genovese, *Roll, Jordan, Roll*, 585–660; and Camp, *Closer to Freedom*.

22. Dower, *War without Mercy*, 11. Dower assesses warfare between Americans and Japanese to argue that racial differences, and outright hate, prompted the atrocities in the Pacific theater.

23. Sylvanus A. Markham to sister, Jan. 29, 1864, Markham Family Papers, CWMC.

24. Thomas Claybrook Elder to wife, Dec. 21, 1862, Thomas Claybrook Elder Papers, VHS.

25. Anson B. Shuey to wife, Mar. 25, 1863, Anson B. Shuey Letters, CWMC.

26. John Daniel Follmer, Apr. 6, 1863, diary entry, HSPA.

27. Noe, *Reluctant Rebels*, 100.

28. Phillips, *Diehard Rebels*, 69.

29. Phillips, *Diehard Rebels*, 69.

30. Rotundo, *American Manhood*, 201, 204.

31. John Dooley, Dec. 11, 1862, diary entry, in Dooley, *John Dooley's Civil War*, 96.

32. Marten, *Sing Not War*, 5; Harris, *Across the Bloody Chasm*; Jordan, *Marching Home*.

33. Robertson, *Soldiers Blue and Gray*, 139.

1. Fraternity and Resistance

James McBeth to Billy, May 1, 1864, William Conrow Letters, NYHS.

1. Private Wilbur Fisk to *The Green Mountain Freeman*, June 17, 1863, in Fisk, *Hard Marching Every Day*, xiv, 66–67, 102–4.
2. Sellers, *Market Revolution*, 32, 396; Howe, *What Hath God Wrought*, 211, 223; Larson, *Market Revolution in America*, 9.
3. Foner, *Free Soil, Free Labor, Free Men*, 16–17.
4. McCurry, *Masters of Small Worlds*, 85–86.
5. Kimmel, *Manhood in America*, 7.
6. Rotundo, *American Manhood*, 19.
7. Kimmel, *Manhood in America*, 6.
8. Historians have shown that slavery was the primary cause of the Civil War. They have demonstrated the irrepressibility of the sectional crisis and the inevitability of the Civil War because of differing notions of nationalism and culture and a political economy rooted in the institution of slavery. See Potter, *Impending Crisis*; Holt, *Political Crisis of the 1850s* and *Fate of Their Country*; Freehling, *Road to Disunion I* and *Road to Disunion II*; Stampp, *America in 1857*; Varon, *Disunion! The Coming of the American Civil War*.
9. For common soldier ideology, see McPherson, *What They Fought For* and *For Cause and Comrade*, 104–16. For specifically Confederate soldiers, see Faust, *Creation of Confederate Nationalism*, 6–7 ; Wiley, *Life of Johnny Reb*, 15–17; McCurry, *Masters of Small Worlds*, 304, and *Confederate Reckoning*, 21; Sheehan-Dean, *Why Confederates Fought*, 1–3. For Union soldiers, see Wiley, *Life of Billy Yank*; Gallagher, *The Union War*, 6; Manning, *What This Cruel War Was Over*, 18.
10. Carmichael, *War for the Common Soldier*, 9.
11. Murdoch John McSween, diary entry, July 20, 1864, in McSween, *Confederate Incognito*, 215.
12. Richard Prowse to Catherine, Oct. 27, 1862, Richard Prowse Letters, MDAH.
13. Foote, *Gentlemen and the Roughs*, 10.
14. Glatthaar, *General Lee's Army*, 81.
15. John Shipp, diary entry, July 10, 1862, Shipp Family Papers, VHS.
16. Mitchell, *Civil War Soldiers*, 57.
17. James McBeth to Billy, May 1, 1864, William Conrow Letters, NYHS.
18. Linderman, *Embattled Courage*, 2.
19. Glatthaar, *General Lee's Army*, xv.
20. Glatthaar, *General Lee's Army*, 191.
21. William B. Kidd, diary entry, Dec. 21, 1862, William B. Kidd Diary, VHS.
22. James Montgomery Lanning, diary entry, Oct. 22, 1862, ADAH.
23. Granville W. Belcher to wife, Dec. 14, 1862, Belcher Letters, USM.
24. Edward King Wightman to brother, Jan. 27, 1863, Edward King Wightman Letters, MARBL.
25. J. W. C., "New England and McClellan," *New York Observer and Chronicle (1833–1912)*, February 19, 1863.

26. John Daniel Follmer, diary entry, Feb. 19, 1864, HSPA.
27. Foote, *The Gentlemen and the Roughs*, 5.
28. Foote, *The Gentlemen and the Roughs*, 120.
29. John Price Kepner to Mother, Sept. 3, 1863, John Price Kepner Letters, VHS.
30. James H. Walker, diary entry, Apr. 17, 1863, HSPA.
31. Henry Welch to Aunt and Uncle, May 23, 1863, Henry Welch Papers, USAMHI.
32. John West Haley, diary entry, Dec. 17, 1862, VHS.
33. John Wesley Culpepper to Bob Adair, Feb. 18, 1864, John Wesley Culpepper Letters, USM.
34. William Cross Hazelton to Fannie, Dec. 16, 1862, in Hazelton, *Army of the Potomac*, 91.
35. James McBeth to Billy, May 1, 1864, in William Conrow Letters, NYHS.
36. Silas Auchmoedy to brother Lewis, sister Maria, and parents, Jan. 16, 1863, NYHS.
37. For more on the actions and impact of Copperheads, see Weber, *Copperheads*; and Landis, *Northern Men with Southern Loyalties*, 226–50.
38. Henry Welch to Aunt and Uncle, Apr. 17, 1864, Henry Welch Papers, USAMHI.
39. Joshua Hoyet Frier Memoirs, 17–19, SAF.
40. David Jackson Logan to enquirer, Sept. 1, 1863, in Logan, *"A Rising Star of Promise,"* 124.
41. Joseph W. Griggs to Pa, Dec. 19, 1862, Joseph W. Griggs Papers, VHS.
42. James McBeth to Billy, May 1, 1864, in William Conrow Letters, NYHS.
43. John S. Smith to Julianna Reynolds, Nov. 25, 1862, Tilton C. Reynolds Papers, Library of Congress.
44. William B. Kidd, diary entry, Apr. 20, 1862, William Kidd Diary, VHS.
45. Tally N. Simpson to sister, Dec. 2, 1862, in Everson and Simpson, *Far, Far from Home*, 160.
46. Thomas Bell, diary entry, Mar. 10, 1864, Thomas Bell Diary, CWMC.
47. Rotundo, *American Manhood*, 87.
48. Kimmel, *Manhood in America*, 59.
49. Carnes, *Secret Ritual and Manhood in Victorian America*, 146.
50. Pflugrad-Jackisch, *Brothers of a Vow*, 9.
51. Clawson, *Constructing Brotherhood*, 112–20; Kimmel, *Manhood in America*, 59; Jacobs, *Origins of Freemasonry*, 4; Carnes and Griffen, *Meanings for Manhood*, 260.
52. Richard Prowse to Catherine, Sept. 7, 1862, Richard Prowse Letters, MDAH.
53. Broomall, "We Are a Band of Brothers," 290.
54. Nelson, *National Manhood*, 178–79.
55. Thomas Bell, diary entry, June 1, 1864, Thomas Bell Diary, CWMC.
56. Linderman, *Embattled Courage*, 36.
57. Sheehan-Dean, *Why Confederates Fought*, 57.
58. Court-martial of Private Charles D. Goldenburgh, Twenty-Seventh New Jersey, Aug. 20, 1864, LL3204, RG 153, NA.
59. John West Haley, diary entry, Dec. 14, 1862, John West Haley Papers, VHS.

60. Tally Simpson to Anna, Dec. 25, 1862, in Everson and Simpson, *Far, Far from Home*, 169.

61. Linderman, *Embattled Courage*, 176.

62. William McGlothlin, diary entry, Jul. 21, 1863, William McGlothlin Papers, USAMHI.

63. Johnson, *Roaring Camp*, 151–52.

64. Scott, *Domination and the Arts of Resistance*, 4, 108–35. Scott investigates how traditionally subordinate groups regain agency by tests of power, disobedience, and negotiated spaces and calls this process "hidden transcripts"; see also Lears, "Concept of Cultural Hegemony," 567–93.

65. Lee, *Barbarians and Brothers*, 7.

66. Hess, *Union Soldier in Battle*, 142.

2. Discourse

William Cross Hazelton to Fannie, Aug. 25, 1862, in Hazelton, *Army of the Potomac*, 75.

1. Francis Edward Bayol to sister, Sept. 30, 1861, Francis Edward Bayol Letters, VHS.

2. Ashworth, *Trench Warfare 1914–1918*, 133.

3. Captain Robert Gaines Haile, diary entry, June 10, 1862, Robert Gaines Haile Diary, VHS.

4. John P. Barr, diary entry, Dec. 13, 1862, John P. Barr Diary, HSPA.

5. Rable, *Fredericksburg!*, 267.

6. William Reed Moore, diary entry, "After Fredericksburg," William Reed Moore Diary, HSPA.

7. Riley, *Grandfather's Journal*, 121.

8. Rable, *Fredericksburg!*, 396.

9. Silas Auchmoedy to brother Lewis, sister Maria, and parents, Apr. 27, 1863, Silas Auchmoedy Letters, NYHS.

10. James Montgomery Lanning, diary entry, Nov. 13, 1862, James Montgomery Lanning Diary, ADAH.

11. Charles Griswold to sister Mary, Dec. 16, 1862, Griswold Family Letters, NYPL.

12. Greene, "Morale, Maneuver, and Mud," 190.

13. Greene, "Morale, Maneuver, and Mud," 190.

14. Levi Lewis to mother, n.d., Levi Lewis Letters, USM.

15. George A. Mitchell to parents, Feb. 8, 1863, George A. Mitchell Letters, NYHS.

16. Albert W. Peck, diary entry, Mar. 1863, Albert W. Peck Diary, SAF.

17. James Montgomery Lanning, diary entry, Sept. 29, 1862, James Montgomery Lanning Diary, ADAH.

18. Richard S. Thompson to sister, Apr. 12, 1863, Poriss and Poriss, *While My Country Is in Danger*, 44.

19. William Rhadamanthus Montgomery to mother, Dec. 7, 1862, Montgomery, *Georgia Sharpshooter*, 74.

20. Charles Griswold to Mary, Jan. 3, 1863, Griswold Family Letters, NYPL.

21. Charles Ely to sister Elizabeth Ely Fowler, March 18, 1863, Ely Family Letters, NYPL.

22. Roland E. Bowen to Billy, Apr. 8, 1863, in Bowen, *From Ball's Bluff to Gettysburg*, 150.
23. John West Haley, diary entry, Feb. 20, 1863, John West Haley Papers, VHS.
24. Rotundo, *American Manhood*, 201.
25. Jacob L. Betchel to Candice Betchel, Feb. 10, 1863, Jacob Betchel Letters, FSNMP.
26. William Montgomery to Aunt Frank, Apr. 1863, in Montgomery, *Georgia Sharpshooter*, 97.
27. Jacob Betchel to Candace Betchel, Feb. 10, 1863. The Confederate generals the joke refers to are James Longstreet, Ambrose Powell Hill, Daniel Harvey Hill, and Jonathan Thomas "Stonewall" Jackson.
28. Hill, *British Subject's Recollections of the Confederacy*, 31. The "balloon" pertains to Professor Thaddeus Lowe's hot air balloon used to observe the Confederate position in the spring of 1863.
29. George A. Mitchell to parents and brother, Oct. 8, 1862, George A. Mitchell Letters, NYHS.
30. Mann, *Fighting with the Eighteenth Massachusetts*, 139.
31. George A. Mitchell to parents and brother, Oct. 8, 1862.
32. David Lilley to Anonymous, Nov. 28, 1862, David Lilley Papers, FSNMP.
33. Wyman White, diary entry, Jan. 20, 1863, in White, *Civil War Diary of Wyman S. White*, 120.
34. Robertson, *Soldiers Blue and Gray*, 139–44.
35. Wiley, *Life of Billy Yank*, 178.
36. Edward L. Heinichen, "Winter 1862–63," in *Memoirs*, in Edward Heinichen Papers, FSNMP.
37. Robertson, *Soldiers Blue and Gray*, 140.
38. Joseph Hopkins Twichell to father, Nov. 17, 1861, in Twichell, *Civil War Letters of Joseph Hopkins Twichell*, 85.
39. Henry Martin Truehart to family, Sept. 8, 1863, in Williams, *Rebel Brothers*, 169–70.
40. Edgeworth Bird to Sallie, Sept. 25, 1861, in Bird and Bird, *Granite Farm Letters*, 33.
41. Woodworth, *Six Armies in Tennessee*, xiii–xiv.
42. Hess, *Civil War in the West*, xi.
43. Isaac Jackson to Ethan A. Jackson, Mar. 19, 1863, in Jackson, *"Some of the Boys,"* 73.
44. Woodworth, *Nothing but Victory*, 293.
45. Woodworth, *Nothing but Victory*, 313.
46. Isaac Jackson to Ethan A. Jackson, Mar. 19, 1863, in Jackson, *"Some of the Boys,"* 73.
47. George C. Burmeister, diary entry, June 1, 1863, George C. Burmeister Diary, CWMC.
48. John A. Loveless to "beloved companion," July 30, 1863, John A. Loveless Papers, USAMHI.
49. George K. Pardee to wife, Feb. 14, 1863, in Pardee, *My Dear Carrie*, 48.
50. John V. Oliver to Polly, May 6, 1863, Boucher Family Papers, USAMHI; "southern" meaning the Union Army of the Tennessee that fought in the Deep South.
51. Douglas Richie Bushnell to wife, May 24, 1863, Douglas Richie Bushnell Letters, CWMC.
52. Woodworth, *Nothing but Victory*, 350–425.

53. John Guilford Earnest, diary entry, May 18, 1863, in Earnest, *All Right Let Them Come*, 95.

54. William Pitt Chambers, diary entry, Jul. 5, 1863, in Chambers, *Blood and Sacrifice*, 88.

55. J. P. Cannon, diary entry, June 1863, in Cannon, *Bloody Banners*, 35.

56. Felix Walthall to sister Mary L. Lyons, July 4, 1863, Felix Walthall Letters, USM.

57. Larkin Weaver to father, July 15, 1863, Weaver and Gray Family Papers, ADAH.

58. William Pitt Chambers, diary entry, May 18, 1863, in Chambers, *Blood and Sacrifice*, 80.

59. Emma Balfour, diary entry, May 21, 1863, Civil War Diary of Emma Balfour, MDAH.

60. Chesley A. Mosman, diary entry, June 26, 1863, in Mosman, *Rough Side of War*, 60.

61. Theodore F. Upson, July 27, 1863, in Upson, *With Sherman to the Sea*, 62.

62. Theodore D. Fisher, diary entry, June 6, 1864, Theodore D. Fisher Diary, MHM.

63. Woodworth, *Six Armies in Tennessee*, xiv, 4–6.

64. George S. Lea to father, Aug. 18, 1863, George S. Lea Family Papers, USAMHI.

65. Francis Sherman to father, Aug. 12, 1863, in Sherman, *Quest for a Star*, 59.

66. Jabez Banbury, diary entry, Nov. 24, 1863, Jabez Banbury Diary, CWMC.

67. Frederick Hess to wife, Nov. 3, 1863, in Hess, *Letters to Tobitha*, 86–87.

68. Joshua K. Callaway to wife, Oct. 13, 1863, in Callaway, *Civil War Letters of Joshua K. Callaway*, 147.

69. Phillips, *Diehard Rebels*, 6.

70. Linderman, *Embattled Courage*, 3.

71. John Kennerly Farris to Mary, Nov. 11, 1863, in Farris, *Letters to Mary*, 122.

72. James Henry McBride to brother, Dec. 4, 1863, James H. McBride Papers, CWMC.

73. Woodworth, *Six Armies in Tennessee*, 217.

74. John Kennerly Farris to Mary, Dec. 2, 1863, in Farris, *Letters to Mary*, 129.

75. Edward Norphlet Brown to Fannie, Dec. 25, 1863, Edward Norphlet Brown Letters, ADAH.

76. John Kennerly Farris to Mary, Dec. 26, 1863, in Farris, *Letters to Mary*, 136.

77. William Pitt Chambers, diary entry, Feb. 12, 1864, in Chambers, *Blood and Sacrifice*, 119.

78. McMurray, *Atlanta 1864*, 32.

79. McPherson, *Battle Cry of Freedom*, 744–47.

80. Richard T. Van Wyck to mother, July 14, 1864, in Van Wyck, *A War to Petrify the Heart*, 220.

81. Joseph Miller Rand, diary entry, July 13, 1864, Joseph Miller Rand Diary, MDAH.

82. Charles A. Houghton to wife, July 15, 1864, Charles A. Houghton Papers, USAMHI.

83. Hess, *Civil War in the West*, 225–30.

84. J. P. Cannon, diary entry, July 18, 1864, in Cannon, *Bloody Banners*, 83.

85. James W. Watkins to wife, Aug. 8, 1864, James W. Watkins Letters, MARBL.

86. Hess, *Civil War in The West*, 227.

87. George S. Lea to father, Aug. 12, 1864, George S. Lea Family Papers, USAMHI.

88. George S. Lea to father, Aug. 12, 1864, George S. Lea Family Papers, USAMHI.

89. Trudeau, *The Last Citadel*, 22, 25.

90. Trudeau, *The Last Citadel*, 24.
91. Council A. Bryan, diary entry, June 10, 1864, Council A. Bryan Papers, SAF.
92. Greene, *Final Battles of the Petersburg Campaign*, 49–50.
93. William Reed Moore, diary entry, Aug. 1864, William Reed Moore Diary, HSPA.
94. Council A. Bryan, diary entry, June 10, 1864, Council A. Bryan Papers, SAF.
95. James Beard to brother and sister, Aug. 17, 1864, James Beard Letters, CWMC.
96. Daniel Emerson Hurd, "My Experiences in the Civil War," 8, William Marvel Collection, USAMHI.
97. William F. Winkleman to parents, Oct. 17, 1864, William F. Winkleman Papers, USAMHI.
98. James Thomas Perry, diary entry, Oct. 28, 1864, James Thomas Perry Diary, VHS.
99. George Hubbard, diary entry, Aug. 18, 1864, George Hubbard Papers, NYPL.
100. William R. Ray, Oct. 11, 1864, in Ray, *Four Years with the Iron Brigade*, 327.
101. John L. Smith to mother, Aug. 12, 1864, John L. Smith Papers, HSPA.

3. Trade

LeGrand James Wilson, June 7, 1864, in Stubbs, *Duty, Honor, Valor*, 578; Tally N. Simpson to Mary, Apr. 30, 1862, in Everson and Simpson, *Far, Far from Home*, 121.
1. Captain Robert Gaines Haile, diary entry, June 10, 1862, Robert Gaines Haile Diary, VHS.
2. David Jackson Logan to enquirer, Oct. 21, 1863, in Logan, *"A Rising Star of Promise,"* 124.
3. Walter Fabius Maximus Moring, diary entry, Sept. 23, 1863, Walter Fabius Maximus Moring Diary, VHS.
4. Franklin Riley, diary entry, Jan. 14–15, 1863, in Riley, *Grandfather's Journal*, 121.
5. Egbert M. Rogers, diary entry, Feb. 26, 1863, Egbert Rogers Papers, FSNMP.
6. Anson B. Shuey to wife, Mar. 25, 1863, Anson B. Shuey Letters, CWMC.
7. Tally Simpson to Mary, Apr. 10, 1863, in Everson and Simpson, *Far, Far from Home*, 211.
8. James B. Sheeran, Apr. 26, 1863, in Sheeran, *Confederate Chaplain*, 41.
9. James B. Sheeran, Apr. 26, 1863, in Sheeran, *Confederate Chaplain*, 41.
10. Reeves, *History of the Twenty-Fourth Regiment, New Jersey Volunteers*, 30.
11. Henry P. Garrison to Cousin, Jan. 27, 1863, H. P. Garrison Letters, FSNMP.
12. J. D. Cribbs to Miss Jane, Mar. 6, 1863, William B. and Hugh L. Honnoll Papers, MARBL.
13. Henry B. Wood to Sarah, Jan. 27, 1863, in Wood, *Marble Valley Boys*, 46.
14. W. A. Johnson, "Winter Quarters at Fredericksburg 1862–1863," *Atlanta Journal*, November 30, 1901.
15. John Dooley, diary entry, Dec. 11, 1862, in Dooley, *John Dooley's Civil War*, 96.
16. Tally Simpson to sister Mary, Apr. 10, 1863, in Everson and Simpson, *Far, Far from Home*, 211–12.
17. Murdoch John McSween, diary entry, Jan. 25, 1863, in McSween, *Confederate Incognito*, 88.
18. U.S. War Department, 56th and 57th Articles of War, *Rules and Articles*, 16.

19. Court-martial of Lt. George Kessel, Sixty-Second New York, Apr. 25, 1863, LL 234, Records of the Office of the Adjutant General (Army), RG 153, NA.

20. Murdoch John McSween, diary entry, Jan. 25, 1863, in McSween, *Confederate Incognito*, 88.

21. Richard S. Thompson to sister, Apr. 12, 1863, in Poriss and Poriss, *While My Country Is in Danger*, 44.

22. Carmichael, *War for the Common Soldier*, 7.

23. Ballard, *Vicksburg*, 348.

24. Robert Caldwell Dunlap, diary entry, May 23, 1863, in Dunlap, *As the Mockingbird Sang*, 80.

25. Robert Caldwell Dunlap, diary entry, May 25, 1863, in Dunlap, *As the Mockingbird Sang*, 81.

26. Emma Balfour, diary entry, May 31, 1863, Civil War Diary of Emma Balfour, MDAH.

27. Theodore F. Upson, diary entry, May 29, 1863, in Upson, *With Sherman to the Sea*, 112–13.

28. Theodore F. Upson, diary entry, June 17, 1863, in Upson, *With Sherman to the Sea*, 61.

29. T. H. Kemp to wife, Jane, Mar. 5, 1863, in Kemp, *Letters to Jane*.

30. James Palmer, diary entry, July 13, 1863, James Palmer Civil War Diary, MDAH.

31. William Pitt Chambers, diary entry, June 14, 1863, in Chambers, *Blood and Sacrifice*, 83–84.

32. Woodworth, *Nothing but Victory*, 453.

33. Theodore D. Fisher, diary entry, July 5, 1864, Theodore D. Fisher Diary, MHM.

34. Isaac Jackson to Moses and Phoebe Jackson, July 13, 1863, in Jackson, *"Some of the Boys,"* 111.

35. Isaac Vanderwarker III, diary entry, July 7, 1863, Isaac Vanderwarker III Diary, CWMC.

36. Albert H. Merrifield, diary entry, July 7, 1863, Albert H. Merrifield Diary, CWMC.

37. Cozzens, *Shipwreck of Their Hopes*, 15.

38. John Kennerly Farris to Mary, Nov. 11, 1863, in Farris, *Letters to Mary*, 122.

39. Chesley Mosman, diary entry, Oct. 12, 1863, in Mosman, *Rough Side of War*, 101.

40. Chesley Mosman, diary entry, Oct. 14, 1863, in Mosman, *Rough Side of War*, 101.

41. Woodworth, *This Grand Spectacle*, 24.

42. David Ayers to wife, Oct. 24, 1863, David Ayers Letters, CWMC.

43. Cozzens, *Shipwreck of Their Hopes*, 48.

44. James Henry McBride, diary entry, October 1863, James Henry McBride Papers, CWMC.

45. Frederick Hess to wife, Nov. 3, 1863, in Hess, *Letters to Tobitha*, 86.

46. Frederick Hess to wife, Oct. 19, 1863, in Hess, *Letters to Tobitha*, 81.

47. John West Haley, diary entry, Sept. 5, 1864, John West Haley Papers, VHS.

48. Gannon, *Irish Rebels, Confederate Tigers*, 301.

49. James F. Jones to mother, Oct. 15, 1864, James F. Jones Civil War Letters, ADAH.

50. Jordan, *Red Diamond Regiment*, 214.

51. Charles Wellington Reed to mother, June 28, 1864, in Reed, *"A Grand Terrible Drama,"* 236.

52. Marion Hill Fitzpatrick to Amanda, July 10, 1864, in Fitzpatrick, *Letters to Amanda*, 158–59.

53. John West Haley, diary entry, Sept. 5, 1864, John West Haley Diary, VHS.

54. John West Haley, diary entry, Aug. 29, 1864, John West Haley Diary, VHS.

55. Francis Edward Bayol to Sister, Sept. 30, 1861, Francis Edward Bayol Letters, VHS.

56. Henry Martin Truehart to family, Sept. 8, 1863, in Williams, *Rebel Brothers*, 169–70.

57. John West Haley, diary entry, Sept. 5, 1864, John West Haley Diary, VHS.

58. John L. Smith to mother, Aug. 12, 1864, John L. Smith Papers, HSPA.

59. Marion Hill Fitzpatrick to Amanda, July 10, 1864, in Fitzpatrick, *Letters to Amanda*, 158–59.

60. Court-martial of Corporal Albert C. Berry, Fourth New Hampshire, and Albert D. W. Emerson, Fourth New Hampshire, Jan. 18, 1863, LL140, RG 153, NA. Tom and Beverly Lowry compiled a database indexing more than 80,000 Court Martial Records. Tom and Bev Lowry, founders and researchers of The Lowry Project, Inc., were central in helping me to locate the cases where soldiers were brought up on charges of fraternization. See http://www.theindexproject.com/.

61. Court-martial of Private. James Wait, Sixty-Seventh Ohio, May 2, 1863, MM 480, RG 153, NA.

62. Court-martial of Private John H. Longbottom, Feb. 22, 1865, 126th Ohio, OO 707, RG 153, NA.

63. Court-martial of Second Lieutenant Charles A. Roberts, Eighty-Second New York, Oct. 1, 1863, NN 486; Private Marshall St. Germaine, First Vermont Cavalry, Jan. 25, 1864, LL1728, RG 153, NA.

64. Court-martial of Private G. F. Baum, Ninety-Ninth Pennsylvania, June 26, 1864, NN2282, RG 153, NA.

65. Court-martial of Private Paul Frank, Sixty-Ninth Pennsylvania, Nov. 11, 1865, NN3360, RG 153, NA.

66. Court-martial of Private John O'Dell, 105th Pennsylvania, Aug., 29, 1864, NN2644, RG 153, NA.

67. Court-martial of Private McDonough Harmes Twentieth Indiana and Private Charles W. Homan Twentieth Indiana, Oct. 20, 1864, LL2828, RG 153, NA.

68. "Incidents in Picket Life," private letter, Sept. 15, 1864, in Styple, *Writing and Fighting the Civil War*, 299.

69. James Beard to brother and sister, Aug. 17, 1864, James Beard Letters, CWMC.

70. John L. Smith to mother, Aug. 12, 1864, John L. Smith Papers, HSPA.

71. John L. Smith to mother, Aug.12, 1864, John L. Smith Papers, HSPA.

72. Rotundo, *American Manhood*, 201.

73. William F. Winkleman to parents, Oct. 17, 1864, William F. Winkleman Papers, USAMHI.

74. George Henry Ewing to Parents, Dec. 24, 1864, in Ewing, *Ewing Family Civil War Letters*, 33.

75. Ashworth, *Trench Warfare 1914–1918*, 143.

76. "The Army of the Potomac: Our White Oak Church Correspondence," *New York Herald*, January 1, 1863.

77. Samuel Brooks to wife, Feb. 4, 1863, Samuel Brooks Letters, CWMC.

78. Robert A. Moore, Jan. 14, 1863, diary entry, in Moore, *A Life for the Confederacy*, 129; Austin Dobbins, January 14–15, 1863, Austin Dobbins Journal, FSNMP.

79. George Mitchell to parents, Jan. 25, 1863, George A. Mitchell Letters, NYHS.

80. Lucius B. Shattuck to Gill and Mary, Dec. 16, 1862, in Sutherland, *Fredericksburg and Chancellorsville*, 81.

81. John West Haley, diary entry, Sept. 1–3, 1864, John West Haley Diary, VHS.

82. Ashworth, *Trench Warfare 1914–1918*, 134.

83. Joseph Banks Lyle, diary entry, Aug. 4, 1864, Joseph Banks Lyle Papers, VHS.

84. John L. Smith to mother, Oct. 22, 1864, John L. Smith Papers, HSPA.

4. Information

John Dooley, diary entry, Dec. 11, 1862, in Dooley, *John Dooley's Civil War*, 96.

1. Milton Barrett to brother and sister, Feb. 21, 1863, in Barrett, *The Confederacy Is on Her Way up the Spout*, 90.

2. John Martin Steffan to Fred, Mar. 2, 1863, John Marin Steffan Letters, CWMC.

3. Private Wilbur Fisk to *The Green Mountain Freeman*, June 10, 1863, in Fisk, *Hard Marching Every Day*, 102–3.

4. George Huntley to sister, June 10, 1863, in Taylor, *The Cry Is War, War, War*, 111.

5. Bowen, *From Ball's Bluff to Gettysburg*, 101.

6. Walter S. Poor to sister Mary Poor Fox, Jan. 14, 1863, Water S. Poor Correspondence, NYHS.

7. McPherson, *For Cause and Comrades*, 121.

8. Burrage Rice, diary entry, Jan. 4, 1863, Burrage Rice Diary, NYHS.

9. Charles Edward Bates to parents Sept. 22, 1862, Charles Edward Bates Papers, VHS.

10. McPherson, *For Cause and Comrades*, 122.

11. George A. Mitchell to parents, Jan. 4, 1863, George A. Mitchell Letters, NYHS.

12. J. W. C., "New England and McClellan," *New York Observer and Chronicle (1833–1912)*, February 19, 1863.

13. Rable, *Fredericksburg!*, 393.

14. Rable, *Fredericksburg!*, 422–23.

15. William Montgomery to mother, Dec. 7, 1862, in Montgomery, *Georgia Sharpshooter*, 74.

16. Egbert M. Rogers, diary entry, Feb. 26, 1863, Egbert Rogers Papers, FSNMP.

17. Anson B. Shuey, to wife, Jan. 11, 1863, Anson B. Shuey Letters, CWMC.

18. Tally Simpson to Sister Mary, Apr. 10, 1863, in Everson and Simpson, *Far, Far from Home*, 212.

19. John L. Street to family, Mar. 16, 1863, John L. Street Letters, FSNMP.

20. Private Wilbur Fisk to *The Green Mountain Freeman*, June 17, 1863, in Fisk, *Hard Marching Every Day*, 102–4.

21. Sutherland, *Fredericksburg and Chancellorsville*, 101.

22. Court-martial of Private George Vanderpool, Fourth United States, June 11, 1863, NN55, RG 153, NA.

23. Court-martial of Sergeant B. Belzonne and Private Frederick Meyer, Seventh New York, Mar. 21, 1863, LL70, RG 153, NA.

24. Court-martial of Private Samuel Post and Private Parley Post, Sixth New York, Feb. 26–27, 1863, NN3820, RG 153, NA.

25. George H. Alverson to family and friends, Oct. 28, 1863, George H. Alverson Letters, CWMC; some of the men called General Rosecrans "Rosey" and wrote his name as "Roseycrans" and so on in their letters home.

26. McPherson, *Battle Cry of Freedom*, 675.

27. William Montgomery to Aunt, Oct. 16, 1863, in Montgomery, *Georgia Sharpshooter*, 93.

28. Cozzens, *Shipwreck of Their Hopes*, 24.

29. John Kennerly Farris to Mary, Oct. 7, 1863, in Farris, *Letters to Mary*, 109.

30. John Kennerly Farris to Mary, Nov. 11, 1863, in Farris, *Letters to Mary*, 122.

31. Henry Welch to father, Nov. 14, 1863, Henry Welch Papers, CWMC.

32. Henry Gilliam to Susie, Nov. 16, 1863, Gilliam-Chason Family Papers, MDAH.

33. Edward Norphlet Brown to Fannie, Sept. 26, 1863, Edward Norphlet Brown Letters, ADAH.

34. Joseph Miller Rand, diary entry, Oct. 10, 1863, Joseph Miller Rand Diary, MDAH.

35. Phillips, *Diehard Rebels*, 187.

36. Frank Phelps to friends, Dec. 2, 1863, in Tapert, *The Brothers War*, 181.

37. Court-martial of Private Henry Eich, Second Missouri, Oct. 26, 1863, LL2645, RG 153, NA.

38. Woodworth, *This Grand Spectacle*, 40.

39. Woodworth, *This Grand Spectacle*, 56, 68.

40. Woodworth, *This Grand Spectacle*, 82.

41. Woodworth, *Six Armies in Tennessee*, 194.

42. John T. Cheney, diary entry, Nov. 28, 1863, John T. Cheney Collection, USAMHI.

43. James Henry McBride to brother, Dec. 4, 1863, James Henry McBride Letters, CWMC.

44. Cozzens, *Shipwreck of Their Hopes*, 391.

45. Cozzens, *Shipwreck of Their Hopes*, 343.

46. Edward Norphlet Brown to Fannie, Dec. 25, 1863, Edward Norphlet Brown Letters, ADAH. Underlining in original.

47. Thomas Bell, diary entry, June 1, 1864, Thomas Bell Diary, CWMC.

48. Harvey Reid to sisters, June 12, 1864, in Reid, *Uncommon Soldiers*, 159.

49. Hamlin Alexander Coe, diary entry, June 9, 1864, in Coe, *Mine Eyes Have Seen the Glory*, 150.

50. Henry Welch to Aunt and Uncle, June 9, 1864, Henry Welch Papers, CWMC.

51. General Alpheus S. Williams to daughter, June 10, 1864, Williams, *From the Cannon's Mouth*, 315–16.

52. Noe, *Reluctant Rebels*, 206.

53. Grimsley, *And Keep Moving on*, 1–23; Trudeau, *Bloody Roads South*, 10–40.
54. McPherson, *Tried by War*, 209–29.
55. McPherson, *Tried by War*, 231.
56. Rhea, *In the Footsteps of Grant and Lee*, 1–18.
57. Sommers, *Richmond Redeemed*, 3.
58. Phillips, *Diehard Rebels*, 7–8, 73–80.
59. Valentine C. Randolph, May 30, 1864, in Randolph, *A Civil War Soldier's Diary*, 211–12; Julius Whitney, diary entry, July 16, 1864, Julius Whitney Diary, William Marvel Collection, USAMHI.
60. Killian van Rensselaer to mother, Mar. 5, 1865, Killian van Rensselaer Papers, NYHS.
61. Attached with Court-martial of Second Lieutenant John Andrews, 179th New York, June 9, 1864, NN55, RG 153, NA.
62. Special Order No. 167, July 18, 1864, Robert Edward Lee Headquarters Papers, No. 54, Army of Northern Virginia, VHS.
63. Court-martial of Private Isaac Brown, Second Pennsylvania Artillery, Sept. 4, 1864, LL3013, RG 153, NA.
64. Court-martial of Lieutenant Loring Farr, Nineteenth Maine, Oct. 11, 1864, NN486, RG 153, NA.
65. Court-martial of Lieutenant Presley Cannon, Second Pennsylvania Heavy Artillery, Aug. 28, 1864, NN3934, RG 153, NA.
66. Court-martial of Private John Vaughn, Tenth New Hampshire, Sept. 5, 1864, NN3981, RG 153, NA.
67. Court-martial of Private I. L. G. Crandall, Ninety-Eighth New York, July 11, 1864, LL2233, RG 153, NA.
68. Court-martial of Lieutenant Charles Goldenburgh, Thirty-Seventh New Jersey, Aug. 20, 1864, NN2496, RG 153, NA.
69. Court-martial of Major Lyman Knapp, Seventeenth Vermont, Second Lieutenant John Andrews, 197th New York, and Sergeant John Vandermark, 197th New York, Feb. 17, 1865, LL3204, RG 153, NA.
70. U.S. War Department, *War of the Rebellion*, Series I, vol. 42, pt. 3:722.
71. U.S. War Department, *War of the Rebellion*, Series I, vol. 42, pt. 3:753.
72. Weber, *Copperheads*, 83.
73. John Price Kepner to parents, Mar. 28, 1863, John Price Kepner Papers, VHS.
74. Henry C. Matrau to mother, Nov. 17, 1864, Matrau, *Letters Home*, 100.
75. Weber, *Copperheads*, 196.
76. George P. McClelland to Lizzie, Sept. 20, 1864, McClelland, *Your Brother in Arms*, 222.
77. Zerah Coston Monks to parents, Sept. 13, 1864, Zerah Coston Monks Letters, MARBL.
78. Samuel B. Pierce, diary entry, July 4, 1864, Samuel B. Pierce Papers, MARBL.
79. James F. Jones to mother, Oct. 15, 1864, James F. Jones Civil War Letters, ADAH.
80. Glatthaar, *General Lee's Army*, 242.
81. John A. Everett to wife, Feb. 7, 1865, John A. Everett Letters, MARBL.

82. Weitz, *A Higher Duty*, 171.
83. U.S. War Department, *War of the Rebellion*, Series I, vol. 42, pt. 2:828–29.
84. Elisha Hunt Rhodes, Feb. 25, 1865, in Rhodes, *All For the Union*, 216.
85. Jordan, *Red Diamond Regiment*, 214.
86. Franklin Boyts to Josiah, Feb. 28, 1865, Franklin Boyts Papers, HSPA.
87. Wesley Gould to brother, Sept. 18, 1864, in Gould, *Dear Sister*, 141.
88. U.S. War Department, *War of the Rebellion*, Series I, vol. 46, pt. 2:1292–93.
89. Captain Charles Minor Blackford to wife, July 17, 1864, in Blackford, *Letters from Lee's Army*, 267.

5. Ceasefires

John L. Smith to mother, July 10, 1864, John L. Smith Papers, HSPA.

1. Ashworth, *Trench Warfare 1914–1918*, 19. Scholars of World War I have studied and analyzed fraternization between Germans and British troops in the trenches, most notably during the Christmas Eve truce of 1914. See Leed, *No Man's Land*, 109–10; Weintraub, *Silent Night*.
2. Hess, *Trench Warfare under Grant and Lee*, xiii–xvii. For more on the strategic and tactical changes of siege war, see Michael Ballard, *Vicksburg*, 358–95; Peter Cozzens, *Shipwreck of their Hopes*, 1–7; Richard M. McMurray, *Atlanta 1864*, 121–60; Richard Sommers, *Richmond Redeemed*, 1–4; Noah Andre Trudeau, *The Last Citadel*; A. Wilson Greene, *The Final Battles of the Petersburg Campaign*, 37–40.
3. James McBeth to Billy, July 16, 1862, William Conrow Letters, NYHS.
4. George Bryan to Jennie, Oct. 2, 1863, in Bryan, *Friend Jennie*, 105.
5. John Guilford Earnest, diary entry, May 18, 1863, in Earnest, *All Right Let Them Come*, 95.
6. Richmond V. Black to wife, May 24, 1863, Richmond V. Black Papers, USAMHI.
7. Isaac Jackson to Sarah, June 28, 1863, in Jackson, *"Some of the Boys,"* 108.
8. William M. Stone, diary entry, June 18, 1863, William M. Stone Papers, MDAH.
9. Alfred A. Rigby, diary entry, May 25, 1863, Alfred A. Rigby Papers, MARBL.
10. William Pitt Chambers, diary entry, May 25, 1863, in Chambers, *Blood and Sacrifice*, 78.
11. James K. Newton to mother, May 29, 1863, in Newton, *Wisconsin Boy in Dixie*, 72.
12. Alfred A. Rigby, diary entry, May 25, 1863, Alfred A. Rigby Papers, MARBL.
13. W. D. Willett, diary entry, May 25, 1863, W. D. Willett "Pickens Planters" Diary, ADAH.
14. George Pardee to wife, May 26, 1863, in Pardee, *My Dear Carrie*, 93.
15. George C. Burmeister, diary entry, May 25, 1863, George C. Burmeister Diary, CWMC.
16. George C. Burmeister, diary entry, May 21, 1863, George C. Burmeister Diary, CWMC.
17. William Pitt Chambers, diary entry, May 25, 1863, in Chambers, *Blood and Sacrifice*, 78.
18. Charles Edwin Cort, Sept. 8, 1863, in Cort, *"Dear Friends,"* 102–3.
19. Charles Edwin Cort, Sept. 3, 1863, Tomlinson, *"Dear Friends,"* 103.
20. King, *Three Years with the 92nd Illinois*, 110.

21. Benjamin Abbott to Green Haywood, Sept. 26, 1863, in Mills, *"Dear Mother,"* 275.
22. Woodworth, *Six Armies in Tennessee*, 134.
23. Chesley Mosman, diary entry, Sept. 27, 1863, in Mosman, *Rough Side of War*, 93.
24. Chesley Mosman, diary entry, Sept. 27, 1863, in Mosman, *Rough Side of War*, 93.
25. Chester H. Southworth, diary entry, May 29, 1864, Southworth Family Papers, USAMHI.
26. Taylor Lester Dewitt, diary entry, June 30, 1864, Taylor Lester Dewitt Diary, CWMC.
27. J. P. Cannon, diary entry, June 18, 1864, in Cannon, *Bloody Banners*, 76.
28. Hamlin Alexander Coe, diary entry, June 9, 1864, in Coe, *Mine Eyes Have Seen the Glory*, 150.
29. Hess, *Kennesaw Mountain*, 52.
30. Hess, *Civil War in the West*, 216.
31. William C. Buchanan, diary entry, June 29, 1864, William C. Buchanan Diary, CWMC.
32. Hess, *Kennesaw Mountain*, 167.
33. John Hill Ferguson, diary entry, June 29, 1864, in Ferguson, *On to Atlanta*, 54.
34. Chesley Mosman, diary entry, June 29, 1864, in Mosman, *Rough Side of War*, 228; John Hill Ferguson, diary entry, June 29, 1864, in Ferguson, *On To Atlanta*, 54.
35. Theodore F. Upson, diary entry, June 27, 1864, in Upson, *With Sherman to the Sea*, 116–17.
36. J. P. Cannon, diary entry, June 29, 1864, in Cannon, *Bloody Banners*, 79–80.
37. Mitchell, *Civil War Soldiers*, 38.
38. Hess, *Kennesaw Mountain*, 216–18.
39. Richard T. Van Wyck to mother, July 14, 1864, in Van Wyck, *War to Petrify the Heart*, 220. Kelly's Ford was a major crossing on the Rappahannock River both used and guarded by troops throughout the war.
40. Van Wyck, *War to Petrify The Heart*, 220.
41. J. P. Cannon, diary entry, July 16, 1864, in Cannon, *Bloody Banners*, 83.
42. J. P. Cannon, diary entry, July 17, 1864, in Cannon, *Bloody Banners*, 83.
43. John Hill Ferguson, diary entry, July 11, 1864, in Ferguson, *On to Atlanta*, 66.
44. Hamlin Alexander Coe, diary entry, July 12, 1864, in Coe, *Mine Eyes Have Seen the Glory*, 174.
45. Simeon McCord to sister, July 8, 1864, Earl M. Hess Collection, USAMHI.
46. George Edwin Dalton to wife, July 14, 1864, in Dalton, *Path of Patriotism*, 139.
47. Harvey Reid to sisters, July 16, 1864, in Reid, *Uncommon Soldiers*, 168–69.
48. General Williams to daughter, July 15, 1864, in Williams, *From the Cannon's Mouth*, 330.
49. Carter, *Siege of Atlanta*, 273.
50. James W. Watkins to wife, Aug. 8, 1864, James W. Watkins Papers, MARBL.
51. Hess, *Civil War in The West*, 227.
52. George S. Lea to father, Aug. 12, 1864, George S. Lea Family Papers, USAMHI.
53. George S. Lea to father, Aug. 12, 1864, George S. Lea Family Papers, USAMHI.
54. George S. Lea to father, Aug. 12, 1864, George S. Lea Family Papers, USAMHI.

55. Chester H. Southworth, diary entry, Aug. 22, 1864, Southworth Family Papers, USAMHI.

56. Thomas Bell, diary entry, July 30, 1864, Thomas Bell Diary, CWMC.

57. Thomas Bell, diary entry, Aug. 12, 1864, Thomas Bell Diary, CWMC.

58. John Hill Ferguson, diary entries, Aug. 12–17, 1864, in Ferguson, *On to Atlanta*, 74–76.

59. Hess, *Civil War in the West*, 252–57.

60. Noe, *Reluctant Rebels*, 206.

61. Hess, *Trench Warfare under Grant and Lee*, xiii–xvii. Hess demonstrates how the new tactics used in Petersburg finally caught up to the rifle and artillery technological innovations that caused so many casualties throughout the war. Hess's coalescence of Grant's persistence and its effects on Union troops coupled with the Confederate starvation in the city provides the context in which fraternization took place.

62. Glatthaar, *General Lee's Army*, 376.

63. Leed, *No Man's Land*, 110.

64. James Thomas Perry, diary entry, Dec. 16, 1864, James Thomas Perry Papers, VHS.

65. Joseph Banks Lyle, diary entry, June 19, 1864, Joseph Lyle Banks Papers, VHS.

66. Small, *Road to Richmond*, 153.

67. Unidentified soldier, diary entry, June 28, 1864, J. L. Power Scrapbook, MDAH.

68. Samuel B. Pierce, diary entry, July 4, 1864, Samuel B. Pierce Papers, MARBL.

69. Valentine C. Randolph, May 30, 1864, in Randolph, *Civil War Soldier's Diary*, 211–12.

70. Gannon, *Irish Rebels*, 306–7.

71. Joseph Banks Lyle, diary entry, Oct. 5, 1864, Joseph Banks Lyle Papers, VHS.

72. Private Letter, "Incidents in Picket Life," Sept. 15, 1864, in Styple, *Writing and Fighting the Civil War*, 299.

73. Joseph Miller Rand, diary entry, July 13, 1864, Joseph Miller Rand Diary, MDAH.

74. Charles Wellington Reed to mother, June 18, 1864, Reed, *"A Grand Terrible Drama,"* 236.

75. Charles Wellington Reed to Helen, July 7, 1864, Reed, *"A Grand Terrible Drama,"* 243.

76. Joseph R. Ward, Jan. 7, 1865, in Ward, *An Enlisted Soldier's View of the Civil War*, 195–96.

77. John West Haley, diary entry, Aug. 27, 1864, John West Haley Diary, VHS.

78. William Ray, July 1, 1864, in Ray, *Four Years with the Iron Brigade*, 286.

79. William Ray, July 1, 1864, in Ray, *Four Years with the Iron Brigade*, 286.

80. Franklin Lafayette Riley, Dec. 26–28, 1864, in Riley, *Grandfather's Journal*, 226.

81. Glatthaar, *Forged in Battle*, 165–66, 195–200.

82. Lavender Ray to Father, Feb. 14, 1865, in Lane, *"Dear Mother,"* 345.

83. James Thomas Perry, diary entry, Dec. 24, 1864, James Thomas Perry Papers, VHS.

84. John West Haley, diary entry, July 2, 1864, John West Haley Diary, VHS.

85. George P. McClelland to Lizzie, Aug. 5, 1864, in McClelland, *Your Brother in Arms*, 214.

86. Samuel B. Pierce, July 4, 1864, Samuel B. Pierce Letters, MARBL.

87. Marion Hill Fitzpatrick to Amanda, Sept. 24, 1864, in Fitzpatrick, *Letters to Amanda*, 170.

88. Greene, *Civil War Petersburg*, 208.

89. Edmund Fitzgerald Stone to Uncle Samuel Marion Stone, Dec. 7, 1864, Edmund Fitzgerald Stone Papers, VHS.

90. Greene, *Civil War Petersburg*, 20.

91. Enos Bennage, diary entry, June 7, 1865, Enos Bennage Papers, MARBL.

6. Memory

Mann, *Fighting with the Eighteenth Massachusetts*, 139.

1. Isaac Van Houten, "Speech Given at 55th Anniversary of the Battle of Fredericksburg," Isaac Van Houten Papers, CWMC.

2. After the war, Southerners constructed a narrative that absolved them from guilt, ignored the issue of slavery, championed military heroes, and attributed Northern victory to their seemingly endless supply of men and their manufacturing capabilities. This narrative, commonly known as the "Lost Cause," had a monumental impact in shaping Civil War memory, the experience of African Americans, and the Jim Crow South. For more on the Lost Cause, see Gallagher and Nolan, *The Myth of the Lost Cause and Civil War History*. In the past thirty years historians have expanded their studies of the postwar era to understand how groups and individuals came to terms with the memory of war, including the role of the Lost Cause. An essential contribution to memory studies is Nina Silber's *The Romance of Reunion*. Silber suggests that, in an effort to resolve differences, Northerners and Southerners alike celebrated the war as the true height of their respective manhoods. Each man praised the bravery of his worthy opponent. These notions of the ultimate forms of masculinity and manliness during wartime facilitated the bridging of the sectional gap. In the definitive work *Race and Reunion: The Civil War in American Memory*, David Blight argues that the processes of reconciliation and emancipation were mutually dependent after the war . However, due to hostilities and emotions still tied to the memory of the war and prewar life, sectional reunion trumped racial equality and national efforts to assist African Americans after 1877. Reunion happened because, as Blight claims, "The sections needed one another, almost polar opposites that made the center hold and kept both industrial economy humming and a New South on the course of revival," 139.

In a very similar approach John Neff focuses on commemoration in his book *Honoring the Civil War Dead*. Neff argues that the Northern public sacrificed their ideals of union at the expense of the Lost Cause because they adopted a policy of "cause victorious" that highlighted honor and sacrifice. Since notions of honor, sacrifice, and mourning were not exclusive to the North, Southern and Northern publics participated in joint ceremonies, which aided reconciliation. Recently, Caroline Janney refutes this argument in *Remembering the Civil War*, claiming the North did not capitulate to Southern memory but kept a distinctly Northern version. Janney confronts Blight's argument head on by claiming "reconciliation was never the predominant memory of the war among its participants," 5–6.

3. Marten, *Sing Not War*, 10. Although a few historians of common soldiers track their subjects into the postwar or focus their studies of memory solely on veterans, James

Marten in *Sing Not War* is the first to make veteran soldiers the primary focus. While other historians have based their conclusions on the perspectives of politicians, capitalists, and journalists and have not focused on veterans aside from their membership in the Grand Army of the Republic/United Confederate Veteran chapters and their presence at reunions, Marten considers the voices of members of these chapters in addition to those who lived in disabled veteran homes and remained isolated altogether. He reveals, "Veteran is not a single concept but a social construction with multiple meanings and uses," 30.

4. Linderman, *Embattled Courage*, 266–73. Initially, soldiers' letters and diaries fizzled out after surrender and their return to their homes. For fifteen years after the war, a period termed by Gerald Linderman as "hibernation" ensued. He argues that between 1865 and 1880 soldiers privately struggled to make sense of their sacrifice while they integrated back into civilian society. Blight agrees that veterans did feel a disconnect on their return but argues it was a period of "incubation" because soldiers still thought and talked about their experiences. Blight, *Race and Reunion*, 139.

5. Marten, *Sing Not War*, 7–8; Blight, *Race and Reunion*, 18–19.

6. Janney, *Remembering the Civil War*, 166–67.

7. Daniel Emerson Hurd, "My Experiences in the Civil War," in Daniel Emerson Hurd Diary, William Marvel Collection, 1861–1864, USAMHI.

8. Beatty, *Memoirs of a Volunteer*, 257.

9. William C. Burge, "Through the Civil War," in William C. Burge Papers, CWMC, 5.

10. Darby, *Civil War Memoirs of Sergeant George W. Darby*, 80.

11. Seymour, *Civil War Memoirs of Captain William J. Seymour*, 102.

12. Seymour, *Civil War Memoirs of Captain William J. Seymour*, 102.

13. Seymour, *Civil War Memoirs of Captain William J. Seymour*, 102.

14. Blanchard, *I Marched with Sherman*, 99.

15. James Flint Merrill, "Petersburg," in James Flint Merrill Memoirs, CWMC.

16. Frank M. Smith, "Civil War Reminiscences," in Frank M. Smith Reminiscences, CWMC, 29.

17. Hartzell, *Ohio Volunteer*, 131.

18. Hartzell, *Ohio Volunteer*, 141.

19. Jones, "Rank and File of Vicksburg," 24.

20. Clark, *A Glance Backward*, 29.

21. James Flint Merrill, "Petersburg," in James Flint Merrill Memoirs, CWMC.

22. Wickman, *"We Are Coming Father Abra'am,"* 389.

23. Jones, "Rank and File of Vicksburg," 24.

24. Clark, *A Glance Backward*, 17.

25. Mann, *Fighting with the Eighteenth Massachusetts*, 139.

26. Clark, *A Glance Backward*, 29.

27. Darby, *Civil War Memoirs of Sergeant George W. Darby*, 80.

28. Seymour, *Civil War Memoirs of Captain William J. Seymour*, 44.

29. Howard Malcolm Walthall, "Memoir of Civil War Service," 1913, CWMC.

30. Howard Malcolm Walthall, "Memoir of Civil War Service," 1913, CWMC.

31. Jones, "Rank and File of Vicksburg," 23.

32. Jones, "Rank and File of Vicksburg," 24.

33. John Oliver Andrews, "War Record of John Andrews," in John Oliver Andrews Memoirs, CWMC.

34. Seymour, *Civil War Memoirs of Captain William J. Seymour*, 44.

35. Comey, *Legacy of Valor*, 186–87.

36. Darby, *Civil War Memoirs of Sergeant George W. Darby*, 80.

37. Darby, *Civil War Memoirs of Sergeant George W. Darby*, 82–83.

38. Blight, *Race and Reunion*, 164.

39. Polley, *A Soldier's Letters to Charming Nellie*, 96.

40. M. A. Ryan, "Battle of Nashville," 1910, in M. A. Ryan Memoir, MDAH.

41. Jones, "Rank and File of Vicksburg," 23.

42. Holt, *Mississippi Rebel*, 267.

43. Holt, *Mississippi Rebel*, 267.

44. Holt, *Mississippi Rebel*, 269.

45. Holt, *Mississippi Rebel*, 275.

46. Holt, *Mississippi Rebel*, 275.

47. Rhea, *To the North Anna River*, 338–41. The Forty-Eighth New York was at Petersburg, but they were part of Butler's Army of the James, which was not stationed at the Anna Rivers (North or South.) There was also a Forty-Eighth Pennsylvania, but they were part of the Army of the Potomac's Ninth Corps, who were opposite the Sixteenth Mississippi's Third Amy Corps on the river.

48. Janney, *Remembering the Civil War*, 166.

49. Blight, *Race and Reunion*, 199.

50. Blight, *Race and Reunion*, 173.

51. Colonel John S. Mosby, "A Bit of Partisan Service," in Johnson and Buel, *Battles and Leaders of the Civil War*, 3:148.

52. Thomas T. Roche, "Fighting for Petersburg," in Johnson and Buel, *Battles and Leaders of the Civil War*, 5:531.

53. Roche, "Fighting for Petersburg," 5:531–32.

54. Roche, "Fighting for Petersburg," 5:532.

55. General J. B. Kershaw, "Richard Kirkland, The Human Hero of Fredericksburg," *Southern Historical Society Papers* 3, no. 4 (April 1880): 186–88.

56. Kershaw, "Richard Kirkland," 186–88.

57. Kershaw, "Richard Kirkland," 186–88.

58. Richard Kirkland Memorial Dedication Folder, 1965, FSNMP.

59. John B. Gordon, "They Would Mix on the Picket Line. Anecdote of the War by General Gordon," *Southern Historical Society Papers* 10, nos. 8–9 (1882): 422.

60. Captain John C. Featherston, "Brilliant Page in History of War," *Southern Historical Papers* 36 (1908): 170–73.

61. M. J. Smith, President of the Association of the Defenders of Port Hudson, "Fortification and Siege of Fort Hudson," *Southern Historical Society Papers* 14 (1886): 334–35.

62. Smith, "Fortification and Siege of Fort Hudson," 334–35.

63. J. G. Law, "In diary," *Southern Historical Society Papers* 12, nos. 10–12 (1884): 540–41.

64. Smith, "Fortification and Siege of Fort Hudson," 334–35.

65. "Phi Gamma in War—Instances of Restoration of Good Will and Fraternity," *Southern Historical Society Papers* 28 (1900): 309.

66. "Phi Gamma in War," 309.

67. "Phi Gamma in War," 310.

68. "Phi Gamma in War," 311.

69. "Phi Gamma in War," 311.

70. "Phi Gamma in War," 312.

71. Gallagher, introduction to *The Southern Bivouac*, 23.

72. W. A. Day, "Life Among Bullets—The Siege of Petersburg, VA," *Confederate Veteran* 29, no. 4 (1921): 140.

73. Captain A. C. Jones, "Inaugurating the Picket Exchange," *Confederate Veteran* 26, no. 4 (April 1918): 154–55.

74. J. M. Tydings, "Why the Pickets Ceased Firing at Each Other," *Southern Bivouac* 1 (Feb. 1883): 268.

75. "Military Memoirs—At the Gate of Atlanta," *National Tribune*, May 28, 1885.

76. "Recitals and Reminiscences," *National Tribune*, Dec. 30, 1909.

77. "Untitled," *National Tribune*, March 20, 1884.

78. Walker Y. Page, "The Old Log Cabin on the Rapidan," *Blue and Gray; The Patriotic American Magazine* 2 (July–Dec. 1893): 292.

79. Page, "Old Log Cabin on the Rapidan," 292.

80. Page, "Old Log Cabin on the Rapidan," 294.

81. "Fraternity along the Rappahannock," *Blue and Gray; The Patriotic American Magazine* 2 (July–Dec. 1893): 189.

82. "Fraternity along the Rappahannock," 189.

83. "Fraternity along the Rappahannock," 189.

Conclusion

1. Gallagher, *Causes Won, Lost, and Forgotten*, 14.

2. See, for example, the Fredericksburg and Spotsylvania National Military Park; Confederate Whitehouse in Richmond, Virginia.

3. Grey, *The 2nd City of London Regiment (Royal Fusiliers) in the Great War, 1914–1919*, 33.

4. MacGill, *The Red Horizon*, 84.

5. Morgan, *Leaves from a Field Note-Book*, 270–71.

6. Jordan et al., *Understanding Modern Warfare*, 301–19.

Bibliography

Archives and Manuscript Materials

Alabama Department of Archives and History—Montgomery, Alabama
    Edward Norphlet Brown Letters
    Weaver and Gray Family Papers
    James Montgomery Lanning Diary
    McCullough Family Letters
    Mark Lyons Letters
    James F. Jones Civil War Letters
    William R. Jones Diary
    Paul Turner Vaughn Diary
    W. D. Willett "Pickens Planters" Diary
Emory University, Manuscripts and Rare Book Library— Atlanta, Georgia
    Enos Bennage Papers
    John A. Everett Letters
    William B. and Hugh L. Honnoll Papers
    Zerah Coston Monks Letters
    Samuel B. Pierce Papers
    Sue Richardson Papers
    Alfred A. Rigby Papers
    James W. Watkins Letters
    Edward King Wightman Letters
Fredericksburg and Spotsylvania National Military Park—Fredericksburg, Virginia
    Jacob Betchel Letters
    Austin Dobbins Journal
    H. P. Garrison Letters
    Edward Heinichen Papers
    Richard Kirkland Memorial Dedication Folder
    David Lilley Papers
    Egbert Rogers Papers
    John L. Street Letters

Historical Society of Pennsylvania—Philadelphia, Pennsylvania
    John P. Barr Diary
    Franklin Boyts Papers
    John Daniel Follmer Diary
    James Milton McGown Diary
    William Reed Moore Diary
    John L. Smith Papers
    William Stackhouse Diary
    James H. Walker Diary
Library of Congress—Washington DC
    Tilton C. Reynolds Papers
Mississippi Department of Archives and History—Jackson, Mississippi
    Emma Balfour Civil War Diary
    Gilliam-Chasom Family Papers
    James Palmer Civil War Diary
    J. L. Power Scrapbook
    Richard Prowse Letters
    Joseph Miller Rand Diary
    M. A. Ryan Memoir
    William M. Stone Diary
Missouri History Museum Library and Research Center—St. Louis, Missouri
    Theodore D. Fisher Diary
National Archives—Washington DC
    Court-Martial Case Files, Records of the Office of the Adjutant General (Army)
New York Historical Society—New York City
    Silas Auchmoedy Letters
    William Conrow Letters
    George A. Mitchell Letters
    Walter S. Poor Correspondence
    Killian van Rensselaer Papers
    Burrage Rice Diary
    David Roche Letters
    Margaret Scott Correspondence
    Southard Family Correspondence
    David Ludlow Thompson Letters
    Loren W. Tuller Papers
    John Wagner Correspondence
    James M. Willet Correspondence
New York Public Library—New York City
    Albert V. C. Collier Diary
    Ely Family Letters
    Griswold Family Letters
    George Hubbard Papers

    Smith Family Papers
    George S. Stone Diary
    John C. Whiting Letters
State Archives of Florida—Tallahassee, Florida
    Council A. Bryan Papers
    Joshua Hoyet Frier Memoirs
    Albert W. Peck Diary
University of Southern Mississippi Special Collections—Hattiesburg, Mississippi
    Granville W. Belcher Letters
    John Wesley Culpepper Letters
    Levi Lewis Letters
    John Leroy "Lee" Robinson Letters
    Felix Walthall Letters
U.S. Army Military History Institute Carlisle, Pennsylvania
    Richmond V. Black Papers
    Boucher Family Papers
    Butler Family Papers
    Civil War Miscellaneous Collection
        George H. Alverson Letters
        John Oliver Andrews Memoirs
        David Ayers Letters
        Jabez Banbury Diary
        James Beard Letters
        Thomas Bell Diary
        Samuel Brooks Letters
        William C. Buchanan Diary
        Douglas Richie Bushnell Letters
        William C. Burge Papers
        George C. Burmeister Diary
        Taylor Lester Dewitt Diary
        Markham Family Papers
        James Henry McBride Papers
        Albert H. Merrifield Diary
        James Flint Merrill Memoirs
        Anson B. Shuey Letters
        George Sinclair Letters
        Frank M. Smith Reminiscences
        John Martin Steffan Letters
        Isaac Vanderwarker III Diary
        Isaac Van Houten Papers
        Howard Malcolm Walthall Memoir
    John T. Cheney Collection
    Earl M. Hess Collection

Simeon McCord Letters
  Charles A. Houghton Papers
  George S. Lea Family Papers
  John A. Loveless Papers
  William Marvel Collection
    Daniel Emerson Hurd Papers
    Julius Whitney Diary
  William McGlothlin Papers
  Southworth Family Papers
  Henry Welch Papers
  Clark W. M. Whitten Papers
  William F. Winkleman Papers
Virginia Historical Society—Richmond, Virginia
  Charles Edward Bates Papers
  Francis Edward Bayol Letters
  John Hampden Chamberlayne Papers
  William Harris Clayton Papers
  Robert Edward Lee Headquarters Papers
  Thomas Claybrook Elder Papers
  Robert Gaines Haile Diary
  John West Haley Papers
  Joseph W. Griggs Papers
  John Price Kepner Papers
  William B. Kidd Diary
  Joseph Banks Lyle Papers
  Walter Fabius Maximus Moring Diary
  James Thomas Perry Papers
  Shipp Family Papers
  Edmund Fitzgerald Stone Papers

Published Works

Ashworth, Tony. *Trench Warfare 1914–1918: The Live and Let Live System*. New York: Holmes & Meier Publishers, 1980.

Ballard, Michael B. *Vicksburg: The Campaign That Opened the Mississippi*. Chapel Hill: University of North Carolina Press, 2004.

Baptist, Edward E. *The Half Has Never Been Told: Slavery and the Making of American Capitalism*. New York: Basic Books, 2016.

Barrett, Milton. *The Confederacy Is on Her Way up the Spout: Letters to South Carolina, 1861–1864*. Edited by J. Roderick Heller III and Carolynn Ayres Heller. Athens: University of Georgia Press, 1992.

Beatty, John. *Memoirs of a Volunteer: 1861–1863*. Edited by Harvey S. Ford. New York: W. W. Norton, 1946.

Berry, Daina Ramey. *The Price for Their Pound of Flesh: The Value of a Slave, From Womb to Grave, in the Building of a Nation*. Boston: Beacon Press, 2017.

Berry, Stephen W., II. *All That Makes a Man: Love and Ambition in the Civil War South*. New York: Oxford University Press, 2005.

Bird, Edgeworth, and Sallie Bird. *Granite Farm Letters: The Civil War Correspondence of Edgeworth and Sallie Bird*. Edited by John Rozier. Athens: University of Georgia Press, 1988.

Blackford, Charles Minor. *Letters from Lee's Army*. Edited by Susan Leigh Blackford. New York: Charles Scribner's Sons, 1947.

Blanchard, Ira. *I Marched with Sherman: Ira Blanchard Civil War Memoirs of the 20th Illinois Infantry*. Edited by Nancy Mattingly. iUniverse, 2000.

Blight, David. *Race and Reunion: The Civil War in American Memory*. Cambridge MA: Harvard University Press, 2001.

Bowen, Roland E. *From Ball's Bluff to Gettysburg . . . And Beyond: The Civil War Letters of Private Roland E. Bowen, 15th Massachusetts Infantry, 1861–1864*. Edited by Gregory A. Coco. Gettysburg PA: Thomas Publications, 1994.

Broomall, James J. "'We Are a Band of Brothers': Manhood and Community in Confederate Camps and Beyond." *Civil War History* 60, no. 3 (2014): 270–309.

Bryan, George. *Friend Jennie: The Civil War Letters of Lt. George Bryan, 125th NY State Volunteers*. Edited by Joseph Stickelmyer. Shelbyville KY: Wasteland Press, 2009.

Callaway, Joshua K. *The Civil War Letters of Joshua K. Callaway*. Edited by Judith Lee Hallock. Athens: University of Georgia Press, 1997.

Camp, Stephanie M. H. *Closer to Freedom: Enslaved Women and Everyday Resistance in the Plantation South*. Chapel Hill: University of North Carolina Press, 2004.

Cannon, J. P. *Bloody Banners and Barefoot Boys: A History of the 27th Regiment Alabama Infantry CSA: The Civil War Memoirs and Diary Entries of J. P. Cannon, M.D.* Shippensburg PA: Burd Street Press, 1997.

Carmichael, Peter S. *The War for the Common Soldier: How Men Thought, Fought, and Survived in Civil War Armies*. Chapel Hill: University of North Carolina Press, 2018.

Carnes, Mark C. *Secret Ritual and Manhood in Victorian America*. New Haven CT: Yale University Press, 1989.

Carnes, Mark C., and Clyde Griffen. *Meanings for Manhood: Construction of Masculinity in Victorian America*. Chicago: Chicago University Press, 1990.

Carter, Samuel, III. *Siege of Atlanta, 1864*. New York: Bonanza Books, 1973.

Chambers, William Pitt. *Blood and Sacrifice: The Civil War Journal of a Confederate Soldier*. Edited by Richard A. Baumgartner. Huntington WV: Blue Acorn Press, 1994.

Clark, George A. *A Glance Backward; Or, Some Events in the Past History of My Life*. Houston: Press of Rein & Sons, 1914.

Clawson, Mary Ann. *Constructing Brotherhood: Class, Gender, and Fraternalism*. Princeton NJ: Princeton University Press, 1989.

Clayton, William Henry Harrison. *A Damned Iowa Greyhound: The Civil War Letters of William Henry Harrison Clayton*. Edited by Donald C. Elder. Iowa City: University of Iowa Press, 1998.

Coe, Hamlin Alexander. *Mine Eyes Have Seen the Glory: Combat Diaries of Union Sergeant Hamlin Alexander Coe*. Edited by David Coe. Rutherford NJ: Fairleigh Dickinson University Press, 1975.

Comey, Henry Newton. *A Legacy of Valor: The Memoirs and Letters of Captain Henry Newton Comey, 2nd Massachusetts Infantry*. Edited by Lyman Richard Comey. Knoxville: University of Tennessee Press, 2004.

Confederated Southern Memorial Association, Sons of Confederate Veterans, United Confederate Veterans, and United Daughters of the Confederacy. *Confederate Veteran*. Nashville TN: S. A. Cunningham, 1893–1932.

Copp, Colonel Elbridge J. *Reminiscences of the War of Rebellion, 1861–1865*. Nashua NH: self-published, printed by the Telegraph Publishing Company, 1911.

Cort, Charles Edwin. *"Dear Friends": The Civil War Letters and Diary of Charles Edwin Cort*. Edited by Helyn W. Tomlinson. Madison: University of Wisconsin Press, 1962.

Cozzens, Peter. *The Shipwreck of Their Hopes: The Battles for Chattanooga*. Urbana: University of Illinois Press, 1994.

Dalton, George Edwin. *The Path of Patriotism: Civil War Letters of George Edwin Dalton* Edited by Theodore A. Dalton. Palo Alto CA: Theodore A. Dalton, 2003.

Darby, George W. *The Civil War Memoirs of Sergeant George W. Darby, 1861–1865*. Edited by Rogan H. Moore. Bowie MD: Heritage Books, 1999.

Dooley, John. *John Dooley's Civil War: An Irish American's Journey in the First Virginia Infantry Regiment*. Edited by Robert Emmett Curran. Knoxville: University of Tennessee Press, 2012.

Dower, John W. *War without Mercy: Race and Power in the Pacific War*. New York: Pantheon Books, 1986.

Du Bois, W. E. B. *Black Reconstruction in America*. New York: Harcourt, Brace, 1935.

Dunlap, Robert Caldwell. *As the Mockingbird Sang: The Civil War Diary of Pvt. Robert Caldwell Dunlap, C.S.A.* Edited by Susanne Staker Lehr. St. Joseph MO: Platte Purchase Publishers, 2005.

Dunning, William. *Reconstruction, Political and Economic 1865–1877*. New York: Harper and Brothers, 1907.

Earnest, John Guilford. *All Right Let Them Come: The Civil War Diary of an East Tennessee Confederate*. Edited by Charles Swift Northern III. Knoxville: University of Tennessee Press, 2003.

Everson, Guy R., and Edward W. Simpson, Jr. *Far, Far from Home: The Wartime Letters of Dick and Tally Simpson, 3rd South Carolina Volunteers*. New York: Oxford University Press, 1994.

Ewing, George Henry. *The Ewing Family Civil War Letters*. Edited by John T. Greene. East Lansing: Michigan State University Press, 1994.

Farris, John Kennerly. *Letters to Mary: The Civil War Diary of John Kennerly Farris*. Edited by John Abernathy Smith. Winchester TN: Franklin County Historical Society, 1994.

Faust, Drew Gilpin. *The Creation of Confederate Nationalism: Ideology and Identity in the Civil War South*. Baton Rouge: Louisiana State University Press, 1988.

Ferguson, John Hill. *On to Atlanta: The Civil War Diaries of John Hill Ferguson, Illinois Tenth Regiment of Volunteers*. Edited by Janet Correll Ellison. Lincoln: University of Nebraska Press, 2001.

Fisk, Wilbur. *Hard Marching Every Day: The Civil War Letters of Private Wilbur Fisk, 1861–1865*. Edited by Emil and Ruth Rosenblatt. Lawrence: University of Kansas Press, 1992.

Fitzpatrick, M. Hill. *Letters to Amanda: The Civil War Letters of Marion Hill Fitzpatrick, Army of Northern Virginia*. Edited by Jeffrey C. Lowe and Same Hodges. Macon GA: Mercer University Press, 1998.

Foner, Eric. *Free Soil, Free Labor, Free Men: The Ideology of the Republican Party before the Civil War*. Oxford: Oxford University Press, 1970.

Foote, Lorien. *The Gentlemen and the Roughs: Manhood, Honor, and Violence in the Union Army*. New York: New York University Press, 2010.

Freehling, William. *Road to Disunion I: Secessionists at Bay*. New York: Oxford University Press, 1990.

——— . *Road to Disunion II: Secessionists Triumphant*. New York: Oxford University Press, 2007.

Gallagher, Gary W. *Causes Won, Lost, and Forgotten: How Hollywood and Popular Art Shape What We Know about the Civil War*. Chapel Hill: University of North Carolina Press, 2008.

——— . Introduction to *The Southern Bivouac*. Wilmington NC: Broadfoot Publishing, 1992.

——— . *The Union War*. Cambridge MA: Harvard University Press, 2011.

Gallagher, Gary W., and Alan T. Nolan, eds. *The Myth of the Lost Cause and Civil War History*. Bloomington: Indiana University Press, 2010.

Gannon, James P. *Irish Rebels, Confederate Tigers: The 6th Louisiana Volunteers, 1861–1865*. Campbell CA: Savas Publishing, 1998.

Genovese, Eugene D. *Roll, Jordan, Roll: The World the Slaves Made*. New York: Vintage Books, 1976.

Glatthaar, Joseph. *Forged in Battle: The Civil War Alliance of Black Soldiers and White Officers*. New York: Free Press, 1990.

——— . *General Lee's Army: From Victory to Collapse*. New York: Free Press, 2008.

Gould, Wesley. *Dear Sister: The Civil War Letters of the Brothers Gould*. Edited by Robert F. Harris and John Niflot. Westport CT: Praeger, 1998.

Greene, A. Wilson. *Civil War Petersburg: Confederate City in the Crucible of War*. Charlottesville: University of Virginia Press, 2006.

——— . *The Final Battles of the Petersburg Campaign: Breaking the Backbone of the Rebellion* Knoxville: University of Tennessee Press, 2008.

——— . "Morale, Maneuver, and Mud." In *The Fredericksburg Campaign: Decision on the Rappahannock*. Edited by Gary Gallagher, 171–228. Chapel Hill: University of North Carolina Press, 1995.

Grey, W. E. *The 2nd City of London Regiment (Royal Fusiliers) in the Great War, 1914–1919*. Published from the headquarters of the Regiment, 1929.

Grimsley, Mark. *And Keep Moving on: The Virginia Campaign, May–June 1864.* Lincoln: University of Nebraska Press, 2002.

———. *The Hard Hand of War: Union Military Policy toward Southern Civilians, 1861–1865.* Cambridge: Cambridge University Press, 1995.

Haley, John West. *The Rebel Yell & the Yankee Hurrah: The Civil War Journal of a Maine Volunteer.* Edited by Ruth Silliker. Camden ME: Down East Books, 1985.

Harris, M. Keith. *Across the Bloody Chasm: The Culture of Commemoration among Civil War Veterans.* Baton Rouge: Louisiana State University Press, 2014.

Hartzell, John Calvin. *Ohio Volunteer: The Childhood and Civil War Memoirs of Captain John Calvin Hartzell, OVI.* Edited by Charles I. Switzer. Athens: Ohio University Press, 2005.

Hazelton, William Cross. *Army of the Potomac: The Civil War Letters of William Cross Hazelton of the Eighth Illinois Cavalry Regiment.* Edited by Peter G. Beidler. Seattle WA: Coffeetown Press, 2013.

Heller, J. Roderick III, and Carolynn Ayres Heller, eds. *The Confederacy Is on Her Way up the Spout: Letters to South Carolina, 1861–1864.* Athens: University of Georgia Press, 1992.

Hess, Earl J. *The Civil War in the West: Victory and Defeat from the Appalachians to the Mississippi.* Chapel Hill: University of North Carolina Press, 2012.

———. *Kennesaw Mountain: Sherman, Johnston, and the Atlanta Campaign.* Chapel Hill: University of North Carolina Press, 2013.

———. *Trench Warfare under Grant and Lee: Field Fortifications in the Overland Campaign.* Chapel Hill: University of North Carolina Press, 2007.

———. *The Union Soldier in Battle: Enduring the Ordeal of Combat.* Lawrence: University of Kansas, 1997.

Hess, Frederick. *Letters to Tobitha: A Personal History of the Civil War, Letters by Frederick Hess.* Edited by David Primrose. New York: iUniverse, 2006.

Hill, Mary S. *A British Subject's Recollections of the Confederacy While a Visitor and Attendant in Its Hospitals and Camps.* Baltimore MD: Trumbull Brothers, 1875.

Holt, David. *A Mississippi Rebel in the Army of Northern Virginia: The Civil War Memoirs of Private David Holt.* Edited by Thomas D. Cockrell and Michael B. Ballard. Baton Rogue: Louisiana State University Press, 1995.

Holt, Michael. *The Fate of Their Country.* New York: Hill & Wang, 2004.

———. *The Political Crisis of the 1850s.* New York: Norton, 1978.

Howe, Daniel Walker. *What Hath God Wrought: The Transformation of America, 1815–1848.* New York: Oxford, 2007.

Jackson, Isaac. *"Some of the Boys...": The Civil War Letters of Isaac Jackson, 1862–1865.* Edited by Joseph Orville Jackson. Carbondale: Southern Illinois University Press, 1960.

Jacobs, Margaret C. *The Origins of Freemasonry: Facts and Fictions.* Philadelphia: University of Pennsylvania Press, 2006.

Janney, Caroline. *Remembering the Civil War: Reunion and the Limits of Reconciliation.* Chapel Hill: University of North Carolina Press, 2013.

Johnson, Robert Underwood, and Clarence Clough Buel, eds. *Battles and Leaders of the Civil War*. 8 vols. New York: Century Co., 1884.

Johnson, Susan Lee. *Roaring Camp: The Social World of the California Gold Rush*. New York: W. W. Norton, 2000.

Johnson, Walter. *River of Dark Dreams: Slavery and Empire in the Cotton Kingdom*. Cambridge MA: Harvard University Press, 2013.

———. *Soul by Soul: Life Inside the Antebellum Slave Market*. Cambridge MA: Harvard University Press, 1999.

Jones, J. H. "The Rank and File at Vicksburg." In *Publications of the Mississippi Historical Society*. Vol. 7. Edited by Franklin L. Riley. Oxford MS: Printed for the Society, 1903.

Jordan, Brian Matthew. *Marching Home: Union Veterans and Their Unending Civil War*. London: W. W. Norton, 2015.

Jordan, David, James D. Kiras, David J. Lonsdale, Ian Speller, Christopher Tuck, and C. Dale Walton. *Understanding Modern Warfare*. 2nd ed. Cambridge: Cambridge University Press, 2016.

Jordan, William B., Jr. *Red Diamond Regiment: The 17th Maine Infantry, 1862–1865*. Shippensburg PA: White Mane Publishing, 1996.

Kemp, Thomas Henry. *Letters to Jane*. Edited by Joelyn James. Meridian MS: Lauderdale County Department of Archives and History, 1999.

Kimmel, Michael. *Manhood in America: A Cultural History*. New York: Free Press, 1996.

King, John. *Three Years with the 92nd Illinois: The Civil War Diary of John M. King*. Edited by Claire E. Swedberg. Mechanicsburg PA: Stackpole Books, 1999.

Landis, Michael Todd. *Northern Men with Southern Loyalties: The Democratic Party and the Sectional Crisis*. Ithaca NY: Cornell University Press, 2014.

Lane, Mills, ed. *"Dear Mother: Don't Grieve about Me. If I Get Killed, I'll Only Be Dead." Letters from Georgia Soldiers in the Civil War*. Savannah GA: Beehive Press, 1990.

Larson, John Lauritz. *The Market Revolution in America: Liberty, Ambition, and the Eclipse of the Common Good*. Cambridge: Cambridge University Press, 2010.

Lears, T. J. Jackson. "The Concept of Cultural Hegemony: Problems and Possibilities." *American Historical Review* 90, no. 3 (1985): 567–93.

Lee, Wayne E. *Barbarians and Brothers: Anglo-American Warfare, 1500–1865*. New York: Oxford University Press, 2011.

Leed, Eric J. *No Man's Land: Combat and Identity in World War I*. London: Cambridge University Press, 1979.

Linderman, Gerald. *Embattled Courage: The Experience of Combat in the American Civil War*. New York: Free Press, 1987.

Logan, David Jackson. *"A Rising Star of Promise": The Civil War Odyssey of David Jackson Logan: 17th South Carolina Volunteers, 1861–1864*. Edited by Samuel N. Thomas Jr. and Jason Silverman. Campbell CA: Savas Publishing, 1998.

MacGill, Patrick. *The Red Horizon*. New York: George H. Doran, 1916.

Mahood, Wayne. *Fight All Day, March all Night: A Medal of Honor Recipient's Story*. New York: New York University Press, 2012.

Mann, Thomas H. *Fighting with the Eighteenth Massachusetts: The Civil War Memoir of Thomas Mann*. Edited by John J. Hennessy. Baton Rouge: Louisiana State University Press, 2000.

Manning, Chandra. *What This Cruel War Was Over: Soldiers, Slavery, and the Civil War*. New York: Alfred Knopf, 2007.

Marten, James. *Sing Not War: The Lives of Union and Confederate Veterans in Gilded Age America*. Chapel Hill: University of North Carolina Press, 2011.

Matrau, Henry C. *Letter Home: Henry Matrau of the Iron Brigade*. Edited by Marcia Reid-Green. Lincoln: University of Nebraska Press, 1998.

McClelland, George P. *Your Brother in Arms: A Union Soldier's Odyssey*. Edited by Robert C. Plumb. Columbia: University of Missouri Press, 2011.

McCurry, Stephanie. *Confederate Reckoning: Power and Politics in the Civil War South*. Cambridge MA: Harvard University Press, 2010.

———. *Masters of Small Worlds: Yeoman Households, Gender Relations, and the Political Culture of the Antebellum South Carolina Low Country*. New York: Oxford University Press, 1995.

McDonald, William, Richard W. Knott, and Basil W. Duke. *The Southern Bivouac*. Louisville KY: Southern Historical Association of Louisville, 1882–1887.

McMurray, Richard M. *Atlanta 1864: Last Chance for the Confederacy*. Lincoln: University of Nebraska Press, 2000.

Miller, R. M., Harry S. Stout, and Charles Reagan Wilson, eds. *Religion and the American Civil War*. New York: Oxford University Press, 1998.

Mitchell, Reid. *Civil War Soldiers: Their Expectations and Their Experiences*. New York: Viking Press, 1988.

McPherson, James. *Battle Cry of Freedom: The Civil War Era*. New York: Oxford University Press, 1988.

———. *For Cause and Comrades: Why Men Fought in the Civil War*. New York: Oxford University Press, 1997.

———. *Tried by War: Abraham Lincoln as Commander in Chief*. New York: Penguin Press, 2008.

———. *What They Fought For, 1861–1865*. Baton Rouge: Louisiana State University Press, 1995.

McSween, Murdoch John. *Confederate Incognito: The Civil War Reports of "Long Grabs," a.k.a Murdoch John McSween, 26th and 35th North Carolina Infantry*. Edited by E. B. Munson. Jefferson NC: McFarland, 2013.

Molyneux, Joel. *Quill of the Wild Goose: Civil War Letters and Diaries of Private Joel Molyneux, 141st P.V.* Edited by Kermit Molyneux Bird. Shippensburg PA: Burd Street Press, 1996.

Montgomery, William Rhadamanthus. *Georgia Sharpshooter: The Civil War Diary and Letters of William Rhadamanthus Montgomery*. Edited by George Montgomery Jr. Macon GA: Mercer University Press, 1997.

Moore, Robert A. *A Life for the Confederacy: As Recorded in the Pocket Diaries of Pvt. Robert A. Moore, Co. G 17th Mississippi Regiment*. Edited by James W. Silver. Wilmington NC: Broadfoot Publishing, 1991.

Morgan, J. H. *Leaves from a Field Note-Book*. London: Macmillan, 1916.
Morton, Joseph W., and Benjamin Rush Davenport. *Blue and Gray: The Patriotic American Monthly Magazine*. Philadelphia: Patriotic Pub. Co., 1893.
Mosman, Chesley A. *The Rough Side of War: The Civil War Journal of Chesley A. Mosman, 1st Lieutenant, Co. D, 59th Illinois Vol. Infantry Regiment*. Edited by Arnold Gates. New York: Basin Publishing, 1987.
The National Tribune. Washington DC: G. E. Lemon & Co., 1877–1917.
Neff, John. *Honoring the Civil War Dead: Commemoration and the Problem of Reconciliation*. Lawrence: University of Kansas Press, 2005.
Nelson, Dana D. *National Manhood: Capitalist Citizenship and the Imagined Fraternity of White Men*. Durham NC: Duke University Press, 1998.
Newton, James K. *A Wisconsin Boy in Dixie: Civil War Letters of James K. Newtown*. Edited by Stephen E. Ambrose. Madison: University of Wisconsin Press, 1961.
New York Observer and Chronicle. New York: Morse, Hallock & Co., 1833–1912.
Noe, Kenneth. *Reluctant Rebels: The Confederates Who Joined the Army after 1861*. Chapel Hill: University of North Carolina Press, 2010.
O'Reilly, Francis Augustin. *The Fredericksburg Campaign: Winter War on the Rappahannock*. Baton Rouge: Louisiana State University Press, 2006.
Pardee, George K. *My Dear Carrie: The Civil War Letters of George K. Pardee and Family*. Edited by Robert H. Jones. Akron OH: Summit County Historical Society Press, 1994.
Parker, Robert W. *Lee's Last Casualty: The Life and Letters of Sgt. Robert W. Parker, Second Virginia Cavalry*. Edited by Catherine M. Wright. Knoxville: University of Tennessee Press, 2008.
Pflugrad-Jackisch, Ami. *Brothers of a Vow: Secret Fraternal Orders and the Transformation of White Male Culture in Antebellum Virginia*. Athens: University of Georgia Press, 2010.
Phillips, Jason. *Diehard Rebels: The Confederate Culture of Invincibility*. Athens: University of Georgia Press, 2007.
Polley, J. B. *A Soldier's Letters to Charming Nellie by J. B. Polley of Hood's Texas Brigade*. Edited by Richard B. McCaslin. Knoxville: University of Tennessee Press, 2008.
Potter, David. *The Impending Crisis*. New York: Harper Collins, 1977.
Power, J. Tracy. *Lee's Miserables: Life in the Army of Northern Virginia from the Wilderness to Appomattox*. Chapel Hill: University of North Carolina Press, 1998.
Rable, George C. *Fredericksburg! Fredericksburg!* Chapel Hill: University of North Carolina Press, 2002.
———. *God's Almost Chosen People: A Religious History of the American Civil War*. Chapel Hill: University of North Carolina Press, 2010.
Randolph, Valentine C. *A Civil War Soldier's Diary: Valentine C. Randolph, 39th Illinois Regiment*. Edited by David Roe. DeKalb: Northern Illinois University Press, 2006.
Ray, William R. *Four Years with the Iron Brigade: The Civil War Journals of William R. Ray, Co. F, Seventh Wisconsin Infantry*. Edited by Lance Herdegen and Sherry Murphy. Cambridge MA: Da Capo Press, 2002.
Reed, Charles Wellington. *"A Grand Terrible Drama": From Gettysburg to Petersburg: The Civil War Letters of Charles Wellington Reed*. Edited by Eric A. Campbell. New York: Fordham University Press, 2000.

Reeves, James J. *History of the Twenty-Fourth Regiment, New Jersey Volunteers*. Camden NJ: S. Chew, Printer, 1889.

Reid, Harvey. *Uncommon Soldiers: Harvey Reid and the 22nd Wisconsin March with Sherman*. Edited by Frank L. Byrne. Knoxville: University of Tennessee Press, 2001.

Rhea, Gordon. *In the Footsteps of Grant and Lee: The Wilderness through Cold Harbor*. Baton Rouge: Louisiana State University Press, 2007.

———. *To the North Anna River: Grant and Lee, May 13–25, 1864*. Baton Rouge: Louisiana State University Press, 2000.

Rhodes, Elisha Hunt. *All for the Union: A History of the 2nd Rhode Island Volunteer Infantry*. Lincoln RI: Andrew Mowbray, 1985.

Riley, Franklin Lafayette. *Grandfather's Journal: Company B, Sixteenth Mississippi Infantry Volunteers, Harris' Brigade, Mahone's Division, Hill's Corps, A.N.V., May 27, 1861–July 15, 1865*. Dayton OH: Morningside, 1988.

Robertson, James I. *Soldiers Blue and Gray*. Columbia: University of South Carolina Press, 1998.

Rotundo, E. Anthony. *American Manhood: Transformations in Masculinity from the Revolution to the Modern Era*. New York: Basic Books, 1993.

Ruegmer, Edward B. *Slave Law and the Politics of Resistance in the Early Atlantic World*. Cambridge MA: Harvard University Press, 2018.

Scott, James C. *Domination and the Arts of Resistance: Hidden Transcripts*. New Haven CT: Yale University Press, 1990.

Sellers, Charles. *The Market Revolution: Jacksonian America*. New York: Oxford University Press, 1991.

Seymour, William J. *The Civil War Memoirs of Captain William J. Seymour: Reminiscences of a Louisiana Tiger*. Edited by Terry L. Jones. Baton Rouge: Louisiana State University Press, 1991.

Sheehan-Dean, Aaron, ed. *The View from the Ground: Experiences of Civil War Soldiers*. Lexington: University of Kentucky Press, 2006.

———. *Why Confederates Fought: Family and Nation in Civil War Virginia*. Chapel Hill: University of North Carolina Press, 2007.

Sheeran, James B. *Confederate Chaplain: A War Journal of Rev. James B. Sheeran, c.ss.r., 14th Louisiana, C.S.A.* Edited by Joseph T. Durkin. Milwaukee WI: Bruce Publishing, 1960.

Sherman, Francis T. *Quest for a Star: The Civil War Letters of Colonel Francis T. Sherman of the 88th Illinois*. Edited by C. Knight Aldrich. Knoxville: University of Tennessee Press, 1999.

Silber, Nina. *The Romance of Reunion: Northerners in the South, 1865–1900*. Chapel Hill: University of North Carolina Press, 1997.

Small, Abner R. *The Road to Richmond: The Civil War Memoirs of Major Abner R. Small of the 16th Maine Volunteers*. Edited by Harold Adams Small. Berkley: University of California Press, 1957.

Sommers, Richard J. *Richmond Redeemed: The Siege at Petersburg*. New York: Doubleday, 1981.

Southern Historical Society, R. A. Brock, and Virginia Historical Society, eds. *Southern Historical Society Papers*. Richmond: Virginia Historical Society, 1876–1959.

Stampp, Kenneth. *America in 1857*. New York: Oxford University Press, 1990.

———. *The Era of Reconstruction, 1865–1877*. New York: Knopf, 1965.

Sutherland, Daniel. *Fredericksburg and Chancellorsville: The Dare Mark Campaign*. Lincoln: University of Nebraska Press, 1998.

Stubbs, Steven H. *Duty, Honor, Valor: The Story of the Eleventh Mississippi Infantry Regiment*. Philadelphia MS: Dancing Rabbit Press, 2000.

Styple, William B., ed. *Writing and Fighting the Civil War from the Army of Northern Virginia*. Kearny NJ: Belle Grove Publishing, 2003.

Tapert, Annette, ed. *The Brothers War: Civil War Letters to Their Loved Ones from the Blue and Gray*. New York: Times Books, Random House, 1988.

Taylor, Michael W., ed. *The Cry Is War, War, War: The Civil War Correspondence of Lts. Burwell Thomas Cotton and George Job Huntley, 34th Regiment North Carolina*. Dayton OH: Morningside, 1994.

Thompson, Richard S. *While My Country Is in Danger: The Life and Letters of Lieutenant Richard S. Thompson*. Edited by Gerry Hatcher Poriss and Ralph G. Poriss. Hamilton NY: Edmonston Publishing, 1994.

Trudeau, Noah Andre. *Bloody Roads South: The Wilderness to Cold Harbor, May–June 1864*. Boston: Little, Brown, 1989.

———. *The Last Citadel: Petersburg, Virginia June 1864–April 1865*. Boston: Little, Brown, 1991.

Twichell, Joseph Hopkins. *The Civil War Letters of Joseph Hopkins Twichell*. Edited by Peter Messent and Steve Courtney. Athens: University of Georgia Press, 2006.

Upson, Theodore F. *With Sherman to the Sea: The Civil War Letters Diaries and Reminiscences of Theodore F. Upson*. Edited by Oscar Osburn Winther. Baton Rouge: Louisiana State University Press, 1943.

U.S. War Department. 56th and 57th Articles of War. In *Rules and Articles for the Government of the Armies of the United States*. Washington DC: A. O. P. Nicholson, Public Printer, 1857.

———. *The War of Rebellion: A Compilation of the Official Records of the Union and Confederate Armies*. 128 vols. Washington DC: Government Printing Office, 1880–1901.

Van Wyck, Richard T. *A War to Petrify the Heart: The Civil War Letters of a Dutchess, N.Y. Volunteer*. Edited by Virginia Hughes Kennedy. Hensonville NY: Black Dome Press, 1997.

Varon, Elizabeth. *Disunion! The Coming of the American Civil War*. Chapel Hill: University of North Carolina Press, 2008.

Ward, Joseph R. *An Enlisted Soldier's View of the Civil War: The Wartime Papers of Joseph R. Ward, 39th Illinois Volunteer Infantry*. Edited by D. Duane Cummins and Daryl Hohweiler. West Lafayette IN: Belle Publications, 1981.

Weber, Jennifer L. *Copperheads: The Rise and Fall of Lincoln's Opponents in the North*. Oxford: Oxford University Press, 2006.

Weintraub, Stanley. *Silent Night: The Story of the World War I Christmas Truce*. New York: Free Press, 2001.

Weitz, Mark A. *A Higher Duty: Desertion among Georgia Troops during the Civil War*. Lincoln: University of Nebraska Press, 2000.

White, Wyman Silas. *The Civil War Diary of Wyman S. White: First Sergeant Company F, 2nd United States Sharpshooter Regiment*. Edited by Russell C. White. Baltimore: Butternut and Blue, 1991.

Wickman, Don. *"We Are Coming Father Abra'am": The History of the Ninth Vermont Volunteers Infantry*. Lynchburg VA: Schroeder Publications, 2005.

Wiley, Bell Irvin. *The Life of Billy Yank: The Common Soldier of the Union*. New York: Bobbs-Merrill Company, 1952.

———. *The Life of Johnny Reb: The Common Soldier of the Confederacy*. New York: Bobbs-Merrill Company, 1943.

Williams, Alpheus S. *From the Cannon's Mouth: The Civil War Letters of General Alpheus S. Williams*. Edited by Milo M. Quaife. Detroit MI: Wayne State University Press, 1959.

Williams, Edward B, ed. *Rebel Brothers: The Civil War Letters of the Trueharts*. College Station: Texas A&M University Press, 1995.

Wood, Henry B. *The Marble Valley Boys*. Edited by Wayne Wood. Hoover AL: Interface Printing, 1986.

Woodward, C. Vann. *Origins of the New South, 1877–1913*. Baton Rouge: Louisiana State University Press, 1951.

Woodworth, Steven E., ed. *The Chickamauga Campaign*. Carbondale: Southern Illinois University Press, 2010.

———. *This Grand Spectacle: The Battle of Chattanooga*. Abilene TX: McWhiney Foundation Press, 1999.

———. *The Music of the Mocking Birds the Roar of the Cannon: The Civil War Diary and Letters of William Winters*. Lincoln: University of Nebraska Press, 1998.

———. *Nothing but Victory: The Army of the Tennessee, 1861–1865*. New York: Alfred A. Knopf, 2005.

———. *Six Armies in Tennessee: The Chickamauga and Chattanooga Campaigns*. Lincoln: University of Nebraska Press, 1998.

Index

Page numbers in italics indicate illustrations.

Abbott, Benjamin, 116–17
Ackerman, William, 67
Adairsville GA, 55
African Americans, 5, 7–8, 14, 132–34, 138, 185n2. *See also* race; United States Colored Troops (USCT)
Alabama regiments, 21, 36, 42
Albany NY, 142
alcohol abuse, 23–24, 55, 95
Allatoona Creek, 99, 123
Alverson, George H., 93–94
amnesty, 116–17, 146, 147, 148, 149, 152, 161–63
Anderson, R. H., 103
Andrews, John Oliver, 105, 146
Angel of Marye's Heights, 153–54
Antietam, 37, 127
antiwar sentiment, 46, 47
Appalachian Mountains, 72
Army of Northern Virginia: at Chickamauga, 45; commander of, 21; fraternization by, 6, 11, 168; morale of, 57, 107–8; at Petersburg, 127; at Richmond, 54; soldiers' individualism in, 20; studies of, 5; in Tennessee, 51; trading of newspapers, 88–91, 106, 108–9; William Harris Clayton in, 2; winter encampment of, 37–38
Army of Tennessee: at Atlanta, 55, 118, 127; at Chattanooga, 51, 52, 73, 97–98; at Chickamauga, 45, 117; fraternization by, 6, 12, 14; at Jackson MS, 48, 51; at Kennesaw Mountain, 119; morale of, 54–56
Army of the Cumberland: to Atlanta, 98, 141; at Chickamauga, 45, 117; command of, 54, 94, 99; crossing of Tennessee valley, 72; fraternization by, 6, 12, 51, 52, 56, 168; at Missionary Ridge, 97; shortage of food, 73
Army of the Department of the Mississippi, 6, 12, 45, 48, 51, 71, 112, 168
Army of the James, 6, 187n47
Army of the Ohio, 6, 54, 56, 98
Army of the Potomac: at Chancellorsville, 45; command of, 94, 102; compassion for enemy, 74; fictional story about, 151; fraternization by, 6, 11, 17; at Fredericksburg, 37; morale of, 57; Morris Brown with, 1, 2; at Petersburg, 58, 74, 187n47; in Richmond, 54; in Tennessee, 51; trading of newspapers, 88–91, 108–9
Army of the Tennessee: and antiwar sentiment, 46, 47; to Atlanta, 98, 121; ceasefires agreed to, 112; at Chickasaw Bayou, 46; command of, 54, 94, 95; fraternization by, 6, 12, 50, 56, 168; hardships of, 47–48; trading of newspapers, 99; at Vicksburg, 45, 48, 49, 51, 69, 124
artillery: attack of Union at Atlanta, 56; attacks by Confederate, 37, 48, 76, 113, 119; casualties caused by, 184n61; during ceasefires, 122;

artillery (*cont.*)
   during trench and siege warfare, 13, 111, 113, 127. *See also* soldiers
Ashworth, Tony, 81, 111, 182n1
Association of the Defenders of Port Hudson, 155
Atlanta: battle in, 55–57, 124, 127; ceasefires at, 118, 122, 128; control of roads to, 73; fraternization before and during battle in, 14, 52, 68, 98, 141; General Sherman's advance on, 14, 55, 98–100, 102, 121, 123–24, *125*; newspapers from, 70; soldiers' memories of battle in, 160; terrain near, 72
Auchmoedy, Silas, 24–25
Augusta GA, 96
Ayers, David, 73

Balfour, Emma, 50, 70
Ballard's Farm, 47
balloon, reconnaissance, 43
Baltimore Sun, 89
Banbury, Jabez, 53
Barnett, Captain, 116
Barrett, Milton, 85
Battle of Bull Run, 157
Battle of Chancellorsville, 17, 23, 45
Battle of Chickamauga, 12, 45, 51, 73, 93–95, 116–17, 141, 168
Battle of Chickasaw Bayou, 46
Battle of Cold Harbor, 57, 100, 102
Battle of Spotsylvania, 57, 149–50
Battle of the Crater, 132, 134
Battle of the Wilderness, 57
Battle on the Jerusalem Plank Road, 130
Battles and Leaders of the Civil War (Johnson and Buel), 152, 158
Baum, G. F., 78
Bayol, Francis Edward, 36, 76
Beard, James, 59, 79–80
Beatty, John, 141
Belcher, Granville, 22
Bell, Thomas, 28, 98, 125–26
Belzonne, B., 93
Bennage, Enos, 135
Bermuda Hundred, 58, 104
Berry, Albert C., 78
Bird, Edgeworth, 45
Black, Richmond V., 112–13

Blackford, Charles, 110
Blanchard, Ira, 142
Blight, David, 148, 151, 185n2, 186n4
Blue and Gray, 158, 161–62
boats: soldiers' transportation by, 78, 81, 90–91; trading by, 65, 67, 77, 78, 82, 85–86, 90, 91, 93, 144, 145
Boisseau, Dr., 105
Boston Post, 86
Bowen, Roland E., 42, 86
Boydton Plank Road, 135
Boyts, Franklin, 109–10
Bragg, Braxton: at Chattanooga, 72; command of, 52, 94, 98; control of roads to Atlanta and Nashville, 73; desertion under, 95; fraternization of men of, 12, 51; at Jackson MS, 51; at Missionary Ridge, 97
breastworks. *See* trench warfare
British Army, 166–67, 182n1
British Royal Fusiliers, 166
Brown, Edward Norphlet, 55, 95, 98
Brown, Isaac, 104
Brown, Morris, Jr., 1
Bryan, A., 58
Bryan, George, 112
Buchanan, William C., 120
Buel, Clarence Clough, 152, 158
Burge, William, 141
Burmeister, George C., 47, 115
Burns, Ken, 165
Burnside, Ambrose E., 11, 37, 88, 89, 133, 153
Bushnell, Douglas Richie, 48
Butler, Benjamin F., 57, 60

Callaway, Joshua, 53
Calvert, William H., *140*
Camp Fuller, 29
Cannon, J. P., 49, 56, 119, 121, 122
Cannon, Presley, 104
card games, 117, 118, 131
Carmichael, Peter, 5, 20, 68
Carnes, Mark, 28
Carney, Dick, 38
Carr, Charley, 64
ceasefires: agreements to, 8, 17, 44–45, 116, 118–20, 122, 124, 126, 128, 130, 131, 141, 143–44, 147, 148, 159–60; frequency of, 118, 127; regulations regarding, 102–3; results of, 122,

130–31; during siege warfare, 13–14, 111, 112, 115, 119, 124–26, 128; soldiers' and officers' memories of, 146, 147, 159; as test for Reconstruction, 132; trading during, 68, 81, 86, 114, 115, 118, 120, 122–24, 126, 131, 142, 152, 155; treatment of black soldiers during, 133; veterans' memories of, 143–44; during WW I, 111, 166, 182n1. *See also* truces; burial

Chambers, William Pitt, 49, 55, 71, 113–15

Chandhore Valley Railroad, 59

Chantilly VA, 157

chaplains, 65–66. *See also* religious services

Charleston SC, 90, 143

Chattahoochee River, 14, 118, 121–23

Chattanooga Creek, 143

Chattanooga TN, 12, 45, 51–54, 68, 72–74, 94–98, 117, 141, 148

Cheatham's Hill, 119–20

Cheney, John T., 97

Chicago IL, 47

Chickamauga Creek, 117

civil rights movement, 154

Civil War: battle tactics during, 111, 127, 182n2, 184n61; casualties of, 100, 182n2; causes of, 19, 139, 148, 171n8; comparison to WW I, 159; goals of, 89, 100, 107; memories of, 14–15, 138–39, 151, 163, 185n2; nativism among troops in, 148–49; nature of fraternization during, 6, 29, 165, 167–68; newspaper coverage of, 87, 106; scholarship on fraternization during, 3–6, 9, 10, 16, 170n15; social dynamics after, 135, 152; soldiers' adaptation to life during, 20; Southern term for, 153; talk about end of, 12–13, 38, 55, 64, 66, 82–84, 100, 106, 107, 114, 122, 139, 162

The Civil War (documentary), 165

Civil War Soldiers (Mitchell), 4

Claibourne, General, 124

Clark, George A., 143, 144

Clayton, William Harris, 2

clothing, 73–77, 82, 94, 118

Coe, Hamlin Alexander, 99, 122

coffee, sharing of, 9, 71

coffee trading: by boat, 65, 67, 145; in siege environment, 75, 99, 122; for sugar, 155; for tobacco, 12, 63–67, 73, 76, 79, 82, 118–20, 123, 126, 141, 142, 145, 150, 152; after Vicksburg surrender, 72; for whiskey, 70

Collins, Michael, 67

Comey, Henry Newton, 147

Compromise of 1877, 137

Confederacy, 25, 100, 127, 132, 134–35, 164, 185n2. *See also* Southerners

Confederate Army: attitudes toward enemy, 10, 99, 116–17, 121; attitudes toward war, 9, 25–26; casualties of, 26, 69; commanders of, 21, 23, 42–43, 60, 70, 81, 98; coping strategies of, 31; data from soldiers in, 6, 170n15; furloughs in, 21–22; joking with enemy, 42–44, 55, 59–60, 149, 160; knowledge about current events and war, 89–90; morale of, 54–57, 95, 107–10; and non-soldiers, 25; prisoners from, 1; reasons for fighting, 5, 102; strategy and tactics of, 46, 127; supplies and conditions of, 12, 42, 48–50, 57, 64, 65, 71–76, 94–95, 109–10, 142, 145, 156, 182n2, 184n61; surrender of, 135; Union soldiers' attitudes toward, 18, 146. *See also* Army of Northern Virginia; Army of Tennessee; Army of the Department of the Mississippi; Southerners

Confederate Conscription Act (1862), 25. *See also* Conscription Acts

Confederate Veteran, 158, 159

Congressional Medal of Honor, 1–2

Conscription Acts, 13, 25

conversation: during burial truces, 114–15; across Chattahoochee River, 121; common bond through, 64; after Confederate surrender at Vicksburg, 71; environment for, 36–37, 56, 141, 144, 147; joking in, 42–44, 50–52, 55, 56, 59–60, 149, 160; through letters, 44, 79–80; in siege environment, 50, 69, 70; soldiers' memories of, 142, 162; subjects of, 12–13, 81–84; and trade networks, 61, 81; among veterans, 139. *See also* fraternization

Coosaw River, 78

Copperheads. *See* Northern Democrats

Cort, Charles Edwin, 115–16

court-martial sentences, 32, 40, 67, 77–78, 91–93, 96, 104–5

Cozzens, Peter, 73, 97–98, 182n2

Crandall, I. L. G., 104

Culpepper, John Wesley, 24

Cumberland Plateau, 72

Dallas GA, 55, 98, 118–19
Dalton, George, 123
Dalton GA, 54, 55, 56, 118
Darby, George W., 141, 145, 147
Davis, Jefferson, 44, 56, 60, 100, 110, 132
Day, W. A., 159
Dean, Aaron-Sheehan, 4
DeLashmutt, William G., *140*
Democratic Party, 100. *See also* Northern Democrats
desertion: from Confederate Army, 32, 75, 95, 108–10, 124, 142, 145–46; courts-martial for, 96; due to hunger, 75; as form of resistance, 32, 38; seriousness of offense, 68, 78; threats of, 54; in Union Army, 22
Dewitt, Taylor Lester, 119
Dick, Lieutenant, 21
Diehard Rebels (Phillips), 5, 96
Dooley, John, 13, 66–67, 85
Dudley, O., 105–6
Dunlap, Robert Caldwell, 69–70
Durgin, Lieutenant, 105

Early, Jubal, 158–59
Earnest, John Guilford, 48–49, 112
earthworks. *See* picket duty; trench warfare
East Point GA, 124
Eich, Henry, 96
election, presidential (1864), 13, 14, 87, 99, 100, 102, 107, 127
Emancipation Proclamation, 13, 87–89. *See also* slavery
Emerson, Albert D., 78
European immigrants, 149
Everett, John, 108
Everson, Guy, 67
Ewing, George H., 81
Ezra Church, 56

Falmouth VA, 85
Farr, Loring, 104
Farris, John Kennerly, 54–55, 72, 94–95
Featherstone, John C., 155
Ferguson, John Hill, 120, 122, 126
Fisher, Theodore, 50–51, 71
Fisher, William, 78
Fisk, Wilbur, 17–18, 86

Fitzpatrick, Marion Hill, 75, 77, 133–34
Florida regiments, 60
Follmer, John Daniel, 9, 23
Folly Island SC, 78
food, 64, 67, 71–76, 82, 94, 108–10, 146, 160. *See also* sugar
Foote, Lorien, 5, 20, 23
For Cause and Comrades (McPherson), 4
Fort Delaware, 78
Fort Donelson, 148
Fort Stedman, 129–30
Frank, Paul, 78
Franklin-Nashville Campaign, 127
fraternal organizations, 29, 157–58
fraternization: in antebellum society, 11, 18–19, 27–29, 33, 84, 157; common bond through, 68, 82–84, 118, 162; definition of, 6; documentation of, 2, 4, 6, 7, 14, 32, 45, 64, 70, 93, 99, 121–22, 124, 126, 137–39, 144, 145, 163, 165–66; environment for, 35–37, 44, 49–50, 52, 65, 68, 167, 168, 182n2, 184n61; evolution of, 6, 115, 142; as form of resistance, 32, 76; frequency of, 66, 70–71, 106, 141; illegality of, 2, 13, 14, 31, 63, 66–68, 77–79, 86, 91–93, 96, 99, 102–6, 123, 126, 142, 144, 145, 162; influence on postwar society, 135, 137–38, 151–52, 156, 160–61, 162–64; misconceptions about, 161–62, 164; negative consequences of, 145–46; participants in, 7, 10–11, 15; purpose and benefits of, 2, 6, 8–10, 16, 29–30, 32, 51, 61, 74, 77, 79–80, 86, 95, 102, 104, 112, 115, 118, 121–22, 126, 142, 152, 168; qualities promoted by, 152, 154, 158; race issues of, 8, 84, 134, 164; risks of, 52, 102; romanticized accounts of, 148, 149, 151, 156; talk of peace during, 81–84. *See also* conversation; trading
Fredericksburg Centennial Commission, 154
Fredericksburg VA: battle tactics at, 127; fraternization at, 11, 50, 68–69, 137, 152, 168; General Hooker's defensive position near, 45; memories of fraternization at, 153, 154, 159; news of Union defeat at, 46; picket duty at, 41, 66, 137, 143; trading at, 64–66, 93, 144–45; Union casualties at, 37, 89
Freemasons, 29, 157
Frier, Joshua Hoyet, 25
furloughs, 21–22

Gaines Mill VA, 63–64
Gallagher, Gary, 165
Garrison, Henry P., 66
General Lee's Army (Glatthaar), 5
Georgia, 55, 56, 57, 97, 108–9, 118, 122, 127. See also Atlanta
Georgia regiments, 2, 85
German soldiers, 7, 47, 166–67, 182n1
Gettysburg PA, 1, 2, 127, *140*
Gilliam, Henry, 95
Glatthaar, Joseph, 20, 21, 128
Goldenburgh, Charles, 104–5
Gordon, John B., 129–30, 154
Gould, Wesley, 110
Grand Army of the Republic, 139, 160, 185n3
Grand Gulf MS, 48
Grant, Ulysses S.: battle plans of, 96, 182n2, 184n61; battles fought under, 100; at Boydton Plank Road, 135; at Chattanooga, 51, 54; at Chickasaw Bayou, 46; on Confederate deserters, 109; at Missionary Ridge, 96–97; newspaper reports about, 99; at Petersburg, 57, 58; promotion of, 51, 94; pursuit of Confederates in Virginia, 127; refusal to release prisoner, 106; soldiers under, 12, 13, 54, 57; at Vicksburg, 46–50, 69, 113
Greene, A. Wilson, 134, 182n2
Griggs, Joseph, 26
Griswold, Charles, 38, 41

Haile, Robert Gaines, 36–37, 63–64
Haley, John West, 23–24, 31, 42, 74, 75, 76, 82, 131
Halleck, Henry, 51
Hamilton College, 1
handshakes, 44–45
Harmes, McDonough, 79
Harper's Weekly, 90, 108
Hartzell, John Calvin, 143
Hazelton, William Cross, 24, 35
Hess, Earl J., 5, 33, 182n2, 184n61
Hess, Frederick, 53, 74
Hill, A. P., 134
Hill, Mary S., 43
Holt, David, 149–51
Homan, Charles, 79
homesickness, 9, 27, 38, 40
Honoring the Civil War Dead (Neff), 185n2

Hood, John Bell, 14, 56, 124, 127
Hooker, Joseph: chaplain in army of, 65–66; on exchange of newspapers, 92; fighting style of, 99; at Fredericksburg, 45; at Lookout Mountain, 97; prohibition of fraternization, 66; replacement of General Burnside, 89; soldiers under, 22, 54; in Tennessee, 94
Houghton, Charles, 56
Hubbard, George, 60
Huntley, G. J., 86
Hurd, Daniel Emerson, 59, 141

Illinois, 47
Illinois regiments, 48, 52, 115–16, 125–26, 146, 148
illness and injury, 26–27, 47–49, 124, 128
An Incident of War (Lumley), *90*
Indiana, 47
Indiana regiments, 79, 123, 159
infantry, 13, 56, 76, 97, 113, 118, 119, 122, 123. See also soldiers
insubordination, 68
Iowa regiments, 47
Irish soldiers, 7
Iron Brigade, 60

Jackson, David Logan, 25, 64
Jackson, Isaac, 46, 47, 71–72, 113
Jackson, Thomas Jonathan "Stonewall," 21
Jackson MS, 48, 51
James River, 57, 58, 100
Janney, Caroline, 139, 185n2
Jews, 149
Johnson, Robert Underwood, 152, 158
Johnston, Joseph E., 14, 48, 51, 55–57, 98, 119–21
Jones, A. C., 159
Jones, James F., 75, 108
Jones, J. H., 143, 144, 146, 149
Jonesboro GA, 56

Kelly's Ford VA, 121
Kemp, T. H., 71
Kennesaw Mountain, 14, 118–21, 128, 141, 147
Kentucky regiments, 94, 95
Kepner, John Price, 23, 107
Kershaw, Joseph, 153–54
Kessel, George, 67
Kidd, William B., 3, 27

Kimmel, Michael, 19
King, John, 116
Kingston GA, 123
Kirkland, Joseph, 153–54
Knapp, Lyman, 105
knives, 73, 75, 77
Knoxville TN, 94
Kunstler, Mort, 165

Lanier, Richard Nunn, 154
Lanning, James Montgomery, 21
Law, J. G., 156
Lea, George S., 52, 57, 124
Lee, Robert E.: battles fought under, 45, 54, 57, 58, 100, 127, 128, 135; newspaper coverage of, 99, 108; prohibition of fraternization, 66, 103, 154; soldiers under, 11, 12, 21, 57
Lee, Wayne, 32
Leed, Eric, 128
letters, 44, 79–80, 91, 123, 162–63. *See also* fraternization: documentation of
Lewis, Levi, 40
Libby Prison, 154
The Life of Billy Yank (Wiley), 4
The Life of Johnny Reb (Wiley), 4
Lincoln, Abraham: command of army, 54, 94; election of, 30, 100, 127; Emancipation Proclamation of, 87, 89; Northern Democrats' criticism of, 25; soldiers' attitudes toward, 44, 60, 107
Linderman, Gerald, 20, 30, 54, 186n4
Longbottom, John H., 78
Longstreet, James, 21, 94
Lookout Mountain, 54, 72, 73, 94, 97, 141, 157, 158
"Lost Cause" narrative, 138, 156, 158, 159, 185n2
Louisiana regiments, 43
Lovejoy's Station GA, 56
Loveless, John, 47
Lowe, Thaddeus C., 43
Lumley, Arthur, *90*
Lyle, Joseph Banks, 83, 128, 130
Lyons, Mark, 3

Mahone (commander at Petersburg), 152
Maine, Seventeenth, 31, 109
Manassas VA, 45
Mann, Thomas, 43, 137, 144

Manning, Chandra, 5
"March to the Sea," 127
Markham, Sylvanus A., 8–9
Marten, James, 138, 185n3
Marye's Heights, 37, 153–54
Maryland regiments, *140*, 170n15
masculinity: definition and expression of, 4, 18–19; and race, 8, 32, 133; of soldiers' discourse, 43; war accounts promoting, 158, 164, 185n2
Masons. *See* Freemasons
Matrau, Henry, 107
McBeth, James, 20, 24, 26, 112
McBride, James Henry, 54, 74, 97
McClellan, George B., 60, 89, 107
McClelland, George P., 107, 133
McCord, Simeon, 123
McPherson, James, 4, 88, 121
McSween, Murdoch John, 67
Meade, George Gordon, 78, 102–3, 106
Merrifield, Albert, 72
Merrill, James, 142
Merrill, James Flint, 143–44
Meyer, Frederick, 93
Michigan regiments, 150–51, 187n47
"The Miracle," 97
Missionary Ridge, 73, 96–97, 117
Mississippi, 118. *See also* Vicksburg MS
Mississippi regiments, 42, 52, 59, 65, 66, 71, 146, 148, 187n47
Mississippi River, 47, 48, 72
Missouri regiments, 48, 50–51, 96
Mitchell, George, 43
Mitchell, Reid, 4, 121
Monks, Zerah Coston, 107
Montgomery, William, 41, 42, 94
Moore, William Reed, 37, 58
Morgan, J. H., 166
Moring, Walter F., 64
Morris Island SC, 78
Mosby, John S., 152
Mosman, Chesley A., 50, 73, 117–18, 120
"Mud March," 89
music, 44
My Friend, the Enemy (Kunstler), 165

Nashville TN, 73, 148
National Tribune, 158, 160, 161

Neff, John, 185n2
Nelson, Dana D., 30
neutral zones: black soldiers in, 133; effect of battle tactics on, 167; on land, 44, 131; meetings in, 68, 71, 75, 81, 91, 131, 159, 162; rivers as, 36, 121, 123
New Hampshire regiments, 105
New Hope Church GA, 55
New Market Heights, 132
New Orleans LA, 143
newspapers, *87*, *101*; content of, 13, 86–90, 93, 95–96, 108, 109; on legacy of Civil War, 15. *See also* periodicals
newspaper trading, 2, 9, 17, 64, 70, 83, 85–86, *90*, *92*, 108, 141, 168; by black soldiers, 133; by boat, 65, 67, 85–86, 90; during ceasefires, 120, 123, 126, 131; frequency of, 88, 103, 105; memories about, 143, 145, 155; punishment for, 91–93, 96, 104–5; in siege environment, 74, 75, 98–99, 124
Newton, James, 114
New York Herald, 2, 86, 89, 90, 104
New York regiments, 1, 20, 41, 44, 67, 93, 99, 105, 112, 137, 187n47
New York Tribune, 96
Noe, Kenneth, 9–10
North Carolina regiments, 159
Northern Democrats, 25, 100, 106–8, 161. *See also* Democratic Party

Odd Fellows, 29
O'Dell, John, 79
officers: and black soldiers, 134–35; ceasefires arranged by, 114, 115; conduct during truces, 31; drunkenness of, 23–24, 55; and memories of war, 138, 146–47, 151–53, 158–59; and newspaper exchanges, 92, 93, 102, 104–5; and presidential election, 100; reactions to fraternizing, 67–68, 77–79, 85, 93, 96, 99–100, 103, 106, 122, 123, 126–27, 131, 144, 145, 154, 155; soldiers' attitudes toward, 22–24, 31, 49, 55, 81, 89, 91, 93–94, 122; after Vicksburg surrender, 72; withholding information from soldiers, 86
Ohio regiments, 47, 78
Oliver, John V., 48
Orchard Knob, 97
Overland Campaign, 57, 100

Page, Walker Y., 161–62
Palmer, James, 71
Pardee, George K., 47–48, 114–15
Pareture, Ned, 76
Patrick, Brigadier General, 31
Peace Democrats. *See* Northern Democrats
Peck, Albert, 40
Pemberton, John C., 12, 13, 45, 46, 48–49, 51, 69, 71, 113
Peninsula Campaign, 2
Pennsylvania regiments, 23, *140*, 187n47
periodicals, 151. *See also* newspapers
Perry, James Thomas, 59, 128, 133
Petersburg VA: African American soldiers at, 132; ceasefires at, 143–44, 155; court-martial cases during campaign at, 104; fighting style at, 58, 108, 127–28, *129*, 182n2, 184n61; fraternization at, 12, 14, 52, 74, 141; hardships at, 57–59, 74, 75, 108–10, 127–28; importance to Confederates, 127; memories of fraternization at, 152; Morris Brown at, 1–2; political effect of battle at, 100; prisoners after battle at, 134–35; regiments at, 187n47; talk of peace at, 83; as target of Union Army, 57–58; trade at, 68, 78, 103, 105, 150; Union control of, 135; wood cutting at, 152
Pflugrad-Jackisch, Ami, 29
Phelps, Frank, 96
Phi Gamma, 157–58
Philadelphia Enquirer, 90
Philadelphia PA, 60, 161
Phillips, Jason, 5, 10, 96
picket duty, *39*, *41*, *53*; accounts of fraternization during, 1, 2, 9, 162; black soldiers on, 14, 132–34; ceasefires during, 111–12, 116, 122–26, 130, 143, 147, 148, 159–60; at Chattanooga, 52–53; at Chickamauga, 117–18; Confederate desertion during, 95, 109; conversation during, 42–43, 56, 81–84, 102, 149; hardships of, 40, 119; newspaper reading during, 86, *90*, 96, 102, 143; at Petersburg, 58–60, 74–75; prohibition of fraternization during, 31, 67, 77–79, 96, 103–6; proximity to enemy during, 40–41, 44, 73, 77; at Rapidan River, 141, 142; on Rappahannock, 17, 38, 141, 152; as setting for fraternization, 11, 35–36, 81, 167; under siege, 58–59, 61, 111–12;

INDEX 209

picket duty (cont.)
  timing and purpose of, 36; trade during, 63–69, 74, 76, 79–80, *80*, 82, *90*, 92, 96, 98, 99, 143, 160; at Vicksburg, 69; warnings to opposition during, 129–30, 154. *See also* trench warfare
Picket's Mill GA, 55
Pierce, Samuel, 108, 129, 133
politicians, 24, 81–82, 100, 106–7, 161
politics: in antebellum society, 18–19; and fraternal organizations, 29; of military command, 89; newspaper reports about, 99, 106; in postwar society, 137–39, 151, 152; soldiers' discussion of, 83
Polley, J. B., 148
Poor, Walter S., 88
Port Royal SC, 78
Post, Parley, 93
Post, Samuel, 93
Prowse, Richard, 29
Pryor, Roger A., 105–6

Rable, George, 38
race, 8, 14, 32, 84, 133, 134, 164, 170n22. *See also* African Americans; United States Colored Troops (USCT); whites
Race and Reunion (Blight), 185n2
Rand, Joseph Miller, 56, 95
Randolph, Valentine C., 129
Rapidan River, 1, 131, 141, 154
Rappahannock River: as environment for fraternization, 121, 122, 137; fighting style at, 58; memories of fraternization at, 141, 152, 159, 162; picket duty at, 11, 37–41, *41*, 43, 85, 93, 137; trading at, 64, 65, 67, 68, 78, 85, 88, 92, 144; Union campaigns on, 37, 45, 57
Ray, Lavender, 132
Ray, William, 60, 131
Reconstruction, 132, 135, 137
Reed, Charles Wellington, 75, 130–31
Reeves, James J., 66
Reid, Harvey, 98, 123
religious services, 162. *See also* chaplains
Reluctant Rebels (Noe), 9
Remembering the Civil War (Janney), 185n2
Resaca GA, 55
Rhodes, Elisha Hunt, 109
Rice, Burrage, 88

Richmond Dispatch, 2
Richmond Enquirer, 104
Richmond Examiner, 90
Richmond News, 96
Richmond VA: African American soldiers at, 132; anticipation of attack in, 57, 58; newspapers from, 86, 89, 91, 143, 145; Union capture of, 54, 135
Richmond Whig, 86
Rigby, Alfred, 113, 114
Riley, Franklin Lafayette, 131
Roberts, Charles, 78
Robertson, James I., Jr., 16
Roche, Thomas R., 152–53
Rockford IL, 29
Rogers, Egbert, 65, 90
The Romance of Reunion (Silber), 185n2
Rosecrans, William, 51, 72, 73, 94, 117
Rossville Gap, 97
Rotundo, E. Anthony, 11, 28, 42
Ryan, M. A., 148

Saunders, Lieutenant, 21
Savannah GA, 127
secessionists, 25, 30
Seymour, William J., 141–42, 145, 147
Sheehan-Dean, Aaron, 31
Sheeran, James, 65
Shenandoah Valley, 102
Sheridan, Philip Henry, 135
Sherman, Francis, 52
Sherman, William Tecumseh: command of armies, 51, 94, 95, 98; fraternization of men of, 14, 119; in Georgia, 55–56, 97, 99, 102, 118–21, 123, *125*, 127; "hard war" policy of, 108; newspaper coverage of, 108; at Vicksburg, 46
Shipp, John, 20
Shuey, Anson B., 9, 65
siege warfare: ceasefires during, 13–14, 111, 112, 115, 119, 122, 125; nature of fraternization during, 36, 50, 51, 61, 69, 72; in Petersburg Campaign, 58, 128; practice of, 46, 48; soldiers' experience of, 73–74, 98, 112–13, 124, 127, 128; trading during, 68
Silber, Nina, 185n2
Simpson, Tally N., 27, 31, 63, 65, 91
Sinclair, George, 3

Sing Not War (Marten), 185n3

slavery: as cause of Civil War, 171n8; Confederate soldiers' attitudes toward, 8, 13, 19, 83; and fraternal organizations, 29; as reason for avoiding war service, 25; and reconciliation, 185n2; soldiers' avoidance of discussing, 83, 84; Union soldiers' attitudes toward, 5, 13, 17, 19. *See also* Emancipation Proclamation

slaves, 132, 134

Small, Abner R., 128

Smith, Frank M., 142–43

Smith, John L., 60, 77, 83, 111

Smith, J. V., 115

Smith, M. J., 155, 156

Smokey Mountains, 72

social class, 18–19, 21–26, 28, 82, 107, 109

soldiers: agency of, 32, 56, 111, 112, 144, 161, 173n64; attitudes toward non-soldiers, 25, 26, 107, 121, 139, 161–62; battle tactics of, 45–46; common experiences of, 44, 64, 68, 82–84, 114, 118, 159; compartmentalization of relationship to enemy, 60–61, 69, 70, 76, 99–100, 114–15, 120–23, *140*, 143, 152; curiosity about enemy, 77; empathy among, 10, 12, 15, 35, 41–43, 53–54, 59, 60, 61, 64, 66, 81–83, 115–17, 128, 130, 131, 134, 139, 150, 161–63, 167; "friendships" between opposing, 123, 126, 137, 138, 142, 146, 155, 156; hardships of, 9, 19–21, 26–27, 35, 37, 38, 44, 46–48, 54–55, 57, 71, 74, 87–88, 95, 100–102, 106–8, 112–13, 124, 125, 127, 128, 143, 163; knowledge about current events and war, 86–91, 95, 96, 98–99, 102, 106; loyalty of, 67–68, 74, 125, 142; manhood of, 5, 8, 18–19, 23, 32; memories of, 14–15, 138, 141, 142, 146–49, 151, 153–59, 161, 163–64, 185n3, 186n4; proximity to enemy, 36–37, 41–42, 44, 50, 112, *129*, 141, 147; reactions to war experience and military life, 2–5, 10–17, 23, 27–28, 30–33, 64, 81–83, 114, 117, 163; reasons for fighting, 19; respect for opposing, 120–21, 135, 139, 148–49, 156, 160–61, 185n2; restraint and resistance of, 5, 7, 8, 11, 14, 22, 23, 28, 30–32, 38, 67, 68, 144, 160, 168; stereotypes of, 10, 12, 44; warnings to opposing, 128–30, 143, 147, 154. *See also* artillery; infantry

Soloman, Horace G., 159

Sommers, Richard, 100, 182n2

Sons of Temperance, 29

South Anna River, 150, 187n47

South Carolina, 78

South Carolina regiments, 118, 148

Southern Bivouac, 158, 159

Southerners, 138, 158, 160, 163, 164, 185n2. *See also* Confederacy; Confederate Army

Southern Historical Society Papers, 153–58

Southworth, Chester H., 118–19, 124–25

Starr, J. B., 150–51

Steffan, John Martin, 85–86

St. Germaine, Marshall, 78

Stone, Edmund Fitzgerald, 134

Stone, William, 113

Stuart, J. E. B., 43

sugar, 64, 67, 72, 145, 155. *See also* food

Sunday Morning Chronicle, 86

swimming, 116, 122–23, 141–42, 144, 159

Taliaferro, Lieutenant, 21

Taylor, Major, 103

Tennessee, 12, 45, *53*, 54, 76, 94, 115, 118. *See also* Battle of Chickamauga; Chattanooga TN

Tennessee River, 51–52, 72, 115

Tenth U.S. Army Corps, 31

Texas regiments, 148

Thomas, George H., 54, 94, 97, 115, 127

Thompson, Richard S., 40–41

tobacco trading: by boat, 65; for coffee, 12, 63–67, 73, 76, 79, 82, 118–20, 123, 126, 141, 142, 145, 150, 152; memories of, 160; for miscellaneous items, 77; in siege environment, 75, 99, 114, 124; for sugar, 67, 155; for whiskey, 43

trading: during ceasefires, 68, 81, 86, 114, 115, 118, 120–24, 126, 131, 152, 155; after Confederate surrender at Vicksburg, 72; conversation during, 84; methods of, 65, 79–80, 85, 144; of miscellaneous items, 73, 75–77, 143; during picket duty, 63–67, 69, 74, 76, 79–80, *80*, 81–82, *90*, 92, 96, 98, 99, 143, 160; punishment for, 78, 91–93, 144–45; soldiers' memories of, 142, 145, 150, 155, 159–60; value of interaction, 76, 77, 80–81, 91, 143, 145. *See also* coffee trading; fraternization; knives; newspaper trading; sugar; tobacco trading; whiskey

INDEX

trench warfare, 111, 119, 124, *125*, 127–28, *129*, 130, 166–67, 182nn1–2. *See also* picket duty
truces, burial, 13, 31, 113–18, 120, 155, 156. *See also* ceasefires
Truehart, Henry Martyn, 44, 76
Tunnel Hill, 97
Twichell, Joseph Hopkins, 44

Union Army: attitudes toward Northern Democrats, 25; battle tactics of, 46, 182n2, 184n61; casualties of, 26, 37, 69; commanders of, 22–23, 42, 55, 60, 70, 81, 93–94; Confederate deserters with, 109; coping strategies of, 31; data about fraternization of, 6, 45, 170n15; desertions from, 22; enlistments in, 30; integration of, 5, 132–33, 135; at Missionary Ridge, 97; morale of, 54, 73–74; Morris Brown in, 1; motivation for fighting, 5, 100–102, 107; newspaper coverage of, 108; in Petersburg Campaign, 58; on picket at Rappahannock, 38; and presidential election, 100; as prisoners, 134–35; prohibition of fraternization of, 13, 66, 96, 102–4; protection of trade network, 91; race issues in, 14, 88–89; relationship with enemy, 42–44, 59–60, 116–17, 121, 146, 149, 160–61; supplies of, 9, 12, 64, 65, 94; victory of, 156, 185n2. *See also* Army of the Cumberland; Army of the James; Army of the Ohio; Army of the Potomac; Army of the Tennessee
The Union Soldier in Battle (Hess), 5
United Confederate Veterans, 139, 160, 185n3
United States Colored Troops (USCT), 8, 14, 132–35. *See also* African Americans; race
Upson, Theodore, 50, 70, 120
U.S. Army, 6
U.S. Congress, 137
Utoy Creek, 56

Valentine, Randolph, 102
Vallandigham party, 107
Vandermark, John, 105
Vanderpool, George, 92–93
Vanderwarker, Isaac, III, 72
Van Houten, Isaac, 137
Van Orden, Al, 43
van Rensselaer, Killian, 102
Van Wyck, Richard T., 121, 122

Vaughn, John, 104
Vermont regiments, 17, 105
Vicksburg MS: aftermath of siege of, 51, 71–72; ceasefires at, 14, 112, 120; description of siege of, 48, 112–13; desertions after siege of, 32; fraternization during siege of, 12, 45, 49–50, 68–72, 143, 168; memories of fraternization at, 146; participants in siege of, 52, 124; significance of campaign at, 46; troop positions at, *69*, 124, 128; veterans of, 94, 98; weaponry at, 112–13; winter encampments near, 47
Virginia: Army of the Potomac in, 1; ceasefires in, 118; Confederate morale in, 108, 110; fraternal lodges in, 29; fraternization in, 11–12; items traded in, 76; siege warfare in, 128; Ulysses S. Grant's command in, 54, 99, 127. *See also* Fredericksburg VA; Petersburg VA; Richmond VA
Virginia regiments, 22, 44, 105–6

Wait, James, 78
Walthall, Felix, 49
Walthall, Howard Malcolm, 145, 146
Ward, Joseph, 131
War Department, 94, 100
Ware Bottom Church, 59
The War for the Common Soldier (Carmichael), 5
Warwick Creek, 63
Washington DC, 160
water supplies, 47, 49, 58, 74, 153–54, 157
Watkins, James W., 57, 124
Weaver, Larkin, 49
Weber, Jennifer L., 107
Weitz, Mark, 109
Welch, Henry, 23, 95, 99
What This Cruel War Was Over (Manning), 5
Wheaton, Frank, 67
whiskey, 43, 70
White, Wyman, 44
whites: attitudes toward black soldiers, 132–35; effect of Emancipation Proclamation on, 88; enlistment of, 19; fraternization among, 7, 13, 14, 28–30, 84, 134, 152, 154; manliness of, 32; protecting supremacy of, 15, 134, 135, 138, 164. *See also* race
Whitney, Julius, 102

Wickman, Don, 144
Wilcox, Cadmus, 106
Wiley, Bell Irvin, 3–4
Willet, W. D., 114
Willey, Collins, 116
Williams, Alpheus S., 99, 123
Wilson, LeGrand James, 63
Wilson's Brigade, 32

Windsor Journal, 86
Winkleman, William, 59, 81
Wisconsin *State Journal*, 96
Wood, Henry B., 66
wood cutting, 131, 152–53
Woodworth, Steven, 47, 54
World War I, 111, 137, 159, 166–67, 182n1

Yancey, William Lowndes, 81

STUDIES IN WAR, SOCIETY, AND THE MILITARY

Military Migration and State Formation: The British Military Community in Seventeenth-Century Sweden
Mary Elizabeth Ailes

Managing Sex in the U.S. Military: Gender, Identity, and Behavior
Edited by Beth Bailey, Alesha E. Doan, Shannon Portillo, and Kara Dixon Vuic

The State at War in South Asia
Pradeep P. Barua

Marianne Is Watching: Intelligence, Counterintelligence, and the Origins of the French Surveillance State
Deborah Bauer

Death at the Edges of Empire: Fallen Soldiers, Cultural Memory, and the Making of an American Nation, 1863–1921
Shannon Bontrager

An American Soldier in World War I
George Browne
Edited by David L. Snead

Beneficial Bombing: The Progressive Foundations of American Air Power, 1917–1945
Mark Clodfelter

Fu-go: The Curious History of Japan's Balloon Bomb Attack on America
Ross Coen

Imagining the Unimaginable: World War, Modern Art, and the Politics of Public Culture in Russia, 1914–1917
Aaron J. Cohen

The Rise of the National Guard: The Evolution of the American Militia, 1865–1920
Jerry Cooper

The Thirty Years' War and German Memory in the Nineteenth Century
Kevin Cramer

Political Indoctrination in the U.S. Army from World War II to the Vietnam War
Christopher S. DeRosa

In the Service of the Emperor: Essays on the Imperial Japanese Army
Edward J. Drea

American Journalists in the Great War: Rewriting the Rules of Reporting
Chris Dubbs

America's U-Boats: Terror Trophies of World War I
Chris Dubbs

The Age of the Ship of the Line: The British and French Navies, 1650–1815
Jonathan R. Dull

American Naval History, 1607–1865: Overcoming the Colonial Legacy
Jonathan R. Dull

Soldiers of the Nation: Military Service and Modern Puerto Rico, 1868–1952
Harry Franqui-Rivera

You Can't Fight Tanks with Bayonets: Psychological Warfare against the Japanese Army in the Southwest Pacific
Allison B. Gilmore

A Strange and Formidable Weapon: British Responses to World War I Poison Gas
Marion Girard

Civilians in the Path of War
Edited by Mark Grimsley and Clifford J. Rogers

A Scientific Way of War: Antebellum Military Science, West Point, and the Origins of American Military Thought
Ian C. Hope

Picture This: World War I Posters and Visual Culture
Edited and with an introduction by Pearl James

Indian Soldiers in World War I: Race and Representation in an Imperial War
Andrew T. Jarboe

Death Zones and Darling Spies: Seven Years of Vietnam War Reporting
Beverly Deepe Keever

For Home and Country: World War I Propaganda on the Home Front
Celia Malone Kingsbury

I Die with My Country: Perspectives on the Paraguayan War, 1864–1870
Edited by Hendrik Kraay and Thomas L. Whigham

North American Indians in the Great War
Susan Applegate Krouse
Photographs and original documentation by Joseph K. Dixon

Remembering World War I in America
Kimberly J. Lamay Licursi

Citizens More than Soldiers: The Kentucky Militia and Society in the Early Republic
Harry S. Laver

Soldiers as Citizens: Former Wehrmacht Officers in the Federal Republic of Germany, 1945–1955
Jay Lockenour

Deterrence through Strength: British Naval Power and Foreign Policy under Pax Britannica
Rebecca Berens Matzke

Army and Empire: British Soldiers on the American Frontier, 1758–1775
Michael N. McConnell

Of Duty Well and Faithfully Done: A History of the Regular Army in the Civil War
Clayton R. Newell and Charles R. Shrader
With a foreword by Edward M. Coffman

The Militarization of Culture in the Dominican Republic, from the Captains General to General Trujillo
Valentina Peguero

A Religious History of the American GI in World War II
G. Kurt Piehler

Arabs at War: Military Effectiveness, 1948–1991
Kenneth M. Pollack

The Politics of Air Power: From Confrontation to Cooperation in Army Aviation Civil-Military Relations
Rondall R. Rice

Andean Tragedy: Fighting the War of the Pacific, 1879–1884
William F. Sater

The Grand Illusion: The Prussianization of the Chilean Army
William F. Sater and Holger H. Herwig

Sex Crimes under the Wehrmacht
David Raub Snyder

In the School of War
Roger J. Spiller
Foreword by John W. Shy

On the Trail of the Yellow Tiger: War, Trauma, and Social Dislocation in Southwest China during the Ming-Qing Transition
Kenneth M. Swope

Friendly Enemies: Soldier Fraternization throughout the American Civil War
Lauren K. Thompson

The Paraguayan War, Volume 1: Causes and Early Conduct
Thomas L. Whigham

Policing Sex and Marriage in the American Military: The Court-Martial and the Construction of Gender and Sexual Deviance, 1950–2000
Kellie Wilson-Buford

The Challenge of Change: Military Institutions and New Realities, 1918–1941
Edited by Harold R. Winton and David R. Mets

To order or obtain more information on these or other University of Nebraska Press titles, visit nebraskapress.unl.edu.

www.ingramcontent.com/pod-product-compliance
Lightning Source LLC
Chambersburg PA
CBHW022010220426
43663CB00007B/1034